ANCIENT
EGYPT

ANCIENT
EGYPT

EVERYDAY LIFE
IN THE LAND OF THE NILE

BOB BRIER & HOYT HOBBS

STERLING
New York

STERLING
New York

An Imprint of Sterling Publishing
387 Park Avenue South
New York, NY 10016

Please see page 313 for image credits.

This edition published by arrangement ABC-CLIO
130 Cremona Drive Suite C,
Santa Barbara, CA 93117-5505, USA.

ISBN 978-1-4549-0907-1

Distributed in Canada by Sterling Publishing
c/o Canadian Manda Group, 165 Dufferin Street
Toronto, Ontario, Canada M6K 3H6
Distributed in the United Kingdom by GMC Distribution Services
Castle Place, 166 High Street, Lewes, East Sussex, England BN7 1XU
Distributed in Australia by Capricorn Link (Australia) Pty. Ltd.
P.O. Box 704, Windsor, NSW 2756, Australia

For information about custom editions, special sales, and premium and corporate purchases,
please contact Sterling Special Sales at 800-805-5489 or specialsales@sterlingpublishing.com.

Manufactured in China

2 4 6 8 10 9 7 5 3 1

www.sterlingpublishing.com

CONTENTS

INTRODUCTION

ANCIENT EGYPT COMPILED A STUNNING LIST OF ACCOMPLISHMENTS. Its Karnak Temple has never been surpassed in size by any later place of worship, and the Great Pyramid, with a north-south orientation as precise as the most modern surveying instruments could achieve, is still the most massive building ever raised by humankind. The massiveness and precision of its buildings compare favorably with the accomplishments of technological societies almost 5,000 years later. Its form of government, although radically different from modern societies, was sufficiently solid that it sustained the civilization for almost 3,000 years—a record unlikely to ever be broken—and it was comparable in sophistication, complexity and efficiency to the Chinese empire that developed two millennia later. Ordinary citizens in ancient Egypt lived and worked in much the same ways as the average European of the eighteenth century, more than 4,000 years later, but ate better and enjoyed more variety in their food. Their clothing was eminently practical (sandals sold in our department stores still copy ancient Egyptian styles) but could also be as intricate and glamorous as the most stylish modern gown. In architecture, ancient Egyptians invented the column, houses with patios, latrines and the first "air-conditioning" by using roof scoops to circulate breezes through their homes. Their art had no competition for at least 2,500 years, and ancient Egyptian carpenters invented every method of joining wood known today. Medicine in ancient Egypt stood head and shoulders above the rest of the world for 2,700 years until Greece's Late Period. The Egyptian army controlled a larger area than any troops in history until the Persians marched in 1,500 years later, and no nation ever dominated its neighbors for as long.

With a civilization so advanced and in many ways so modern, ancient Egyptians seem very much like ourselves—we feel that if we were somehow

THE PRECINCT OF AMUN-RE, *part of the immense Karnak Temple Complex in Luxor, Egypt, is reflected in the Sacred Lake.*

transported to ancient Egypt we would find kindred souls. The people we would actually encounter, however, provide the great paradox of ancient Egypt. Despite their precociousness in many areas, they were not like us at all in the most fundamental ways. Their buildings, architecture, clothing, food and medicine may have been thousands of years ahead of their time, but their view of the world was closer to a prehistoric caveman's than to ours. They saw the universe as inhabited by a panoply of gods—spirits that controlled every natural phenomenon and left an Egyptian feeling powerless, dependent on prayers and offerings to entice gods to accomplish what he could not do on his own. Rather than individuals, pursuing their own destiny, ancient Egyptians acted like helpless pets waiting for whatever their masters, the gods, might provide. This paradoxical combination of startlingly modern accomplishments with incredibly ancient thought processes, of people who looked both forward and back, is what this book attempts to describe.

That a comprehensive description of the ancient Egyptians is even possible, however, verges on the miraculous. As our second oldest civilization, dating from 3000 B.C.E., Egypt's age is truly incredible. We think of Greeks from the days of Socrates and Plato as primeval, but their fifth century B.C.E. perspective looked back to an Egypt as old as those ancient Greeks are to us today. Only because of three unique factors is specific information available to show what people did so long ago and how they lived: Egyptians' love of writing, their accurate tomb paintings, and the modern fascination with ancient Egyptian culture.

Egyptians were among the first people to develop writing and, luckily, they loved their invention, covering yards of papyrus and temple and tomb walls with words. They made lists of what they owned, recorded court cases, described battles and preserved recipes, wrote books on medicine and religion, and told stories. An inherent conservatism of character caused them to preserve their oldest writings and copy them over and over, increasing the chances that examples would survive. Several hundred rolls of papyrus have endured to our day, along with extensive wall inscriptions.

Since their religion told them that gods would re-create whatever they saw on a tomb wall, Egyptians decorated their tombs with paintings of what they most enjoyed. These walls illustrate the clothing, the conduct of professions and the leisure activities of actual people. Although Egyptians took great pains to hide their tombs from robbers in underground recesses, they seldom succeeded— valuable burial goods spurred looters to great efforts. Still, because a painted wall held no resale value in ancient times, the paintings remain for the most part, even in plundered tombs, subject only to the ravages of time and weather. Here, too, we are fortunate. The greatest natural enemy of a painted plaster wall is moisture, which in Egypt is as slight as anywhere in the world. Numerous painted and carved walls remain vivid today, some as bright and fresh as the day the painter laid down his brush to admire his completed work.

Finally, Egypt has held a deep fascination for diverse groups during our century, from those interested in the Bible, to those attracted by Egyptian art, to those intrigued by the occult. As a result, this country has been investigated more than any other ancient civilization. Because the Bible describes Joseph's sojourn in Egypt, Moses' liberation of the Jews from Pharaoh and a visit by the Holy Family, Egypt retains strong Christian and Jewish connections. Hordes of scholars have sifted the sands of Egypt for two centuries searching for clues that might bear on these sacred events. Another impetus came when Napoleon stormed Egypt with his army in 1798. His fascination with the ancient culture led him to include as part of his entourage France's greatest scientists, savants who roamed the country, sketching temples and artifacts, drawing maps and recording plants and animals. When the army returned to France after Napoleon's defeat, these scientists brought descriptions of an art and architecture outside the classical tradition that excited the first of periodic Egyptomanias. The French Empire style with its Egyptian motifs was one direct result. Egyptomania recurred in 1923 with the discovery of the magnificence inside Tut's tomb. This time the craze spread beyond France and England to the United States and the rest of the world. Such fascination caused generations of young people, dreaming of discovering similar treasures, to set their sights on Egypt. No wonder treasure hunters have combed Egypt for almost two centuries in competition with hordes of scientifically minded Egyptologists, sifting the sands, poking the ground for holes, copying and translating inscriptions.

Thanks to all the recovered objects, inscriptions, paintings, and surviving temples and tombs, we know a great deal today about how these ancient people lived and what they thought. This information fills the remaining pages of this book. Why did tens of thousands of free citizens work like slaves to build a pyramid? Why did Egyptians believe cats, ibises and beetles were sacred? What did people eat long before stores existed, and what did they wear? Surprisingly, few popular books focus on the clothing, food, buildings, government, working conditions and religion of the ancient Egyptians and attempt to answer such questions. Of those that do, many were published fifty or more years ago. So it seems appropriate to revisit the life of the average ancient Egyptian to add the discoveries of modern research to what was known before. Our approach is to describe the historical development of Egypt first, along with its religion and form of government, to pave the way for understanding why Egyptians worked, ate and dressed as they did. Architecture, art, warfare and medical and the other knowledge that Egyptians achieved follow, as a kind of conclusion. The very end of the book consists of an annotated bibliography which we hope will encourage the reader to further investigate this fascinating culture.

New discoveries are made every year in Egyptology so the opportunity to revise our book allows us to update our information based on recent finds. In particular, this second edition gives us a chance to present a new theory about how the massive pyramids were constructed and to generally discuss how ancient Egyptians were able to accomplish their wonders, great and small, so we added a new chapter to explain their methods of construction and the technology they employed. We also took this opportunity to add new illustrations and improve the writing, which can always be bettered. The bibliography has been updated, both to include works that did not exist at the time of original publication and to expand it to include periodicals of general interest.

THE CENTRAL NAVE OF KARNAK'S GREAT HYPOSTYLE HALL *consists of twelve richly decorated, 70-foot-high stone columns.*

ANCIENT EGYPT
TIMELINE

PREDYNASTIC PERIOD (c. 4000–3150 B.C.E.)

Towns in Egypt; early religion; pottery and stone vessels; no unified government or writing.

[c. 3100 B.C.E.: Sumer invents writing.]

EARLY DYNASTIC PERIOD (c. 3150–2686 B.C.E.)

Unified pharaonic government; writing; early tombs.

Dynasty I (c. 3050–2890 B.C.E.). Narmer: the first pharaoh.

Dynasty II (c. 2890–2686 B.C.E.). Pharaohs' tombs grow.

[2700 B.C.E.: approximate date of Biblical flood.]

OLD KINGDOM (c. 2686–2181 B.C.E.)

Dynasty III (c. 2686–2613 B.C.E.). Zoser builds first pyramid.

Dynasty IV (c. 2613–2498 B.C.E.). The three pyramids of Giza.

[c. 2500: rise of Minoan civilization.]

Dynasty V (c. 2498–2345 B.C.E.). Sun temples.

Dynasty VI (c. 2345–2181 B.C.E.). First Pyramid Texts.

FIRST INTERMEDIATE PERIOD (2181–2041 B.C.E.)

Dynasties VII–X. Concurrent pharaohs.

MIDDLE KINGDOM (2040–1782 B.C.E.)

Resurrection of unified government; conquest of Kush.

Dynasty XI (2060–1991 B.C.E.). Capital moved to Thebes.

Dynasty XII (1991–1782 B.C.E.). Portraiture; development of Fayum.

SECOND INTERMEDIATE PERIOD (1782–1570 B.C.E.)

Hyksos control northern Egypt and introduce chariots.

Dynasties XIII–XVII.

NEW KINGDOM (1570–1070 B.C.E.)

Conquest of Canaan, Lebanon and Syria; rise of the god Amun; Akhenaten's monotheism.

Dynasty XVIII (1570–1293 B.C.E.). Conquests; Hatshepsut; monotheism.

[c. 1500 B.C.E.: Stonehenge constructed.]

Dynasty XIX (1293–1185 B.C.E.). Rameses the Great; monumental art.

[c. 1230 B.C.E.: Exodus of the Jews from Egypt.]

Dynasty XX (1185–1070 B.C.E.). Capital moved north.

[c. 1120 B.C.E.: Trojan War.]

LATE PERIOD (1069–332 B.C.E.)

Dynasties XXI–XXXI. Attacks by foreign powers; Persian domination; decline.

[c. 950 B.C.E.: The time of King Solomon of Israel.]

[587 B.C.E.: Destruction of Jerusalem; Babylonian captivity of the Jews.]

[428 B.C.E.: Birth of Plato.]

PTOLEMAIC (332–30 B.C.E.)

Dynasties XXXII–XXXIII. Alexander the Great; Ptolemies; Cleopatra.

Conquest of Egypt by Rome (30 B.C.E.).

EGYPTIAN EMPIRE
B.C. 1450

English Miles

0   100   200   300   400   500

1

HISTORY

WHEN HERODOTUS, THE WORLD'S FIRST HISTORIAN, VISITED
Egypt in the fifth century B.C.E., he asked its priests what was the
key to Egypt's greatness. "Egypt is the gift of the Nile," they said;
and so, from the very beginning, it was. Egyptian civilization would never have
accomplished its wonders had it not been for this gift of nature, so crucial to its
people and so mysterious that they considered it divine.

Like clockwork each spring the usually placid Nile roared—more than
twice as high as during the rest of the year—in a torrent into southern Egypt.
River banks could not contain the increased volume which spilled over—in
some places for as much as a mile—and covered flat plains on either side. As
the flood gradually emptied into the Mediterranean in Egypt's extreme north,
the water receded, leaving behind a residue of millions of tons of fertile silt.
Surrounded as Egypt was by the Sahara Desert, it should have been a desolate,
arid environment, but thanks to the Nile, it enjoyed unrivaled fertility. Not
only did the Nile provide water so Egyptians need not depend on unpredictable
rain, but its annual floods replenished soil that would otherwise be drained of
nutrients by continual planting. Growing more food with less manpower than
any other country in the world, Egypt acquired a surplus to trade and time to
devote to matters other than mere survival.

By the dawn of the third millennium, a population of almost one million
had established communities that nestled close to the Nile, following the river's
long, thin course through the center of the country. Along both banks, a mile
or more of farmland was bordered first by cliffs, then by desert. At Egypt's
southernmost point—modern Aswan—giant boulders clogged the Nile to

MAP OF THE EGYPTIAN EMPIRE *in 1450 B.C.E., showing prominent ancient sites along
the Nile River.*

create one natural boundary; the vast Mediterranean formed its northern border. To the west spread a thousand miles of arid Sahara, while east lay the barren Sinai Peninsula and the deep Red Sea. Nature had created a vast fortress wall that protected Egyptians from hostile neighbors, while nurturing them with unfailing sun, abundant water and bountiful crops.

By 3000 b.c.e. Egypt possessed all the characteristics of a country except one. Her people spoke a common language and shared similar religious beliefs, but no government had yet been created which could unite her separate groups of people into a nation; someone had yet to invent that political mechanism. The new system was created by a man whose unification of Egypt was revered through all its history, but the means by which he accomplished his feat became known only as the result of an archaeological excavation at the beginning of our century.

Excavators working in the ancient town of Hieraconpolis, near the southern end of Egypt, found an unusual object. Among a cache of sacred relics buried in the remains of an early temple lay an oversized slate cosmetic palette, similar to others Egyptians used for grinding malachite which they mixed with fat to produce the green cosmetic worn above their eyes. Instead of the normal six-inch palette, however, this one stood two feet tall—a palette for the gods. With carved pictures and rudimentary writing it told the story of the unification of Egypt. One side shows a large figure grasping an enemy by the hair with one hand while raising a mace menacingly with the

THE NARMER PALETTE *is humanity's oldest recording of an event. On one side (left), Narmer attacks an enemy while wearing the White Crown of Upper Egypt. On the other side (right), he wears the Red Crown to signify his conquest of Lower Egypt.*

other. Hieroglyphs over the scene call the man "Narmer." The reverse side shows Narmer leading a procession of tiny figures carrying banners, while a little man behind him in the outfit of a priest cradles a pair of sandals.

Most significantly, Narmer wears one kind of crown on one side of the palette and a different crown on the other—distinctive royal hats known as the Red Crown of the North ($\leftthreetimes$) and the White Crown of the South ($\langle\!\backslash\rangle$). The pictures narrate Narmer's leadership of a southern confederation (with processional banners representing various communities) to its successful conquest of the north, a conquest that made Narmer the first ruler of a unified Egypt. Except for relatively brief periods of instability, the country remained a single entity throughout its 3,000-year history, but Egyptians never forgot their origins. They always referred to their country as the "Two Lands," and their ruler as the "Lord of Upper and of Lower Egypt," a way of acknowledging the indispensable role of the pharaoh in holding a divided country together. Other Egyptian records assign the original pharaoh the name Menes, a different designation for the same man—every pharaoh had at least two names. Egypt, blessed once by its fortunate geography, achieved additional strength from its unification, forging 2,000 years of artistic excellence and military dominance—achievements unequaled then or since. A century later, Egypt had developed a complex national government, a sophisticated religion and a written language; it was the first country to earn the accolade "civilized."[1] Most of the institutions that would characterize Egypt's civilization throughout its long existence were already in place, not least of which was Narmer's form of government which allowed the all-powerful pharaoh to mobilize an entire population to carry out massive public projects.

Tradition credits Menes/Narmer with establishing Memphis as the capital of Egypt. The first capital of the country, it remained the seat of government throughout most of Egypt's history. For almost two centuries after Narmer, Egypt continued to consolidate power and gather energy. During this time, an idea began to germinate and develop: belief in a pharaoh's divinity and immortality. If, after death, the king resurrected to live again in another world, he would need clothing, food and furniture to sustain him. Providing for their pharaoh's eternal life increasingly became the business of his subjects, as they were called upon to build ever larger tombs to store the food and equipment required for his next existence.

Many ancient cultures held similar beliefs about their ruler's divine afterlife and expended great energy creating special burials for their kings. Egypt's special contribution was a new tomb design first devised in about 2700 B.C.E. Architects for the pharaoh Zoser stacked six decreasingly smaller stone brick rectangles on top of each other to form a towering, 200-foot-high "Step Pyramid." This first large building ever raised in stone by humankind initiated a series of pyramids, structural feats that became the signature of Egypt, dazzling us now as much as they amazed the ancients.

Because of the sheer length of Egypt's history, it is helpful to use the nine eras historians have developed to divide Egypt's 3,000-year history into coherent pieces. Egyptologists refer to the time just before Narmer's unification as "Predynastic" (or "Archaic") and the period from the unification of Egypt up to the raising of the first pyramid as "Early Dynastic." The great age of pyramids that Zoser initiated is known as the "Old Kingdom," after which came a period of anarchy and chaos, the "First Intermediate Period." Egypt reassumed power in the "Middle Kingdom," experienced another decline during the "Second Intermediate Period," and resurrected itself again in a final great era of art and military success in the "New Kingdom" before undergoing a slow decline during the "Late Period," ancient Egypt's final era. Since each period covers many centuries and numerous kings, a later Egyptian priestarchivist named Manetho subdivided each period into groups called "dynasties," to indicate rule by descendants of a single family. He separated the Early Dynastic period into the first two dynasties and the Old Kingdom into the third, fourth, fifth and sixth dynasties, and so on. Additional information about Egypt's oldest times is supplied by its architecture. Architectural changes tell us about engineering advances, economic conditions and political and religious movements, while carved pictures and writing inform us about the events of the times. Beginning with the New Kingdom, surviving papyri provide us with increased details.

THE STEP PYRAMID OF DJOSER *(Zoser) at the Saqqara necropolis is the first large monument raised in stone.*

The Nine Eras Of Egyptian History

PERIOD	DATES	DYNASTIES
Predynastic	to 3150 B.C.E.	
Early Dynastic	3150–26862	I–II
Old Kingdom	2686–2181	III–VI
First Intermediate Period	2181–2040	VII–XI
Middle Kingdom	2040–1782	XI–XII
Second Intermediate Period	1782–1570	XIII–XVII
New Kingdom	1570–1070	XVIII–XX
Late Period	1069–332	XXI–XXXI
Ptolemaic Period	332–30	XXXII–XXXIII

OLD KINGDOM (2686–2181 B.C.E.)

The Third Dynasty, led by Zoser, builder of the Step Pyramid, set the Old Kingdom on an unprecedented building spree, although his two successors built smaller step pyramids near Zoser's at Saqqara. However, the first pharaoh of the next dynasty, Sneferu, attempted to erect an eight-step pyramid thirty miles distant at Meidum which incorporated a significant design advance. For the first time, the steps were filled with polished stone to form smooth slanting sides—the true pyramid shape we know today. Although this first attempt proved structurally unstable, he continued experiments with other true pyramids, and, despite a failed second attempt, raised yet another that stood solidly enough to last thousands of years. Together, Sneferu's three pyramids used more stone than the famous Great Pyramid.

As authors of the world's first history books, the Greeks passed down a great deal of misinformation, including the name of Sneferu's son whom they referred to as "Cheops," although his Egyptian name was Khufu. He must have been infected with his father's passion for pyramids, for near Cairo, on a desert plateau called Giza, he built the most massive stone structure the world has ever seen. The Great Pyramid, which originally rose 481 feet in the air, was the tallest building in the world until the Eiffel Tower finally surpassed it 4,500 years later. Resting on a base 756 feet square—large enough to contain the cathedrals of Milan, Florence and Saint Peter's in Rome, along with Westminster Abbey and Saint Paul's in London—the 2,000,000 stones forming the mass of its structure average two and a half tons each. Since a pharaoh never began his royal tomb until taking the throne and since Khufu reigned for twenty-three years, the entire project—from initial surveying to leveling the land and piling millions of stones upon stones—must have been completed in about two decades. Meeting this schedule meant that, on the average, one two-and-a-half-ton block had to be quarried and moved into place every two minutes of every hour of every work day for those two decades. Inside, a magnificent passageway leads a third of the way up the pyramid to a granite chamber in which a polished granite sarcophagus held Khufu's mortal remains. Complex anti-burglary systems, such as passageways that led to dead-ends and massive stone plugs that sealed the true route to the burial site, sadly proved to no avail: the pyramid was picked clean in ancient times.

Pharaohs of the Old Kingdom

DYNASTY	PHARAOH	DATES (B.C.E.)
III	Setnakhte	2686–2668
III	Djoser	2668–2649
III	Sekhemkhet	2649–2643
III	Khaba	2643–2637
III	Huni	2637–2613
IV	Sneferu	2613–2589
IV	Khufu (Cheops)	2589–2566
IV	Djedefre	2566–2558
IV	Khafre (Chephren)	2558–2532
IV	Menkaure	2532–2504
IV	Shepseskaf	2504–2500
V	Userkaf	2498–2491
V	Sahure	2491–2477
V	Neferirkare	2477–2467
V	Shepseskare	2467–2460
V	Neferefre	2460–2453
V	Niuserre	2453–2422
V	Menkauhor	2422–2414
V	Djedkare	2414–2375
V	Unas	2375–2345
VI	Teti	2345–2333
VI	Pepi I	2332–2283
VI	Merenre	2283–2278
VI	Pepi II	2278–2184
VI	Nitokerti	2184–2181?

In addition to building the largest of all tombs, Khufu constructed a temple where offerings could be made to his immortal soul and a grand causeway leading from his pyramid to yet another temple in the valley below. Five large pits around the pyramid contained the boats intended to transport his remains and funerary goods to the next world. One of these disassembled boats, found almost perfectly preserved in 1954, was built of the finest Lebanese cedar and measured 143 feet from bow to stern.[3]

The Great Pyramid was only the first of three imposing pyramids erected at Giza which earned the Old Kingdom the name "Pyramid Age." Khufu's son Khafra, known to the Greeks as Chephren, took up the challenge at Giza with a massive effort beside his father's Great Pyramid. Since it stands on higher ground, Khafra's pyramid rises even higher than its famous neighbor, although it actually stood ten feet shorter when it was new. Its gleaming casing of white limestone, transported by boats from quarries across the Nile, still covers the top, laid over interior limestone blocks which were cut from the surrounding Giza site. Probably in the course of freeing these interior blocks, quarrymen struck a seam of harder rock they avoided, leaving a small hill. Khafra had this outcrop carved in the shape of a recumbent lion bearing his own face—the famous Sphinx. The Greeks misunderstood this sixty-foot-

KHUFU'S "SOLAR BOAT"—*a ritual vessel intended to transport the king's embalmed body, with the sun god Ra, into the next world—is the world's oldest intact ship.*

THE GREAT SPHINX OF GIZA *depicts the face of Khafra (reign c. 2558–2532 B.C.E.), a Fourth Dynasty pharaoh who built the second largest pyramid.*

high, almost-200-foot-long symbol of power for a woman (perhaps taking its shoulder-length headdress for long hair). In the valley below his pyramid, Khafra constructed a valley temple, as had his father, of monolithic hard granite columns supporting a roof above a polished alabaster floor. Early this century parts of twenty-three realistic, life-sized statues of the king were found inside.

Khafra's son, Menkaura (whom the Greeks called Mycerinus), raised the last of the famous Giza pyramids. Half the size of its neighbors at 218 feet in height, it is distinguished by a lovely casing of hard red granite transported from Aswan, 500 miles to the south. The casing covers only the bottom quarter of the pyramid, however, for Menkaura died unexpectedly after a reign of 28 years, leaving his pyramid and mortuary temple incomplete.

As a result of this spate of pyramid construction, the Giza plateau grew into a virtual city of the dead—laid out in orderly streets lined with smaller pyramids for queens and princesses, along with hundreds of low, rectangular tombs for favored, but nonroyal, courtiers and royal sons. Even today, the magnitude of this project astonishes.

Were it not for the two months every year when the Nile's water covered Egypt's farmland, idling virtually the entire workforce, none of this construction

THIS AERIAL VIEW OF THE GIZA PLATEAU *shows hundreds of subsidiary tombs arranged in orderly rows and divided by "streets."*

would have been possible. During such times, a pharaoh offered food for work and the promise of favored treatment in the afterworld, where he would rule, just as he did in this world. For two months annually, workmen gathered by tens of thousands from all over the country to transport the blocks a permanent crew had quarried during the rest of the year. Overseers organized the men into teams to transport the stones on sleds, devices better suited than wheeled vehicles to moving weighty objects over shifting sand. A causeway, lubricated by water, smoothed the uphill pull. No mortar was used to hold the blocks in place, only a fit so exact that these towering structures have survived for 4,600 years—the only Wonders of the Ancient World still standing today.

As if exhausted from its building frenzy, the glorious Fourth Dynasty simply faded away with a last, short reign. We know little of the origins of the Fifth Dynasty except indications that its founder was born to a royal daughter who married to a nonroyal husband and that his ascendance to the pharaohcy involved a religious revolution over the sun god Ra, who became the great god of Egypt thereafter. Six of the Fifth Dynasty's nine pharaohs incorporate Ra in their names, and all follow them with the phrase "Son of the Sun." Most chose a burial site at modern Abusir, five miles from Giza, where they built a new type of mortuary complex. Because they concentrated on building temples dedicated to the sun, their pyramids were poorly constructed and stood only 200 feet tall or less. Beside each pyramid, however, stood a temple consisting of a football-field-sized open courtyard brilliant in the sun. At one end, beside a squat obelisk—the symbol of the sun's rays—rose an altar for offerings. Inside the open temple stood a slaughterhouse for sacrificial animals, along with storerooms and housing for priests.

These five large sun temples within a mile of each other, far from any city, were obviously intended only for the benefit of their deceased kings. Since the resources to supply temples with offerings and priests with food could not be maintained for every ensuing ruler, the pharaoh Unas, who may have been the last of the Fifth Dynasty or the first of the Sixth, turned away from such temples and built, at Saqqara, a small, sixty-two-foot-tall pyramid, with an innovative concept that compensated for its diminished size. Lovely hieroglyphs, incised in the stone and filled with bright blue pigment, cover the walls of the burial chamber from floor to ceiling. This text is the first ever inscribed inside or outside any pyramid. Called the "Pyramid Texts," this collection of magic spells was intended to ensure the safe passage of the pharaoh to the next world. So powerful were these words believed to be that characters in the shape of birds were drawn with cut wings and those of animals with partial legs, lest the birds fly away and the animals run off.

The next three Sixth Dynasty kings, most of whom enjoyed a long reign, all continued to use Pyramid Texts. The second of these, Pepi I, who died in his fifty-third year on the throne, must have survived into his seventies. He was succeeded by a middle-aged son who reigned only five years and died childless, leaving the throne in turn to a young half-brother, born in his father's twilight years. Pepi II thus began his rule as a child of six and lived to reign for ninety-four years, the record for any monarch in history. When, after almost a century, the doddering old man died, he left a nation weakened and dissipated by years of senile rule and, since his sons had predeceased him, his surviving daughter, Nitokerti, became the first woman to rule Egypt. During the distracted final years of her father's reign, the pharaoh's authority had weakened to the point that representatives who governed various parts of Egypt on the pharaoh's behalf and who had formerly built their own tombs near the pharaoh to acknowledge his dominance, now lived and died in whichever section of the country they administered—a sign of serious disrespect. After Nitokerti's death, the country lay in shambles.

Despite its chaotic end, the glorious Old Kingdom produced the most elegant art of any period in Egypt's long history. Large stone portrait sculptures painted to a lifelike realism incorporated haunting, rock crystal eyes; wall reliefs still delight with their accuracy and elegance of form. The country had grown efficient and powerful enough to import materials for jewelry and construction from as far as Afghanistan for lapis lazuli, Lebanon for cedar wood, the Sinai for turquoise, and Kush (modern Sudan) for gold. Egypt showed signs it was a force to be reckoned with as her armies forged into the Sinai, Palestine, Syrian, Libya and the Sudan. Above all, the wonders of construction accomplished at such an early time in history proved to be the Old Kingdom's outstanding achievement and would awe the world ever after. This single, 500-year era in Egyptian history had enjoyed a longer day in the sun than do most countries during their entire history.

First Intermediate Period (2181–2041 B.C.E.)

One clear sign of the chaos that characterized the First Intermediate Period comes from the ancient historian Manetho who cites more than 140 rulers from four dynasties over a 121-year period, a record possible only if the collapse of central authority allowed several "pharaohs" to rule simultaneously. The fact that various dynasties claimed different capitals supports this view of competing rulers. No great monuments remain from this era, implying that the massive building projects of previous times had been abandoned, presumably because the strong authority to commission them no longer existed. A later papyrus describes the depths to which the country had sunk, how completely law and order had vanished.

> The bowman is ready. The wrongdoer is everywhere. There is no man of yesterday. A man goes out to plow with his shield. A man smites his brother, his mother's son. Men sit in the bushes until the benighted traveler comes, in order to plunder his load. The robber is the possessor of riches. Boxes of ebony are broken up. Precious acacia wood is cleft asunder.[4]

As the authority of the pharaoh weakened, government functionaries gathered more responsibility and power into their own hands. Political offices, previously appointive, became hereditary, insulating the office holder even more from a pharaoh's control. With one powerful person or another proclaiming himself pharaoh—and dressing and acting like one—how was anyone to know which pretender was the true ruler?

While various pretenders called on the population for their allegiance, the mass of the country—its farmers—cared little about who ruled them, for their work remained the same. Life went on, even if more fearful and disrupted. Some art was created, but of a coarser quality than what preceded it; some buildings rose, but smaller and less refined than earlier projects; some expeditions searched for imports, but less frequently and more scaled back than before. It was as though Egypt were marking time, waiting for a resurrection.

MIDDLE KINGDOM (2040–1782 B.C.E.)

It was inevitable that someone would emerge strong enough to overcome the other pretenders and unify the country again. Three times in Egypt's history—at its very beginning, at the end of the First Intermediate Period and at the end of the Second Intermediate Period—such a man came out of the south to impose his will on the nation. Why all three conquests originated in the south poses an interesting question. Perhaps southerners, living far from the foreign cultural influences of the Mediterranean were more ardently patriotic; perhaps a more concentrated population was easier to mobilize; perhaps proximity to rich Kush with its mercenaries and gold gave southern leaders a military edge over opponents. Whatever the reason, it was a southern warrior who succeeded in ending the chaos of the First Intermediate Period and initiating the Middle Kingdom.

The south had long been home to a family with pretension enough to consider themselves royal by enclosing their names in cartouches, an act which caused later record keepers to refer to them collectively as the Eleventh Dynasty. An insignificant town called Waset ("the Scepter"), which the Greeks later designated Thebes, became their capital and, appropriately, the falcon god of war, known as Montu, became their patron god. Since one leader of this dynasty boasted of conquering Abydos, a city only forty miles to the north, their original area of influence could not have been large. Montuhotep I ("Montu Is Pleased") changed all that. In the fourteenth year of his reign, Montuhotep put down an insurrection in Abydos and added the title "Lord of the White Crown"—the king of the south—to his titulary; by the thirty-ninth year of his reign, he had added the title "Uniter of the Two Lands." Like Narmer/Menes before him, he had conquered the north and unified the country.

Montuhotep's achievement in reuniting the country accords him the status of founder of the Middle Kingdom. This southern king made his hometown, Thebes, the capital of his resurrected country, abandoning the old capital Memphis, which had fallen into neglect. With central authority restored and a powerful pharaoh to commission construction projects, the arts reawakened and the army strained at the bit—a glorious era dawned.

HATSHEPSUT'S COLONNADED MORTUARY TEMPLE *at Deir al-Bahari ("The Northern Monastery"), with Montuhotep II's smaller temple in the distance.*

Like other pharaohs throughout Egypt's history, Montuhotep began, in what remained of his fifty-one-year reign, to construct his royal tomb. But because he came from a part of Egypt with different funeral traditions from those of the previous Memphite kings, his architect built, in front of sheer cliffs across the river from Thebes, a huge temple on a platform surrounded by columns on all sides except the rear. On top, a hall led back to an open court running to the cliffs, with a shrine at its end for a statue of the king, but a tunnel running under the court ran deep into the cliffs to the actual tomb. To set off the sweeping building, a large garden in front was planted with scores of tamarisk and sycamore trees. This most elegant complex played the sweep of stacked colonnades against the simple ramp and open garden that led up to them. Walls behind the colonnades were carved with scenes of the pharaoh trampling enemies, hunting and planting seeds. But where, in all this architecture, was the traditional pharaonic pyramid? Viewed from the front, the cliffs behind Montuhotep's temple form a natural pyramid shape.

Pharaohs of the Middle Kingdom

DYNASTY	PHARAOH	DATES (B.C.E.)
XI	Montuhotep I	2060–2010
XI	Montuhotep II	2010–1998
XI	Montuhotep III	1997–1991
XII	Amenemhat I	1991–1962
XII	Senusert I	1971–1926
XII	Amenemhat II	1929–1895
XII	Senusert II	1897–1878
XII	Senusert III	1878–1841
XII	Amenemhat III	1798–1786
XII	Sobekneferu	1785–1782

Montuhotep II followed his famous father and namesake in building a similar mortuary complex, but he died after reigning only twelve years and never completed the building. Confusion followed. We have evidence of at least a six-year reign by a third Montuhotep, but hear no more from this family. During his short reign, Montuhotep III employed a man named Amenemhat, the son of a commoner named Senusert, as his vizier. After the dust had cleared, this Amenemhat emerged as Montuhotep's successor, beginning a great new dynasty, whose kings alternated the names Amenemhat and Senusert.

This newly royal family came from a small town in the center of Egypt that worshipped a god named Amun, "the Hidden One," who, from then on, except for a brief period of religious revolution 700 years later, became the chief god of Thebes, and so, in effect, for all Egypt. Amenemhat I established a new capital near modern Lisht, ten miles south of Memphis, which he called It-towe, "Grasping the Two Lands."

The great quantity of temples and tombs constructed during this dynasty testifies to Egypt's renaissance. Once more pyramids—even if only about 200 feet tall—were raised, some now (in homage to Montuhotep II) on terraces reached by an open ramp. Tombs of the pharaoh's courtiers are found clustered around his burial again, showing that the king's influence had regained its former importance. Despite his firm control of the country, however, Amenemhat lacked royal blood. To ensure his family's continuing reign, he initiated a practice adopted by successive rulers and made his son coregent for the last ten years of his thirty-year reign. Senusert I thus automatically became pharaoh when his father passed away, and during his forty-four-year reign he began the subjugation of the upper Sudan—"Kush" to the ancient Egyptians—building forts to maintain control of the gold Egypt consumed so insatiably. His successors solidified this conquest. Senusert I also built an elegant little temple at a place called Karnak, near Thebes, initiating what would become the largest religious complex in the world.

Successive Amenemhats and Senuserts took special interest in an area— called the Fayum today—which surrounds Egypt's one great lake. They substantially raised agricultural productivity there by constructing a thirty-mile canal that carried water from the Nile to increase the lake's size. Art flourished, as demonstrated by a trove of jewelry belonging to two daughters of Amenemhat II—Egyptian goldwork at its exquisite height. His successor Senusert II began the practice of using adobe bricks for the mass of a pyramid before covering them with fine polished stone, making them appear as substantial as the pyramids of old but with far less work. His grandson, Amenemhat III, enjoyed a forty-five-year reign, long enough to watch his own pyramid as it grew over the years. He built a residence nearby around which much of the government clustered, creating a crowded city so complex that the amazed Greeks later mistook it for the famed labyrinth. Although Amenemhat IV served briefly as copharaoh with his father, Amenemhat III, he died without heirs so his sister succeeded him. After a coregency with her father, Sobekneferu reigned at most three years before darkness again descended on Egypt. The line had run out.

Although half as long as the Old Kingdom, the Middle Kingdom was no less important or successful. During its flowering, the Egyptian language attained a level of refinement that ever after made it the model for good prose in ancient Egypt. Art achieved an elegant realism: for the first time, pharaohs' faces were shown with lines of care and age, rather than idealized. Buildings, though not as mammoth as those of the Old Kingdom, possess a refinement that makes them second to none. Egypt also mounted serious military expeditions into the Sudan, forays that would later extend throughout the Middle East. Even a thousand years later, Egyptians looked back on the Middle Kingdom as a glorious time.

SECOND INTERMEDIATE PERIOD (1782–1570 B.C.E.)

As Babylon first stirred, China became unified, and the pillars of Stonehenge rose, Egypt entered its second Dark Age. Repeating the pattern of the First Intermediate Period, more than 160 kings from three different dynasties ruled during a period that lasted only slightly more than a century and governed from three, or perhaps even four, different capitals. Once again the country had split apart into reduced kingdoms ruled by different pharaohs. In its weakened state Egypt became vulnerable to powerful tribes from central Russia, called the Indo-Europeans, who spoke the earliest form of the Greek language and evolved into the Mycenaeans of Homer's Trojan War. Flowing into the Mediterranean basin, the Indo-Europeans also conquered Turkey, later evolving into the Hittites who would become Egypt's rival for Middle Eastern dominance when she became strong again. Key to their conquests was a great new military weapon—the chariot—which, along with the horse, they introduced to Europe and the Middle East.

During this time, immigrants—either Indo-Europeans or those displaced by their raids—increasingly inundated Egypt from the area of modern-day Israel. Egypt's power vacuum permitted the new arrivals to gain control of the northern Delta and establish a capital at Avaris, in the extreme northeast. Called Hyksos ("foreign kings") by the Egyptians, their race is obscure, although some of their names, one of which sounds like "Yakeb-her," suggest Semitic roots. Regardless of their background, the Hyksos took on Egyptian trappings, built temples to Egypt's gods, wore Egyptian clothes and carved tens of thousands of small, beetle-shaped amulets, called scarabs, just as the Egyptians did. No matter; to the natives, these Hyksos remained "vile asiatics" and despised occupiers.

A Theban family, later referred to as the Seventeenth Dynasty, began the long effort to win Egypt back for the Egyptians. Since the mummy of the next to last leader of this family shows massive head wounds, it is obvious their effort did not go smoothly. Kamose, the final ruler of the dynasty, described the situation:

> What serves this strength of mine, when a chieftain is in Avaris, and another in Cush, and I sit united with an Asiatic and a Nubian, each man in possession of his slice of this Egypt, and I cannot pass by him as far as Memphis. See, he holds Khmun, and no man has respite from spoliation through servitude to the Setyu. I will grapple with him and slit open his belly. My desire is to deliver Egypt and smite the Asiatics.[5]

Kamose describes Egypt as divided into at least two kingdoms, with Kush ruled by a third king. He boasts, in his continuation of the story, of his march north with an army, his siege and destruction of Avaris and his safe return to Thebes. The facts, however, must have been somewhat different since the next Theban king also attacked Avaris, making Kamose's campaign appear more a raid than a conquest. Vanquishing the Hyksos became the task of his brother (or, possibly, nephew), Ahmose, who, during his twenty-five years of rule, not only captured Avaris but continued across the Egyptian border into Gaza to conquer a Hyksos stronghold. Ahmose returned to the south of Egypt and successfully recaptured Kush and its gold mines to complete the reunification of Egypt.

NEW KINGDOM (1570–1070 B.C.E.)

However pleased the Egyptians may have been to evict the Hyksos, they owed a great debt to their former occupiers. Egypt learned about chariots and horses from the Hyksos along with the secret of producing bronze, a metal harder than their copper. Battles against the Hyksos also led Egypt to look beyond its northern borders for the first time and, with a better-equipped army, eventually to dominate the Middle East. Each military success and the plunder that accompanied it encouraged successive pharaohs to donate temples to the god Amun of Thebes, raising that city to co-capital status with Memphis and its god to first place in Egypt's pantheon.

Ahmose is counted as the founder of the Eighteenth Dynasty, the beginning of the New Kingdom, which consisted of the Nineteenth and Twentieth dynasties as well. After twenty-five years spent in conquests, he passed the scepter to his son Amenhotep I who drove even farther south into Kush and began the custom of designating a government official as the "King's Son of Kush," to demonstrate this southern territory's annexation by Egypt. His successor, Tuthmosis I, was a commoner who attained the throne by marrying the eldest royal princess, for the Egyptian throne was passed through the female side. Tuthmosis forged south but took his army northeast as well, through modern Israel into Syria, even crossing the Euphrates River into Iran—the first major incursion into an area which would soon fall within Egypt's sphere of power.

Noteworthy as well were Tuthmosis' funerary preparations. By this time, Egyptians had learned the hard way that burying a royal body inside pyramids visible for miles only served as a challenge to tomb robbers: all the Old and Middle Kingdom pharaonic pyramids had been plundered. Tuthmosis attempted to foil the robbers by hiding his tomb. A desolate spot was found across the Nile from Thebes in a small valley that became known in Arabic as Wadi el Malook, the "Valley of the Kings." Here a great underground cave with halls and storage rooms was constructed into which Tuthmosis' body was laid to rest after his ten-year reign. The entrance was sealed, dirt was heaped over it, and all who had participated in the construction were sworn to secrecy. Hiding one tomb might have succeeded, but when scores of successive monarchs tried the same trick in the same three-acre valley, thieves soon caught on. All, except the tomb of Tutankhamen, were thoroughly robbed in ancient times.

Tuthmosis I's successor, Tuthmosis II, the son of a lesser wife, earned the throne by marrying his father's eldest daughter by his principal wife—that is, his half-sister. His death ended an undistinguished eighteen-year reign, and he

STATUE OF FEMALE PHARAOH HATSHEPSUT *(reign c. 1498–1483 B.C.E.) at her mortuary temple, with the characteristic crook, flail, and crown of Osiris, god of the afterlife.*

left a widow with no sons. Again the son of a lesser wife was chosen for the crown. Since Tuthmosis III was a child of only nine or ten when selected pharaoh, someone had to act as regent until the young king attained maturity. Hatshepsut, widow of the recently deceased king, seized the role and, in one of the stranger interludes in Egypt's history, was crowned as coruler two years into her regency, after which she appropriated all of the paraphernalia of a pharaoh. The fact that one pharaonic insignia was a beard gave Hatshepsut no hesitation: she is portrayed in statues and wall carvings with a delicate oval face ending in an incongruously false royal goatee. Scribes also had a problem, since the word for "pharaoh" was masculine and titles and common phrases were all designed for a male king. Referring to her, they as often wrote "his majesty" as they did "her majesty."

Pharaohs of the New Kingdom

DYNASTY	PHARAOH	DATES (B.C.E.)
XVIII	Ahmose	1570–1546
XVIII	Amenhotep I	1551–1524
XVIII	Tuthmosis I	1524–1518
XVIII	Tuthmosis II	1518–1504
XVIII	Tuthmosis III	1504–1450
XVIII	Hatshepsut	1498–1483
XVIII	Amenhotep II	1453–1419
XVIII	Tuthmosis IV	1419–1386
XVIII	Amenhotep III	1386–1349
XVIII	Akhenaten	1350–1334
XVIII	Smenkare	1336–1334
XVIII	Tutankhamen	1334–1325
XVIII	Ay	1325–1321
XVIII	Horemheb	1321–1293
XIX	Rameses I	1293–1291
XIX	Seti I	1291–1278
XIX	Rameses II	1279–1212
XIX	Merenptah	1212–1202
XIX	Amenmesses	1202–1199
XIX	Seti II	1199–1193
XIX	Siptah	1193–1187
XIX	Twosret	1187–1185
XX	Setnakhte	1185–1182
XX	Rameses III	1182–1151
XX	Rameses IV–XI	1151–1070

Her male garb was not intended to fool the citizens into believing their pharaoh was male. Statues unequivocally portray a female, whose sex, in any case, would have been obvious to any Egyptian from her name, "She Is First Among Noble Women." Rather than denying her femininity, she was proclaiming that she was also a pharaoh, an office that traditionally had been held by a man.

Hatshepsut proceeded to feminize Egypt. Her reign included no great military conquests; the art produced under her authority was soft and delicate; and she constructed one of the most elegant temples in Egypt against the cliffs outside the Valley of the Kings. Built beside the famous mortuary temple of Montuhotep I, Hatshepsut's version elongated the original design to produce a different aesthetic. A long ramp ascended to a wide terrace from a courtyard filled with pools and trees. Bordered by a sweeping wall of columns, the terrace stretched the length of Montuhotep's entire temple, and held a ramp that ascended to a second terrace, also lined by a sweeping wall of columns. Atop its columned halls, whose walls were covered with lovely carvings, stood the temple proper whose smaller rooms contained statues of the queen. Some wall scenes showed her birth as a divine event in which the god Amun disguised as her father Tuthmosis I impregnated her mother, indicating that the god had personally placed her on the throne. Another series depicts a large expedition she sent to Punt, probably modern-day Somalia on Africa's northeast coast, and the ships' return bearing myrrh, ebony, ivory, gold, baboons and leopard skins. Hatshepsut erected two huge obelisks in Karnak temple and claimed she had restored numerous temples throughout Egypt. Her tomb, where she was buried in the twentieth year of her rule, is located deep inside the cliffs that form the Valley of the Kings behind her temple. It also contained the sarcophagus of her father.

After Hatshepsut's death, her stepson and coruler, Tuthmosis III, came into his own. A year later he led a large army into the Middle East to reestablish the authority lost during Hatshepsut's reign. After a brilliant campaign, he returned with 2,000 horses, 1,000 chariots and assorted additional plunder. In one ten-year period, Tuthmosis conducted eight campaigns in this area, capturing all its major cities and crossing the Euphrates where records claim he took time to enjoy an elephant hunt in which he killed 132 of them. Tuthmosis carried Egypt's standard as far as it would ever reach, and, for this reason, he is considered Egypt's Napoleon. He also built extensively at Karnak and added his own obelisks near those of Hatshepsut.

Tuthmosis was also responsible for almost obliterating Hatshepsut's name from Egyptian history because as a female pharaoh she had upset *maat*—the normal order. Stone carvers were dispatched throughout the land to erase her name and face wherever they were found, and official lists of pharaohs claimed that Tuthmosis II was followed by Tuthmosis III, with no mention of Hatshepsut in between. Tuthmosis III, regarded as one of the greatest of all pharaohs, joined his ancestors in the next world in the fifty-fourth year of his reign.

In what had become custom, Tuthmosis III had associated his son with him on the throne before his death, so Amenhotep II came unquestioned to his crown. One would expect a son raised by a military father to seek approval through warrior skills—certainly he bragged about his strength and athletic prowess: according to one story, he shot an arrow through a metal plate as thick as the palm of a hand is wide. Nonetheless, after his father's death, Amenhotep II engaged in only two military campaigns during a twenty-five-year reign. His successor, Tuthmosis IV, boasted that he had received the throne as a reward from the Sphinx in return for uncovering it from the sand. Although the story is intriguing and the actual events are unknown, the need for such a story reveals that Tuthmosis IV's ascendance required some kind of serious intervention—thus the claim of divine assistance. In any case, although the young king reigned for thirty-three years, he conducted only one military expedition into Nubia.

His son, Amenhotep III, "the Magnificent," came to the throne when Egypt stood at the apex of its power and wealth, and he set out to enjoy his position to the fullest. His impeccable pedigree—pharaoh for a father and pharaoh's principal wife for a mother—allowed him to marry whomever he wished. He chose Tiye, the daughter of two commoners, then proclaimed throughout the land that she was now officially royal, his "great royal wife." Amenhotep III did whatever he wanted, and what he wanted most was to enjoy life and build monuments. Across the Nile from Thebes, where open land remained available, he built a splendid palace compound consisting of separate sumptuous buildings for himself and his staff and for the harem and its staff, as well as a kitchen, stables and barracks for his royal guards. There was also a festival hall for celebrating coronation anniversaries and an artificial lake, large enough to sail a royal barge. He also built a mammoth funerary temple, of which only two sixty-five-foot-tall seated statues of Amenhotep—the famed Colossi of Memnon—survive today, and he erected an entire temple, the largest built by any single person, in Thebes.

Despite a sybaritic life, personal tragedy struck near the end of his thirty-eight years as pharaoh. His eldest and favorite son died, leaving only a malformed younger son to carry on. After his father's death, this new pharaoh, Amenhotep IV, made a bid to change his world.

He began worshipping the visible sun, which he called the Aten, and he changed his own name to Akhen*aten* (Beneficial to the Aten). He added a new kind of temple within Karnak, the previous precinct of Amun. This temple, unlike Amun's dark and mysterious chambers, lay open to the sun. Finally, in a truly revolutionary move, Akhenaten decided that his god was the only god and that he could not worship his god in a place where other, false gods were celebrated. He moved his entire court to a desolate location in the middle of Egypt, near the modern city of Tel Amarna, where, since no town existed at the time, neither did temples to other divinities. There he built a large city from scratch—Akhetaten,

AMENHOTEP III'S COLOSSI OF MEMNON *statues at the Theban necropolis, across the Nile River from Luxor, Egypt.*

the "Horizon of the Aten"—complete with housing projects for workmen and government functionaries, temples and a magnificent palace. Surrounding the perimeter of the town, boundary markers proclaimed that he would never leave his new city. All those who could afford to do so began constructing their tombs in the hills nearby.

Not the least of Akhenaten's innovations was to change the art of Egypt. Before, art had been generic—individuals were portrayed by standard images of a man or of a woman—such that, even if the owner of a tomb were an old man, he was pictured as a perfectly formed, young person, indistinguishable from the owner of the next tomb. Scenes also were standard. Over and over we see the same pictures of a tomb owner seated at a table overflowing with food or we see him overseeing workers in a field. Intimacies are never displayed. All this changes radically with Akhenaten's reign.

New scenes appear. Now the pharaoh sits with a child on his lap, his wife rubs his chin, the pharaoh rubs noses with a daughter. (Egyptians did not kiss.) Contrasted with the intimacy that the pharaoh displays with those near and dear, commoners regularly now include a scene of the pharaoh rewarding them with honors.

The very picture of the royal body changes. Faces become unnaturally long and thin, eyes narrow to slits, the nose grows long, lips swell to bulbous masses, and a strange growth seems to bulge from the back of the head. The neck becomes swanlike, shoulders narrow along with arms, chests seem to grow breasts, stomachs swell as do thighs, but calves and ankles shrink. Nothing like this had been seen before or since. However, this new aesthetic did not survive its patron, Akhenaten.

Theories abound to attempt to explain this artistic revolution. Some see these strange images as realistic portrayals of a diseased Akhenaten. Indeed, an affliction called Marfan's Syndrome causes similar bodily changes. Yet Akhenaten's wife, Nefertiti, is similarly displayed, although, having a different mother and father, it is unlikely that she was similarly afflicted. Also, the famous and beautiful head of the queen shows a face normal in shape. Another theory, based on the fact that only royals were portrayed in this manner, sees the new artistic canon as a way to visually distinguish royals from commoners. Yet another theory points to

EIGHTEENTH DYNASTY PHARAOH AKHENATEN *(reign c. 1350–1334 B.C.E.) appears in this relief with his queen, Nefertiti, and three of their daughters.*

Akhenaten's break from the past in religion and sees a similar break in art based on non-Egyptian sources. However, no foreign art seems similar. All we can be sure of is that Akhenaten wanted to break as sharply with the past in how the world and its people were displayed as he had broken with the old religion. The specific standards of his new aesthetics, however, remain a mystery.

Akhenaten's religion is history's first recorded example of monotheism, and it did not fare well. Although Akhenaten worshipped his one god in Akhetaten, Egyptians elsewhere continued to celebrate all their traditional gods. Dismayed by their actions, Akhenaten sent stone carvers throughout Egypt to obliterate the names of the other divinities and close their temples, a gesture which changed few people's religious practices but forced them angrily underground. Unhappy too were the thousands of priests of the old gods who had, in effect, been thrown out of work by this revolutionary pharaoh, as well as the army who stood idle while the visionary Akhenaten preached a message of love and peace and Egypt's subject territories rebelled. It was an experiment that lasted only for the seventeen years of Akhenaten's reign and died with him.

Akhenaten's beautiful wife Nefertiti and five of their six daughters died before him, leaving only one daughter to carry on the line. Although she was only about nine years old, this daughter was married to the one surviving royal male—a half-brother roughly the same age—to give him a solid claim to the throne. The young couple moved back to Thebes, restored the old religion and changed their "Aten" names to Ankesenamen and Tutankhamen.

Obviously, two nine-year-old royals could not make these political decisions themselves. The power behind the throne was an aged vizier named Ay, who orchestrated a publicity campaign to present the new pharaoh as a friend of the old gods. He had Tutankhamen order the repair of the temples damaged during his father's religious revolution, add decoration to his grandfather's temple in Thebes and donate the largest gold idol ever of Amun, so heavy that thirteen priests were needed to transport it.[6] After only ten years of rule, at age nineteen, Tutankhamen died under highly suspicious circumstances.[7] Evidence points to the old vizier Ay who proceeded to marry Tutankhamen's widow in order to qualify himself for the pharaohcy. Whatever the circumstances surrounding his ascension, Ay lived only four years more, by which time no one of royal blood survived.

The next pharaoh was thus a commoner. The commander-in-chief of the army, Horemheb, used his power base to take control of the country and managed to enjoy an action-filled twenty-seven years on the throne. As can be expected from his background, he campaigned in the Middle East to reestablish Egypt's domination. He also built a splendid pair of pylons at Karnak. His most dubious architectural achievement involved directing workmen to comb all of Egypt to search out and eradicate every reference to Akhenaten, Tutankhamen and Ay and replace their cartouches with his own. He calculated the beginning of his reign from the death of Amenhotep III, pretending that these three subsequent kings had never existed. No wonder Tutankhamen's tomb was lost from sight until its discovery in modern times—officially he never lived.

Since Horemheb had no children, his death again left Egypt leaderless. His vizier, a former army buddy named Rameses, stepped in as Rameses I, the first of many pharaohs to bear that name. Rameses I founded the Nineteenth Dynasty, but since he was of the same generation as Horemheb, he came to his throne as an old man and lasted barely two years. His son, Seti I, hoping to ensure that the throne remained the province of his descendants, built a grand new temple, not at Thebes, but thirty miles north at Abydos, the precinct since primeval times of the old god Osiris. Inside, he constructed chapels for various gods of Egypt, creating a kind of national cathedral, and included a chapel for the worship of himself. His instant divinity notwithstanding, Seti I made certain his son was clearly associated with him before his thirteen years of rule ended. Rameses II, the Great, thus began his sixty-seven-year reign as a teenager.

During his first decade, Rameses the Great warred in the Middle East against Egypt's mighty new rival, the Hittite nation. After three campaigns, a treaty ended hostilities and Rameses's military efforts, but not his telling of them. Rameses inscribed temple after temple with words and scenes of his battles, and in every one his gigantic figure is portrayed single-handedly saving the day. One would think he fought hundreds of times. Since the rest of his long reign was spent building temples for more walls on which to boast of his few victories, his figure appears throughout Egypt and as far south as his imposing temple at

FOUR OF RAMESES II'S FIFTY SONS *are shown in this photograph. Often considered to be Egypt's greatest pharaoh, he probably lived past the age of 90.*

Abu Simbel—all smiting the same enemies over and over. His true talent lay, however, in producing offspring, and he proudly displayed the many names of his one-hundred-plus children. More statues and temples bear his name than that of any other pharaoh, but not because he created more, rather because, following the lead of Tuthmosis III and Horemheb, he substituted his name on whatever already existed.

His thirteenth oldest son, Merenptah—who, being middle aged when Rameses the Great died, reigned for only ten years—took up arms for a campaign in the Middle

THE GREAT TEMPLE AT ABU SIMBEL *consists of four colossal, 67-foot-tall statues of Ramses II carved into the side of a mountain.*

East, claiming to have destroyed all the small kingdoms there, including Israel. His sons, Amenmesses and Seti II, each served short reigns prior to the ascension of a pharaoh who, for some reason, was succeeded by his own father's widow, a queen buried in the Valley of the Kings. A decade of confusion followed before a new dynasty began.

The Twentieth Dynasty began with a king who did little in his two years of power except appropriate the tomb of the last queen of the previous dynasty. His son, Rameses III, who initially took that famous throne name to give himself additional stature, later earned it by saving Egypt. At the time, the whole Mediterranean area had been invaded by a migratory people who had conquered all the countries along their march, including Rameses the Great's enemy, the Hittites, before being turned away by the Egyptians in the Delta after a mighty land and sea battle. With their advance stopped, the invaders disbursed to settle elsewhere around the Mediterranean. (One tribe, called the Peleset, settled in the area thereafter named for them—Palestine; another, the Libu, took Libya; the Danu took Greece.) After the victory, Rameses III built a great temple on the west bank of the Nile opposite Thebes. The temple was unusual both because it annexed a palace and because it was fortified with guard towers and walls sixty feet high and twenty-five feet thick. On the awesome exterior walls of the temple his artists carved florid scenes of his great battle. The rest of Rameses III's reign of thirty-one years included an expedition to Punt for precious incense and another to the Sinai for turquoise.

Problems began to surface during his reign. An inscription reports that workmen in the royal necropolis went on strike because their pay was months in arrears. Another records the arrests of highly placed government officials and ladies of the harem for an attempt to assassinate the pharaoh. Something serious was amiss. Rameses III was succeeded by Rameses IV through Rameses XI, most of whom reigned only briefly. The next dynasty moved the capital to Tanis in the Delta, not far from the earlier Hyksos capital, so rulers could more easily monitor threats from the Mediterranean and the Middle East. As soon as the center of power moved from Thebes, more strikes occurred, tomb robberies increased, and the high priests of Amun grew ever more independent, even donning pharaonic crowns as part of their dress. The New Kingdom, like the Old and the Middle Kingdoms before it, gradually weakened and disappeared.

Never again would Egypt stand as tall as during this last of its great periods. It had achieved its greatest military prowess, dominating an area more than four times its own size and amassing riches such as no country had ever known. An indication of the vastness of its wealth can be measured by the treasures found in the tomb of one of the most insignificant of the era's pharaohs, Tutankhamen: the innermost of his three coffins was solid gold and weighed more than 200 pounds. Gold topped all the obelisks of Egypt, and the sanctuaries of most of the thousands of Egyptian temples were filled with golden idols of the gods. Egypt was rich, strong and proud throughout most of the glorious New Kingdom.

LATE PERIOD (1069–332 B.C.E.)

The Late Period consists of 500 years of ups that never attained the heights of earlier kingdoms and downs that reached the depths of the earlier intermediate periods. Heroic battles were fought and, at times, former glories were reasserted, but, over all, Egypt's dominance gradually weakened as outside forces challenged first its control of the Middle East then its very independence.

The next dynasty, the Twenty-first, after moving the capital north to Tanis, began burying their dead there. Two relatively undespoiled pharaonic tombs were discovered there during the previous century, whose scanty contents demonstrate how substantially Egypt's fortunes had changed. Strange events began toward the end of this dynasty when a Libyan prince living in Egypt somehow compelled the last pharaoh of the Twenty-first Dynasty to marry one of his daughters to his son. This Libyan prince, named Sheshonk (whom the Bible called Shishak when he sacked Jerusalem), became the first pharaoh of the Twenty-second Dynasty, and he used his son's royal connection to breed a line of Libyan pharaohs. In all, eight Libyans ruled for over 200 years, but when the line ran out, affairs in Egypt had reached a stage of chaos, and the next two dynasties ruled concurrently.

In the meantime, Egypt's old vassals in Kush had grown so Egyptianized that they viewed the collapse of traditional values in their mother country with disgust. A Kushite prince who rode north, conquered both of the competing pharaohs and began a Kushite dynasty, the Twenty-fifth Dynasty, had the misfortune of ascending the throne just as a great foreign power challenged its authority. After the warrior-nation Assyria conquered Palestine, it sent army after army against Egypt until it conquered Thebes and chased the Kushite pharaoh south. When the Assyrians returned home after plundering Egypt, the Kushite king came back, this time to meet defeat and death. After the same fate befell his successor, the Kushites decided their original home was a safer place than Egypt.

Rebellion against the Assyrians was finally organized by a family from the Delta town of Sais, who, aided by the distraction of Assyria's new competitor Babylon, expelled the invaders to found the Saite Twenty-sixth Dynasty. Wars between Assyria and Babylon allowed Egypt some breathing room. Pharaohs built monuments again, this time copying the art of the Old Kingdom—even inscribing the old Pyramid Texts in their tombs—to demonstrate their longing for the good old days. Concurrently, refugees from the Assyrian-Babylonian conflict poured into Egypt. There were Greeks in numbers sufficient to build a city of their own and Jews from Palestine.

The second of the Saite kings, Neko II, attempted to revitalize Egypt's economy. He broke ground for a canal to link the Red Sea with the Mediterranean, a forerunner of the Suez Canal, and commissioned a fleet of Phoenician ships to round Africa. But Egypt's period of quiet ceased before either project was completed when enemies came at her from several directions. Phrygian cavalry from the Caucasian Mountains charged up to the border and turned away only when bribed; Medes raided the Middle East; and, most worrisome of all, Babylon, after defeating Assyria, began to feel invincible. Neko died in a clash with the Babylonian king Nebuchadrezzar at Karcamesh in Syria in 605 B.C.E., along with most of his army. A few years and two pharaohs later, Nebuchadrezzar returned, besieging Jerusalem. Apries, the pharaoh at that time, saved it; but in 587 Nebuchadrezzar returned, destroyed Jerusalem and took its citizens captive to Babylon.

A revolt in Egypt brought the dynasty's last pharaoh, Amasis, to the throne. In what at first seemed a fortunate turn of events, the Babylonian threat ended when a new power, the Persians, sacked their city of terraced gardens. But if Persia could conquer mighty Babylon, she must have been powerful indeed. Persia first cleared the field by defeating the Medes and Lydians in Anatolia (Turkey), then turned serious attention to Egypt. King Cambyses brought a mighty army to meet Amasis in a battle that hung in the balance until the Egyptian lines broke. Amasis retreated south to Memphis where, after a long siege, he surrendered his country to the Persian king. The Twenty-seventh Dynasty thus consists of five Persian kings. But the Egyptians were not finished yet. After the Persians had been twice defeated by the Greeks, Egypt seized the opportunity to reassert its independence. Six pharaohs, divided into three brief dynasties, ruled from the Delta for sixty-one years, after which time the Persians, their strength renewed, reinvaded to establish Dynasty Thirty-one. In all, except for the sixty-one-year interlude of Egyptian independence, Persians ruled Egypt from 534 through 332 B.C.E. They met their match in Alexander the Great, the great warrior from Macedonia in northern Greece, who defeated the Persians in Anatolia before turning to Egypt, where he was welcomed as a savior and proclaimed pharaoh.

Alexander stayed only long enough to found Alexandria, his city on the Mediterranean, because the Persian king Darius III had raised another army to contest him. After defeating that army, Alexander made sure Darius would raise no more troops by chasing the Persian king as far as Afghanistan where he was killed by his own men. Far from home, Alexander decided to press on to India, battling his way to its southern shore. After receiving a serious wound in one of the final fights, Alexander made his way back to Babylon where he died in 323 B.C.E. from poison, dysentery or the effects of his wound. His death, which left the "world" he had conquered with no ruler, spurred various generals to lay claim to whatever part of Alexander's dominion they could. The commander of Alexander's personal guard, Ptolemy, seized Egypt to found its final dynasty, the Thirty-second Dynasty, named the "Ptolemaic" after its founder.

Egypt's last rulers were therefore Greeks without a drop of Egyptian blood because they married only other Greeks. The thirteenth of these Ptolemies, the celebrated Cleopatra, became embroiled in Roman politics when she cast her fortune first with Julius Caesar, then, after his death, with his protégé Marc Antony. Roman civil war between Antony, supported by Egypt's troops and fleet, and Julius Caesar's heir, Octavian, at the head of Rome's legions, went hard against Antony, who, in 30 B.C.E., chose suicide over captivity. Cleopatra's own suicide soon after Antony's reduced Egypt to a province of the Roman Empire and ended its independent history until modern times.

CLEOPATRA CONFRONTS CAESAR *after emerging from a rolled-up carpet in this 1866 painting by Jean-Leon Gerome (1824–1904).*

RELIGION

NOTHING AFFECTED THE EVERYDAY LIVES OF ANCIENT EGYPTIANS more than their religion which differed, both in theory and practice, from any we know today. Egyptians worshipped not a single god, but a vast array from which they could pick and choose. Common people took almost no part in religious rituals; that was the sacred responsibility of the priestly class. The afterlife was believed to be not an abstract spiritual realm, but a concrete, real destination mirroring life in this world. Finally, attaining eternal life did not require performing any good acts, but simply doing no wrong.

POLYTHEISM

It is difficult to imagine a time before the existence of science, but such was Egypt's situation throughout her entire 3,000-year history. Because no scientific principles existed to explain natural phenomena, Egyptians believed that whatever occurred in their lives or environment had a supernatural cause. Not understanding why events happened or how to control them, they considered something as familiar and central to their lives as the sun to be more than an astronomical object; it was the falcon god Ra. The Nile was not just a river obeying simple laws of nature, but the god Hapi, depicted as a hermaphrodite—a male with sagging breasts.

Egyptians depended on the good will of their gods to give them what they wanted. The disappearance of the sun each night, for example, frightened them into imagining that it made a dangerous journey past enemies who tried to prevent its reappearance in the morning. So they made offerings to the gods,

EIGHTEENTH DYNASTY PHARAOH TUTHMOSIS III *makes an offering to the falcon-headed god, Horus, in this colored relief at Hatshepsut's mortuary temple.*

prayed, did in general whatever they believed their gods might demand to ensure its return. Lacking scientific laws to explain diverse phenomena, they regarded each natural event as the province of a separate god and assigned that god personal characteristics and a physical form. Of course they did not really believe the sun was a bird or that a river had breasts. Wrestling with the impossible task of representing invisible powers in some concrete manner, they chose to symbolize a particular god as a creature or attribute that exhibited similar abilities: birds fly, breasts produce liquid.

At the peak of their civilization, during the Eighteenth Dynasty, Egyptians worshipped more than a thousand gods. Some were the same deity celebrated under different names in different cities, but most were separate gods.

Ancient Egyptians were not required to choose a single god to worship, unlike later practices of monotheism. In the case of childbirth, for example, several divinities were responsible for different aspects of the process. One, a pregnant hippopotamus called Tauret, the "Great One," protected a woman through the term of her pregnancy. Another, a lion-headed male dwarf named Bes, looked after the child when he was born. When a woman became pregnant, she wore an amulet of Tauret around her neck for protection, much as Christians wear saints' medals. After giving birth, the new mother donned a Bes amulet.

Despite an abundance of special-occasion gods, Egyptians believed that a few chief gods controlled everything in their world, including the lesser deities. In Memphis, the administrative capital of Egypt, priests credited the chief god Ptah, a human figure wearing a skullcap, with creating the world by imagining it in his mind, then uttering the word. Thebes celebrated a different major god—Amun, the "Hidden One"—with powers so great he could not be visualized, yet because he had to be represented in some way in order to pay him homage, he was depicted as a man with a tall ostrich plume crown. To introduce order into their large collection of gods, Egyptians placed each

PRINCIPAL GODS AND GODDESSES *of ancient Egypt.*

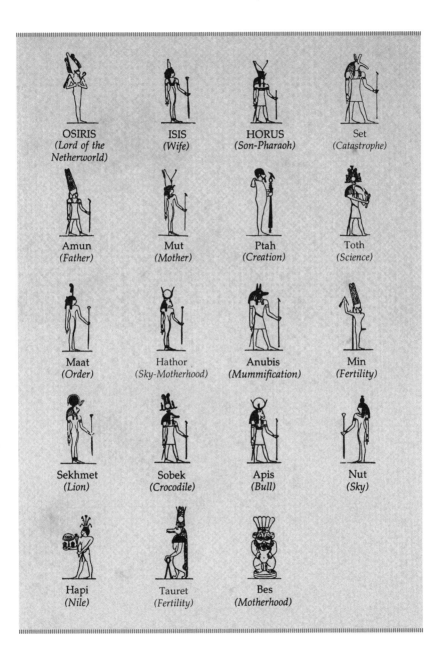

OSIRIS
(Lord of the Netherworld)

ISIS
(Wife)

HORUS
(Son-Pharaoh)

Set
(Catastrophe)

Amun
(Father)

Mut
(Mother)

Ptah
(Creation)

Toth
(Science)

Maat
(Order)

Hathor
(Sky-Motherhood)

Anubis
(Mummification)

Min
(Fertility)

Sekhmet
(Lion)

Sobek
(Crocodile)

Apis
(Bull)

Nut
(Sky)

Hapi
(Nile)

Tauret
(Fertility)

Bes
(Motherhood)

Major Egyptian Gods

NAME	DEPICTION	ATTRIBUTES
Amun	Man with tall crown of ostrich plumes	The "Hidden One," king of the gods, associated with the sun
Anubis	Jackal	God of embalming
Apis	Bull	Power and fertility
Aten	Solar disk	The sun
Bast	Cat or woman with cat head	Goddess of the East and of fire
Bes	Dwarf with feathered headdress, mane and tail	War and childbirth
Hapi	Man with breasts	The Nile
Hathor	Cow or woman with a crown of horns around the sun	Motherhood
Horus	Falcon or man with falcon head	Sky and protector of the pharaoh
Imhotep	Seated man with skullcap	Healing
Isis	Woman with crown, the sun between two horns	Magic
Khnum	Ram or ram-headed man	Creator
Maat	Feather or woman with single feather on her head	Divine order
Min	Man standing with erect penis	Fertility
Nut	Woman stretched across the sky	Sky

Osiris	Standing man wrapped as a mummy	Protector of the dead
Ptah	Man in sheathe with skullcap and staff	Wisdom and writing
Ra	Sun or falcon with sun headdress	Sun
Sekhmet	Woman with lioness' head	Dangers to humans
Seth	Doglike animal with pointed ears and forked tail	Evil
Sobek	Crocodile	Water dangers
Toth	Baboon or man with ibis head	Writing, knowledge

within a hierarchy based on their relative powers. Relying on the familiar, they collected their pantheon into "families" of threes—a father, mother and son—the first trinities, with the superiority of a chief god symbolized by his fatherhood. Memphis' chief god Ptah was paired with Sekhmet, a lioness; their son Nefertum appeared in human form with lotus plants on his head. Similarly, Amun's wife was Mut, a lioness-headed human; their son Khonsu took the form of a ram-headed human. One feature of polytheistic religions is that even if someone lived in Memphis and prayed to Ptah, he could still believe in Amun. The principle is the same as a baseball fan today who roots for the New York Yankees and believes they are the best team, yet knows that the Boston Red Sox are just as genuine. It is not that they don't exist; they just aren't your team.

Religious Practice

Egyptians also practiced their religion differently from modern people whose attendance is expected at a church, temple or mosque for participation in joint prayer, recitation of common beliefs and practice of rituals. Egyptian lives were so filled with gods they felt no need to set aside special times for praying together.

Only on rare festival days might groups congregate outside a temple to witness a performance of holy rites. In every other respect the business of religion was conducted entirely by proxy: only priests were permitted inside temples and only priests were allowed to perform the rituals. In effect, being a believer required no action whatsoever.

An Egyptian temple was a dark, mysterious place considered to be the divine residence of a specific god or god's family, rather than a communal gathering place for worshippers. Far inside, in the "holy of holies," the innermost room of the temple, stood a sacred statue of the temple god. These statues—usually bronze images up to two feet tall inlaid with gold and silver or, occasionally, composed of solid gold—were meticulously served and cared for by specially trained priests as if they were living gods. Each morning the priests opened the doors to the shrine, placed food before the statue for its first meal, painted cosmetics around its eyes, perfumed it, and dressed it in white linen. These rituals complete, they closed the doors to the shrine until it was time for the next rites. The only occasion an average Egyptian might see his cult statue was on important festival days when people crowded into temple courtyards for rare glimpses of their god's image as it was carried outside on portable litters of gilded wood.

According to ancient texts, these cult statues could nod their heads and talk. Perhaps the reality was that priests secretly pulled strings to make the head move, spoke for the god by throwing their voices, or otherwise represented their own words as the deity's. Whatever the illusion employed, statues were consulted for their opinions on a variety of personal problems; one ancient record even credited a statue with solving a crime.

A papyrus in the British Museum describes a theft that took place in Thebes. When, during the festival of Opet, the great statue of Amun was carried from Luxor to Karnak Temple, about a mile and a half away, a citizen named Amunemwia who guarded the storehouse of a nobleman appeared before his local statue to report that five colored shirts had been stolen while he napped one day. Addressing the statue, he asked, "My good and beloved lord, wilt thou give me back their theft?" to which the papyrus states that "the god nodded very greatly." Amunemwia began to read a list of townspeople. The statue, upon hearing the name of the farmer Pethauemdiamun, nodded and said, "It is he who stole them." When the accused farmer was dragged in front of the statue he denied the theft and appealed to the oracle of his own district, Amun of Te-Shenyt, whose judgment agreed with the first statue. Pethauemdiamun again denied the theft and was brought before a third statue, Amun of Bukenen, "in the presence of many witnesses," with the same result. Returning to the original statue of Amun of Pe-Khenty, Pethauemdiamun was forced to ask, "Was it I who took the clothes?" When he received an affirmative nod he finally broke down and confessed. He was beaten a hundred times with a palm-rib and made to swear that, if he went back on his word to return the clothes, he would be thrown to the crocodiles.

A PAINTED CARVING OF A SACRED "BARQUE," *representing the symbolic journey to the afterlife. During the Opet festival, statues of gods were placed in these boats, which were carried by priests from the Precinct of Amun-Re at Karnak to the Luxor Temple.*

Cult statues even served as judges in courts of law. In a case involving a dispute over the ownership of a tomb, an oracle actually—somehow—wrote its decision. A workman named Amenemope had laid claim to a tomb he said belonged to his ancestor Hai, but necropolis officials who inspected the site questioned his claim when they found only a coffin with no name, funerary equipment or offerings. To settle the matter, Amenemope appealed to his local god who, according to his own account, "gave me the tomb of Hai in writing"—a mystery indeed. Perhaps two papyri—one supporting Amenemope's claim, the other denying it—were presented to the statue who indicated his choice with a "nod."

Another case, involving a dispute over a house, is recorded on a pottery fragment in the British Museum. The builder Kenna had found an abandoned house in poor repair and renovated it for himself, but he was prevented from moving in by his neighbor, Mersekhmet, who claimed that he had previously consulted the statue of Amenhotep I and been told that he and Kenna should share the house. Kenna decided to take the case before the same statue in the presence of witnesses. As townspeople assembled outside the temple, the "carriers of the god" paraded the statue for all to see and heard the god say, "Give the dwelling to Kenna its owner again . . . no one shall divide it." Perhaps one of the priests uttered the actual words. In any event, Kenna got his house.

Although temples generally employed groups of priests to tend cult statues, say prayers and conduct temple business, during Egypt's earliest history, pharaohs bore the sole responsibility for maintaining divine order by acting as high priest, in addition to serving as king. As Egypt grew more populous, pharaohs no longer had time to perform all the duties and rituals demanded by the burgeoning numbers of temples. The designees who were selected as stand-ins evolved into Egypt's priestly class. Because they merely represented the pharaoh, these men were not required to hold deep religious convictions; only their duties distinguished them from other government workers. Priests, in fact, often held regular jobs as carpenters, scribes, or goldsmiths in addition to their religious responsibilities because most worked in the temple only a total of three months a year: their tours of duty lasted thirty days, followed by three months of secular life.

Because each temple needed some full-time person to manage its operations, the position of first god's servant evolved. As temples grew more complex and powerful, these men oversaw temple-owned farms, fields, cattle, and orchards and managed the temple staff. The position carried such responsibility and power that parents frequently advised their children to become scribes because it was from these ranks that first god's servants were chosen. In the case of large temples, second and third god's servants existed beneath the first god's servant; beneath them were endless other priests, each performing a specific job.

Regular priests fell into two categories: those directly responsible for the cult statue and those who performed other kinds of religious duties. *Wab* priests, held to the highest standards of cleanliness because they came in contact with the cult statue, shaved all their body hair to avoid lice and wore nothing but pure white linen clothing. Even their internal purity was monitored: they had to swear they had not recently eaten fish, considered ritually unclean, before touching the idol. Other priests, called "scroll carriers," managed the sacred scrolls in the temple library, recorded donations and estate revenues, kept inventory and recited prayers. When the bakers, beer brewers and cooks, who supplied each temple with offerings, and the farmers, herdsmen and overseers of the temple estates were all counted, these thousands and thousands of religious functionaries in ancient Egypt formed the largest bureaucracy, in terms of percentage, the world had ever seen.

Priests were primarily paid—directly or indirectly—from the pharaoh's coffers. When warrior pharaohs returned from conquered foreign lands with gold and other booty, they donated a portion of their plunder to the temples, both in gratitude for the gods' favor and to ensure their continued goodwill. Foreign conquests also supplied Egypt with captives who provided an important source of manpower for temple construction and work on temple estates. Further adding to the wealth of the temples, pharaohs often donated large tracts of their own land to temples as continuing annuities until the holdings of Egypt's religious orders paralleled those of the Roman Catholic Church in Medieval Europe—each growing to rival the wealth of its kings.

Egyptian priests spent little time dealing with the well-being of individuals, seldom advising or counseling those with personal problems, but concentrating instead on cosmic matters such as keeping the sun in the sky and ensuring the fertility of the land. Any individual who desired special favors from the gods could, however, pay for offerings and prayers that priests would perform on their behalf.

The only other personal service priests regularly performed for believers was to interpret their dreams—also for a fee. One might even arrange to spend the night near a temple god, hoping to receive a divine message during sleep. Since all dreams were considered prophetic, the key lay in their interpretation, a service priests performed with the help of special books. Since these books were written thousands of years before the idea of an unconscious mind, they ignore the possibility that a dream might result from the dreamer's experiences.

Along the right-hand margin of one surviving copy of a *Dream Book*[1] run the words, "If a man sees himself in a dream"; an accompanying horizontal line describes a dream and categorizes it as either "good" or "bad" and why, as in these examples:

Dream	Prophecy
Killing an ox	Good. Enemies will be removed from one's presence.
Seeing a large cat	Good. A large harvest is coming to the dreamer.
Climbing a mast	Good. He will be suspended aloft by his god.
Seeing one's face leopard	Good. Authority will be gained over the as a townsfolk.
A dwarf	Bad. Half his life is gone.
Bare backside	Bad. He will soon be an orphan.
Picking dates	Good. He will find food from his god.

A dream's details, not its theme, determined its meaning: Egyptians viewed their dreams as messages from the gods. Regardless of who the dreamer was, dream symbols were universal, carrying the same message for everyone.

LIFE AFTER DEATH

No civilization ever invested more faith, energy or money in attaining life after death than ancient Egypt. Its people loved life, yet made extensive and costly preparations for death because their religion promised they would live again—just as the myth of Isis and Osiris taught.

Isis and Osiris had unusually strong bonds with one another; according to the myth, they were both brother and sister and husband and wife. Isis was a fabled magician and Osiris was credited with bringing civilization first to Egypt—by introducing domesticated animals and farming into the formerly precarious existence along the Nile Valley—and then to the world. When Osiris returned from his travels, his evil brother Seth invited him to a great banquet, after which he offered a prize to whoever could fit inside a wooden chest he had previously constructed to Osiris' exact body measurements. When Osiris climbed inside, Seth immediately sealed the lid, poured molten lead over it, and threw it into the Nile. Isis set out to recover his body, found it in a foreign country and brought it back to Egypt for a proper burial. But Osiris' tribulations were not over. When evil Seth discovered the grave, he hacked the body into fourteen pieces and scattered them throughout Egypt. Undaunted, and trusting in her magic, Isis recovered all the pieces but one—the penis, which had been thrown into the Nile and eaten by fish. She reassembled her deceased husband, fashioned an artificial penis to replace the missing part, then, assuming the form of a bird, hovered over Osiris' body until he came back to life. Thus revived—remember this is a myth—Osiris impregnated his wife before departing to become ruler of the next world.

AN ANCIENT BRONZE *statue of the god Osiris, who presided over the land of the dead.*

No one knows whether this ancient myth gave the Egyptians their first ideas about the hereafter or whether the myth was invented later to explain ideas that already existed. In either case it contains their most basic beliefs about death; even the box that fit Osiris later became their human-shaped coffin. It demonstrates the Egyptians' most important religious belief: resurrection—that a physical body would literally revive in the next world, just as Osiris was magically reanimated. To gain a perfect eternal life required an intact body. Isis went to such lengths to retrieve the corpse of her husband for a proper burial because, if she had not pieced together his dismembered body—the vehicle for eternal life—he could not have been resurrected.

Certain ideas about life after death evolved over time. Originally, immortality was not thought to be parceled out equally: only the pharaoh was assured eternal life, a reasonable assumption given that he alone descended from the gods. It was believed that a nonroyal Egyptian's best chance for eternal life was to be buried near his pharaoh's pyramid in hopes that the king would take some commoners with him to the next world. Our earliest known writings about resurrection were found on the walls of the royal pyramid of Unas, the last king of the Fifth Dynasty, and include hundreds of magical inscriptions in vertical lines running from ceiling to floor. These hieroglyphic "utterances," referred to as Pyramid Texts, detail the three stages of a pharaoh's transition to the next world: awakening in the pyramid, ascending through the sky to the netherworld, and finally being admitted into the company of the gods. The principle behind all the spells is the same: the word is the deed. Saying something, or having it inscribed on a pyramid wall, made it so.

According to these texts, the king's body rested in its burial chamber until it was time to travel through the sky to the next world—somewhere to the west because that was the place where the sun died each day. (Fittingly, Osiris, god of the dead, was called the "Lord of the West" and the dead were referred to as "westerners.") When its journey was complete, a pharaoh's body would be welcomed by Osiris to begin its eternal life, an existence that would continue much as it had in this world. A pharaoh would need clothes, furniture, food and drink, all of which had to be buried with the body.

Next to Unas' pyramid stood a mortuary temple where commissioned priests made offerings of food and drink for the sustenance of his eternal body. The offering of prayers was also considered essential for eternal life. Because Egyptians realized their priests were fallible, often lazy, setting up a fund to pay for the prayers was no guarantee they would be made. In the event the priests did not do their job, some of the prayers were also inscribed on one wall of the pyramid's burial chamber so that the written word could substitute for the spoken:

> Oh Unas, stand up. Sit down to thousands of loaves of bread and thousands of jars of beer. The roast for the double rib is from the slaughter house, thy retch-bread is from the Wide Hall. As a god is supplied with the offering meal, Unas is supplied with his bread.[2]

Although the Pyramid Texts applied only to royalty, during the lawlessness that followed the collapse of the Old Kingdom, pyramids were opened and robbed, allowing commoners to learn about the spells. By the Eleventh Dynasty, with stability restored, nonroyals began inscribing similar writings on the sides of their own coffins to assure their own immortality. Known as "Coffin Texts," they are variations of the Pyramid Texts, with the same concern—the well-being of the deceased. Eventually, these spells became so numerous that they no longer fit on the coffin, which led to their being written on rolls of papyrus that were placed inside the coffin and today are referred to collectively as the *Book of the Dead.*

Although not a book in the sense of a single work but many versions of roughly the same material, each consisted of a collection of spells, incantations, prayers, hymns and rituals. The various versions—among them numbering about 400 different spells—have been standardized and codified by Egyptologists for ease of reference. Any spell dealing with the deceased's heart, for example, is called chapter 30.

As customers eager for immortality increased, books of the dead became a major industry for scribes who made thousands of copies. Naturally, quality varied greatly. Some scrolls stretched as long as ninety feet with beautifully colored paintings to illustrate different spells; others were brief with no illustrations. In general, people got what they paid for. Many of the books were, at least for the period, mass produced. Places for the deceased's name were left blank—the first "forms" in history—until purchase, when a scribe would fill in the appropriate information. Because these scrolls were written before an owner was known, their language had to be general; for example, "Ask the local god of your town for power in your legs" instead of calling the god and the owner by their names. Mistakes were made: a scribe might not understand what he was writing or be careless; sometimes the same spell was repeated in different parts of the same papyrus because two scribes worked simultaneously on different sections of the same book. Even illustrations in mass-produced work could prove problematic. Artists sometimes drew their pictures on the top of sheets before scribes wrote the appropriate text below; if an artist left insufficient room for the words, chapters might be severely abbreviated or condensed, sometimes to the point of unintelligibility, or the picture might illustrate a different spell. Despite all these mistakes and problems, however, such papyri provide abundant information about ancient Egyptians' understanding of life after death.

To achieve an afterlife, Egyptians expected two final judgments, crucial tests to be passed before admittance into the next world. One was beyond the deceased's control; the other was based on his persuasive skill. The first test placed the heart of the deceased on one side of a balance scale whose other pan held a feather. Since the feather hieroglyph (β) stood for the word *maat* or "truth," this test examined the heart to determine how truthful the person had been in life. Osiris is usually depicted presiding over the judgment to ensure fairness while the god of writing, Toth, records the result. If the dead person failed the test, his heart was thrown to a creature with the body of a hippopotamus and the head of a crocodile who destroyed the person by eating his heart. Egyptians sent no one to Hell, only out of existence. After surviving the balance scale test, the deceased would be ushered into the Hall of Double Truth for a second judging by a tribunal of forty-two gods. He would be required to "separate himself from

IN THE "WEIGHING OF THE HEART" *ceremony, the deceased's heart is weighed against the feather of truth, as Toth—the ibis-headed god of writing—records the result.*

evil doings" by making a plea, convincing each god that he had never done a specific wrong.

One purpose of the *Book of the Dead* in guiding the deceased through the judgment process was to reveal the names of the forty-two judging gods, because Egyptians believed that knowing someone's name gave them power over that person. (Amun, for example, was considered so mighty that "only his mother knew his name.") The petitioner was told to gain the upper hand by greeting each god in turn by saying his name, then instructed as to which sin to deny to satisfy that particular deity. For example:

Hail Strider, coming forth from Heliopolis. I have done no wrong.

Hail Eater-of-Shadows, coming forth from the caverns. I have not slain men.

Hail He-Whose-Two-Eyes-Are-on-Fire, coming forth from Sais. I have not defiled the things of the gods.

Hail Breaker-of-Bones, coming forth from darkness. I have not transgressed.

Hail Doubly-wicked, coming forth from Ati. I have not defiled the wife of any man.

Hail Disposer-of-Speech, coming forth from Weryt. I have not inflamed myself with rage.

Hail Provider-of-Mankind, coming forth from Sais. I have not cursed God.

Hail White Teeth, coming forth from Ta-she. I have not slaughtered the divine cattle.

If the deceased passed this second test and was declared "true of voice," he earned passage to the netherworld and became a "westerner," ready to be welcomed by Osiris. Egyptians focused so much attention on the importance of their physical bodies that it may seem as if they lacked any concept of a soul. In fact, however, they had such an abstract concept. In chapter 125 of the *Book of the Dead*, the dead person's soul is represented as a heart, but the fully evolved theory was more sophisticated. A soul was thought to be made up of several parts, the most important of which were the *ba* and the *ka*.

The *ba* was represented as a bird with the head of the deceased. Since the *ba* of a living person was rarely spoken of, we can deduce that it came into independent existence only when someone died and so resembled modern concepts of a soul. But unlike its modern counterpart, an Egyptian *ba* had physical needs. Relatives of the deceased were supposed to leave offerings in front of the tomb to feed the *ba* until it reached the next world; paintings in the *Book of the Dead* even show the *ba* flying around the tomb or outside it. One amusing papyrus tells the story of a man who laments the sad state of the world and considers killing himself while his *ba* ironically argues with him, threatening to desert him in the next

THE SOUL (BA) OF THE DEAD *was represented as a bird, perhaps symbolizing its weightlessness, as shown in this painted relief from the cow goddess Hathor's temple at Dendera.*

world if he commits the deed. A special spell in the *Book of the Dead*, "Causing the Uniting of the *ba* and its body in the Netherworld," ensured that his *ba* would be reunited with the deceased.

> Oh great god, cause that my *ba* may come to me from any place where it is. If there is a problem, bring my *ba* to me from any place where it is. . . . If there is a problem, cause my *ba* to see my body. If you find me Oh Eye-of-Horus, support me like those in the Netherworld. . . . May the *ba* see the body and may it rest upon its mummy. May it never perish, may it not be separated from the body forever.—Say this spell over an amulet of the ba made of gold, inlaid with stone that is placed on the deceased's neck.[4]

The soul's second element was called the *ka*, a kind of spiritual duplicate of the deceased that required a place to dwell—preferably the mummified body. A wealthy Egyptian would be buried with a *ka*-statue, a likeness of himself that the *ka* would recognize and in which it could live, in the event that his body was later destroyed.

MUMMIFICATION

Preserving the physical body after death became, over the centuries, a kind of Egyptian industry. At first, the dead were simply placed in sand pits and covered with more sand. Contact with the hot, dry granules quickly dehydrated the body and created natural mummies. Later, as burials became more elaborate, bodies were placed in rock-cut tombs but, away from the drying sands, they soon decomposed. Artificial mummification was needed to dehydrate the body before burial.

When someone died, a member of his family ferried across the Nile to embalming shops on the west bank where a type of mummification, which varied according to price, was chosen. Much as we hire hearses today, a special funerary boat was rented for the occasion to transport the corpse to the shop where it was deposited for seventy days. Female mourners who

FOUND IN TUTANKHAMEN'S TOMB, *this gilded wooden statue represented his* ka, *or spiritual double.*

accompanied the body were paid to weep, wail and throw sand on their heads in traditional gestures of lament.

The mummification process removed the moist internal organs which cause a body to decompose. In the most expensive method of mummification, the brain was drained out through the nasal passages after a long, needlelike instrument was inserted through the nostril to break into the brain cavity, then a thin tool with a hook, resembling a coat hanger, was pushed into the cranium and rotated to break the brain into pieces. When the cadaver was turned upside down, the mixture ran out through the nostrils. The brain was one of the few parts of the body embalmers discarded because it was thought to serve no useful function. Egyptians believed people thought with their hearts—when thoughts excite us, our hearts beat more quickly.

Embalmers next removed the organs inside the torso through a small abdominal incision in the left side. The stomach, intestines, liver and spleen were all pulled through this hole, but the heart was left in place so the deceased, once resurrected, would be able to think and say the magical spells necessary to become reanimated. Organs were individually stored in one of four jars specially made for the purpose, each with a lid carved in the shape of one of the four sons of Horus: Mesti, the human headed son; Duamutef, the jackal; Hapi, the baboon; and Qebesenef, the hawk. These jars were called "canopic" jars by early Egyptologists because the Greek god Canopus was worshipped in the form of a jar. A fluid, called the "liquid of the children of Horus" was poured over the internal organs to preserve them and the jars were sealed. Finally, priests recited prayers to invoke the protection of Horus' sons.

> Mesti says: I am Mesti, thy son, Osiris. I come so that I may protect thee.
>> I cause thy house to prosper, to be firm, by the command of Ptah, by the command of Re himself.
> Hapi says: I am Hapi, thy son, Osiris. I come so that I may protect thee.
>> I bandage for thee thy head and thy limbs, killing for thee thy enemies under thee. I give to thee thy head forever.
> Duamutef says: I am thy son, Horus, loving thee. I come to avenge my

father, Osiris. I do not permit his destruction to thee. I place it under
thy feet forever and ever.

Qebesenef says: I am thy son Osiris. I have come that I may protect thee.
I gather together thy bones, I collect thy limbs, I bring for thee thy
heart. I place it upon its seat in thy body. I cause thy house to prosper.[5]

Now the body was ready for drying. Natron, a naturally occurring
compound of sodium carbonate, sodium bicarbonate and sodium chloride,
basically baking soda and table salt, was shoveled onto the body until it was
completely covered. Given the human body's large mass and approximately 75
percent water content, more than 600 pounds of natron and forty days were

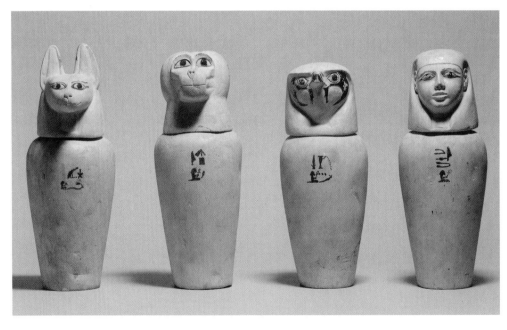

THIS SET OF CANOPIC JARS *(c. 850 B.C.E.) display the four sons of the god Horus. The
jackal-headed Duamutef protected the stomach; the falcon-headed Qebehsenuef, the
intestines; the baboon-headed Hapi, the lungs; and human-headed Imsety, the liver.*

necessary to complete dehydration. The abdominal and chest cavities were then washed with palm wine and aromatic spices and packed with resin-soaked linen that would harden to maintain the body's original contours. For less expensive mummifications, sawdust and onions placed in small linen bags were used as body-packing material, and the face was padded with linen in the cheeks and under the eyelids. (In one instance, onions were even placed in the eye sockets.)

Last, the body was anointed twice from head to toe with oils mixed with frankincense, myrrh and the same lotions used in daily life—cedar oil, Syrian balsam and oil of Libya. (Wealthy Egyptian ladies kept seven small alabaster vases of these oils on their boudoir tables, just as a modern woman might have a selection of perfumes.) A priest wearing a jackal mask recited a prayer while the anointing oils were poured:

> Thou hast received the perfume which shall make thy members perfect. Thou receivest the source (of life) and thou takest the form of it to give enduring form to thy members; thou shall unite with Osiris in the Great Hall. The unguent cometh unto thee to fashion thy members and to gladden thy heart, and thou shalt appear in the form of Ra; it shall spread abroad the smell of thee in the nomes of Aqert. . . . Thou receivest the oil of the cedar in Amentet, and the cedar which came forth from Osiris cometh unto thee.[6]

Next, bandages, which could come from the bedding of the deceased or other linen scraps, were torn into strips as long as fifteen feet by four inches wide and rolled, prior to use, like modern bandages, then applied according to a fixed ritual. First, each finger and toe was wrapped individually, with wealthy clients receiving gold covers for toes and fingers as additional protection—pure gold was the metal of eternity because it does not tarnish. The head was bound tightly to reveal the contours of the face: two bandages wrapped the top of the head, two the mouth, four the neck, and so on, as precisely dictated by ritual, while priests recited a prayer ensuring the deceased's ability to see and breathe in the netherworld:

Grant thou that breathing may take place in the head of the deceased in the under-world, and that he may see with his eyes, and that he may hear with his two ears; and that he may breathe through his nose; and in the underworld.[7]

The arms, feet and torso were bandaged last. Magic amulets were also usually placed within the wrappings to protect the mummy until it was resurrected in the west.

When the mummification was complete, the family returned to the west bank of the Nile with an entourage of friends, mourners and dancers. Servants

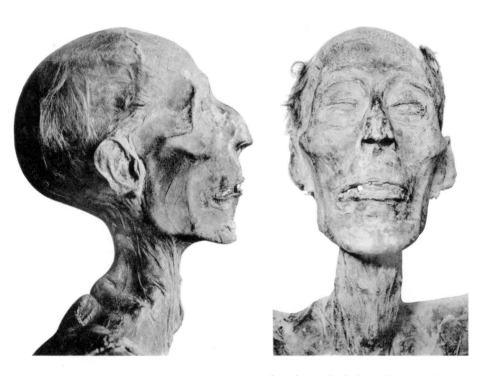

THIS PHOTOGRAPH OF THE RAMSES II MUMMY *shows how well a body can be preserved over thousands of years.*

carried furniture, clothing and food to be placed in the tomb and bore the mummy to its final resting place. Next came the most important of all the resurrection rituals: the "opening of the mouth" ceremony. Involving more than a dozen participants, the ceremony was a play, perhaps the oldest in history, that took place in front of the tomb on the day of burial. The ground on which the play was to be performed was purified with water from four vases representing the corners of the earth. An officiating priest, reading from a papyrus roll, described how the rituals and speeches should proceed. Actresses, often members of the family, portrayed Isis and her sister Nephthys; males acted as the guardians of Horus and a central character called "The-son-who-loved-him." After incense was lit and various gods invoked, a calf was slaughtered to commemorate the battle in which Horus avenged the murder of his father, Osiris. (In the continuation of the Isis and Osiris myth, Seth's conspirators, attempting to escape the avenging Horus by changing into various animals, were caught by Horus and decapitated.) Special animals were ritually killed, including two bulls (one for the north and one for the south), gazelles and ducks. One leg from the bull of the south was cut off and, along with its heart, offered to the mummy.

The play ended with a ceremonial opening of the mouth as a priest touched a special implement, shaped like a miniature adz (↰), to the mummy's mouth as he recited:

> Thy mouth was closed, but I have set in order for thee thy mouth and thy teeth.
> I open for thee thy mouth, I open for thee thy two eyes. I have opened thy mouth with the instrument of Anubis, with the iron implement with which the mouths of the gods were opened. . . .
> You shall walk and speak, your body shall be with the great company of the gods. . . .
> You are young again, you live again.[8]
> You are young again you live again.

AN AMULET-PENDANT OF TAWERET,
*the "Great [Female] One," represented as a
pregnant hippopotamus with lion paws and
a crocodile back and tail. She was believed to
protect pregnant women and small children.*

The mummy was now ready for its resurrection in the West. The tomb was sealed while friends and relatives sat together outside to share a meal in memory of the deceased.

AMULETS

In the face of uncontrollable natural events, the average Egyptian tried to protect himself with magical amulets. The Egyptian word for amulet, *meket*, even meant "protector" and was supposed to gain a god's intervention for the wearer. These small images were usually crafted with tiny holes so they could be strung and worn around the neck.

Amulets could be made of stone (lapis lazuli, carnelian, turquoise, feldspar, serpentine and steatite), metal (silver and gold were the most valuable, but bronze was also prized), or wood and bone (inexpensive substitutes for poorer people). Of all the materials used, the commonest was a ceramic called faience, a paste of ground quartz and water molded into a desired shape, fired solid in a kiln, then covered with a glassy glaze that added color. Faience amulets were produced by the thousands in factories throughout Egypt. A master amulet of some durable material, such as stone, was pressed into soft clay, which, when baked, became a hard mold into which the faience mixture could be placed. Any number of molds could be made from the master amulet, so thousands of duplicate amulets could be easily produced. Holes were made by rolling a string in quartz paste and pressing it into the mold; when fired, the paste hardened into faience and the string burned away, leaving a hole.

Amulets were designed according to strict rules. The MacGregor Papyrus lists seventy-five amulets with their names and functions. Another list inscribed on the walls of the temple of Dendera specifies the materials from which each should be made. Egyptians believed that an amulet made from the wrong material would be ineffective but, if a person could not afford a carnelian amulet, then a faience amulet glazed the same rust color would do.

Amulets invoked the gods; for example, a cat amulet carried the protection of the cat goddess Bastet. One of the most common amulets worn in ancient Egypt was the Udjat ("restored") eye (👁), associated with the falcon god Horus. According to myth, Horus fought his evil uncle Seth to avenge the death of his father, Osiris. During the battle, Horus' eye was torn to pieces, but Toth, the god of writing, assembled the pieces and restored his eye. Thus, amulets depicting the characteristic markings around a falcon's eye became a sign of health and well-being. The most popular amulet of all was associated with the god Khepri, who took the form of a beetle (🪲), Carved in the shape of a species of beetle called *Scarabaeus sacer*, from which the modern word scarab comes, these amulets enjoyed great popularity for a combination of reasons. The Egyptians were fond of puns, and the hieroglyphs for beetle also meant "to exist," so if you wore a scarab amulet, your continued existence was ensured. The scarab was also held in high regard because the ancient Egyptians believed this beetle produced offspring without any union of the male and female of the species. After fertilization the female deposited her eggs in a piece of dung and rolled it into a ball which provided their newborn with food. Since this birth was the only part of this reproductive cycle Egyptians witnessed, they assumed the beetle was somewhat like the god Atum who begot children without a female partner. Further, after the beetle fashioned its dung ball, it rolled it to a sunny place, which, to the ancient mind, resembled the journey of the sun across the sky. The top of a scarab amulet was carved to resemble the beetle's body, the bottom was left flat for an inscription, often merely the owner's name which symbolically requested "keep So-and-So in existence," but frequently a god's or a pharaoh's name was inscribed. Wealthy people set their scarabs in rings so they could be used as seals. The top of a wine jar sealed with moist plaster would be given a scarab imprint to keep thirsty servants at bay; a broken seal could not be repaired undetected.

MONOTHEISM: THE ABBERATION

For almost all of Egypt's 3,000 years of recorded history, the same gods were an integral part of daily life. From the time an Egyptian baby was born under the protection of Bes, until the time he died and went West to Osiris, the old-time religion governed his life. Through thousands of years of constancy only once were the old gods of polytheism banished and replaced with monotheism. For a brief seventeen-year span, every Egyptian, from high official to peasant, was pressured to alter his beliefs.

Egypt had reached its greatest glory by the end of the Eighteenth Dynasty—its temples were wealthy, its people prosperous, its army unrivaled. Amenhotep III luxuriated on his throne at this best of all times, proudly dedicating the greatest temple any pharaoh ever built to the great god of Egypt, Amun. At his death it was assumed that his son would carry on the traditions of his forebears. Yet, after ruling only a few years, the new pharaoh changed his name from Amenhotep IV ("Amun is pleased") to Akhenaten ("It is beneficial to the Aten") and declared there was only one god, the Aten. In history's first recorded instance of monotheism, old temples and thousands of priests were no longer supported by the pharaoh, and Egyptians were told that the gods they had always worshipped had ceased to exist. The effect on society was cataclysmic.

Partly to ease social tensions, Akhenaten moved Egypt's capital from thriving Thebes, the home of Amun, to an uninhabited spot of desert in the middle of Egypt, telling his followers of a mystical vision in which the Aten himself had appeared and instructed Akhenaten to build a new city on this deserted site. Akhenaten called the city Akhetaten, the "Horizon of the Aten," and swore he would never leave.

KUSHITE PHARAOH SHABAKA'S SCARAB AMULET *(c. 715 B.C.E.) included a ram's head for divine support on the beetle's back (left). On its opposite side (right), images of a winged sun disk, solar barque, and cobra were believed to provide additional protection.*

Thousands followed their pharaoh into the desert to help found the new religion and erected temples to the new god which, unlike other temples in the country, were built without roofs so the god's light could shine in. Along with the temples, houses, palaces and office buildings, a complete city was constructed. From his new capital, Akhenaten wrote prayers to his abstract god without human or animal form: there could be no statues of a god who was light itself.

The concept of a single abstract deity that ruled the universe was so far ahead of its time that few Egyptians understood what Akhenaten preached. One prayer he wrote, known as "The Hymn to the Aten," has been compared with the 104th Psalm.

> Splendid you rise in heaven's lightland,
> O living Aten, creator of life!
> When you have dawned in eastern lightland
> You fill every land with your beauty.

AKHENATEN WORSHIPPING THE GOD ATEN, *who appears as a solar disk, radiating hands that hold the ankh, or sign of life.*

You are beauteous, great, radiant,
High over every land;
Your rays embrace the lands,
To the limit of all that you made.
Being Re, you reach their limits,
You bend them (for) the son whom you love;
Though you are far, your rays are on earth,

Though one sees you, your strides are unseen.
When you set in western lightland,
Earth is in darkness as if in death;
One sleeps in chambers, heads covered,
One eye does not see another.
Were they robbed of their goods,
That are under their heads,
People would not remark it.
Every lion comes from its den,
All the serpents bite;
Darkness hovers, earth is silent,
As their maker rests in lightland.

Earth brightens when you dawn in lightland,
When you shine as Aten of daytime;
As you dispel the dark
As you cast your rays,
The Two Lands are in festivity.[9]

As part of his new religion, Akhenaten changed the concept of life after death. No longer was death a continuation of this world; gone was Osiris and the West. Only when the Aten rose in the east could dead souls rise along with the rest of Egypt. Most Egyptians found this shadowy sort of afterlife unsatisfying.

For a dozen years, Akhenaten kept his promise never to leave his holy city. He abandoned the rest of the country to its own devices, while the citizens continued worship of old, familiar gods. Finally, angered, he dispatched teams of workmen throughout the land to chisel out the names of other gods wherever they appeared on statues and temple walls. This was the last act of a revolutionary whose revolution had failed. Soon after Akhenaten's death, his holy city was abandoned and Egypt returned to its old religion and rituals. Its brief experiment with monotheism left no lasting imprint on religion along the banks of the Nile. Not until the birth of Christ would monotheism again have a significant effect on Egypt.

 **3**

GOVERNMENT
AND SOCIETY

RELIGION WAS SUCH A POWERFUL FORCE IN ANCIENT EGYPT THAT it determined both the structure of government and the organization of society. Unlike our modern idea that government and religion should be separate, Egyptians believed their ruler was a god with unlimited power who spoke with divine authority.

Egyptians viewed the pharaoh as their protector, the guardian of the country, and they believed that society's order and prosperity depended on unquestioned obedience to him. Their belief that the pharaoh alone could prevent untold terrors from engulfing the land originated in a primeval myth about the great god Ra who came to earth in human form to rule as the first pharaoh. Egypt prospered during his reign as never before, producing crops in such regular and enormous abundance that life settled into a lazy routine. Free of cares, the people grew lax and neglected to honor Ra for the bounty he had bestowed. Ra, angered by their behavior, decided to teach his subjects a lesson they would never forget. Using powerful magic, he created a blood-thirsty lioness, the feared goddess Sekhmet, who roamed the land by day, terrorizing its inhabitants, devouring thousands, and instilling fear and respect among the survivors. With his goal accomplished, yet now unable to contain the blood-crazed Sekhmet, Ra convened a council of gods to devise a plan to save what remained of humanity. The gods made vast quantities of red-dyed beer and spread the mixture on the ground. Sekhmet, thinking it was blood, drank until she fell into a deep, intoxicated sleep. When she awoke, no longer crazed, Ra—being the most powerful god, after all—was able to change her into Hathor, the goddess of love.

STATUE OF THE BLOOD-CRAZED, LION-FACED GODDESS, SEKHMET, *at Rameses III's mortuary temple, Medinet Habu.*

This tale held a moral clear for every Egyptian: Ra must be honored and obeyed. Although possessing the power to make the people of Egypt prosper, he could, if insufficiently honored, just as easily destroy them. Yet how could mere mortals communicate their devotion to a god? The answer is contained at the end of the Ra myth.

After saving the Egyptian people from Sekhmet, Ra continued to rule as pharaoh until he grew weak—inevitable for any god who assumed human form—and had to return to his home in the netherworld. In his place, he sent his son, the god Horus, to rule over the land and protect its people. From that time on, each pharaoh was called, as one of his five names, "the Horus So-and-So," because each was believed to be the living son and representative of Ra. By honoring Ra's divine son Horus, their pharaoh, Egyptians paid homage to a father whose power provided all that was good in their world.

The Pharaoh

Just as Ra had done, it was up to every pharaoh to ensure that proper order, or *maat*, was maintained. But the Egyptians' view of order was calculated strictly along class lines. If good fortune came to a poor person, it was not considered a blessing or a credit to him, but a sign that something was wrong with the world.

> He who possessed no property now is a man of wealth. The poor man is full of joy. Every town says: let us suppress the powerful among us. He who had no yoke of oxen is now possessor of a herd. The possessors of robes are now in rags. Gold and lapis lazuli, silver and turquoise are fastened on the necks of female slaves. All female slaves are free with their tongues. When their mistress speaks it is irksome to the servant. The children of princes are dashed against the walls.[1]

Similar laments were common in Egyptian literature. As long as the rich and powerful prospered while slaves and the poor remained in their places, *maat* was maintained.

Besides ensuring order, pharaohs performed a unifying function. Egyptians believed that their land had once consisted of a northern and a southern kingdom until Narmer (Menes), a mighty hero from the south, conquered the north, married its queen and, by assuming the crowns of both kingdoms, unified Egypt into a single nation. Even after 2,000 years as a unified country, the title "Lord of the Two Lands" was a pharaoh's most important designation. To the Egyptian mind, their union existed solely in the person of the pharaoh— Narmer and his successors—and it was to him, rather than to country or flag, that all loyalty was owed.

Because Egyptians believed names held power, pharaohs possessed a number of other names and titles. (The designation "pharaoh," however, is not an Egyptian one. It appears in no list of pharaoh's titles, only in the Bible. In the ancient Egyptian language, *per ah* meant simply "the great house," which the Israelites applied to the person who lived in the palace.) A pharaoh's titles consisted of five Great Names. The oldest, the Horus name, dated from the first dynasties when it served as the king's only name. Enclosed in a tall rectangle whose vertical stripes symbolized the palace entryway, and surmounted by Horus' symbol, the falcon, this name asserted that Egypt's pharaoh was Horus, the favorite son of Ra. The next oldest title, "Lord of Upper and Lower Egypt," was represented by the vulture Nekhbet, the emblematic animal of the south, and the uraeus (cobra) Wadjet, symbol of the north, each standing on the hieroglyph for lord (). Because

THE FEMALE DEITIES WADJET (COBRA) *and Nekhbet (vulture), symbolizing the unification of upper and lower Egypt, appear on Tutankhamen's burial mask.*

both were female, this is often called the "Two Ladies Name." The next title, the "Horus of Gold" name, showed a falcon standing on the symbol for gold (🦅).

Last stood the nomen and prenomen, the only names enclosed in cartouches—ovals of rope tied at the bottom to form endless circles that probably symbolized dominion (⬭). The prenomen was the pharaoh's coronation name, introduced by the phrase "Lord of the Sedge and the Bee" (emblems of the south and the north, respectively) often translated as "King of Upper and Lower Egypt" (⚘). The nomen, his birth name, was introduced by the phrase the "Son of Ra" (🦆☉). For example, the nomen Tuthmosis meant "Born of Toth," the god of wisdom; Amenemhat meant "Amun Is Foremost"; Tutankhamen meant "The Living Likeness of Amun." A descriptive name followed each complete title. Because Egyptians believed in the magic of names, these titles not only asserted facts but established them as well. The full titular of the conquering pharaoh Tuthmosis III ran as follows:

$$\text{𓅃𓃾𓈖𓎟𓊸𓋴𓂋𓏏𓊪𓇳𓇳𓅓𓈖𓆼𓊪𓇳𓏏𓇳𓏤𓅆𓇳𓏏𓇳𓆓𓏏𓏏}$$

> The Horus "Strong Bull Risen in Thebes," the Two Ladies "Enduring of Kingship like Ra in Heaven," the Horus of Gold "Powerful Crowns," the King of Upper and Lower Egypt "Establishing the Being of Ra," the Son of Ra "Born of Toth, Beautiful of Forms."[2]

This was not a set of names to be taken lightly. As both a god and the embodiment of Egypt, a pharaoh wielded far greater power than any other monarch in history. Were he to ask his subjects to build an impossibly massive tomb, they would toil for decades to make the impossible real, receiving no pay, just enough food to sustain them. They believed praise from their pharaoh when he joined his ancestors in the netherworld would be their ample reward, just as later people devoted vast time and resources to raising cathedrals to the glory of their God and to ensure their personal salvation.

A pharaoh was regarded with awe and fear. Ordinary citizens prostrated themselves in his presence, and upper classes knelt and bowed until their heads touched the ground, waiting for permission to stand. Those closest to the pharaoh might, as a singular honor, be allowed to bow from the waist, but this was an innovation of the more "democratic" New Kingdom. All except his most favored courtiers feared looking directly on the pharaoh's face, and no one spoke unless he granted them that right.

His authority was boundless with every government position filled by his appointee, at least in theory. In fact, given the hundreds of appointments a pharaoh had to make, it was often expedient simply to replace a father with his son. In this way, more and more government positions became hereditary over time and outside a pharaoh's control. As the pharaoh's authority waned, so did Egypt's power, as exemplified by the First and Second Intermediate Periods. When strong pharaohs regained control, they consolidated their power base by reverting to the practice of making their own appointments.

As the lineal descendant of the conqueror Menes, the pharaoh owned Egypt[3]—all of it: the land, the livestock and the people—and governed by a feudal system like that of Medieval Europe. Private property did not exist in such a system because one person controlled everything. The king alone granted the right to manage a farm, town or pond, and whoever received that right exercised it on the king's behalf—what was produced belonged to his lord and master. So it was in the beginning in Egypt: whoever tilled an acre, fished the Nile or mined for gold did so with the pharaoh's permission. Yet, over centuries, the landholdings of the pharaoh gradually diminished. If a farm had been worked by a family for several generations, tradition eventually ceded them a title that could be upheld by the courts, creating a new category of land separate from a pharaoh's estates, although he could levy whatever tax he wished on these farms. Pharaohs themselves contributed to the decrease in their own estates by transferring land in perpetuity to certain temples by designating plots "pious foundations,"[4] a practice which enriched the temples but diminished the pharaoh's landholdings. They further decreased their estates by using land as incentives to service, awarding acreage to those who pleased them. Once land came into the possession of a private citizen he controlled its use and bequeathed it to whomever he pleased. Decreasing royal landholdings added private property to the economy, sometimes, but not always, subject to a pharaoh's national tax. What began as a pharaoh's literal ownership of the country slowly evolved into his right to tax and otherwise distribute the produce, so that, by the end of the New Kingdom, although the pharaoh remained Egypt's largest single landholder, temples collectively controlled more land than he did, and even more acreage was held by small farmers.

Because a pharaoh represented the soul of Egypt, determining a successor assumed great importance. Although succession followed bloodlines, pharaohs could marry whomever they wished and as often, and they used marriages to foreign royalty to seal international treaties. While harems assured pharaohs an abundance of royal heirs, they also created abundant confusion about who would succeed the reigning king. To sort out the priorities of potentially scores of heirs—in the case of Rameses the Great, more than fifty sons—one wife was designated the "great royal wife," possibly referring to the queen of the north Narmer had married to become Egypt's first pharaoh. Her children were accorded privileged status, and her name, at least from the New Kingdom on, was enclosed in a cartouche like the pharaoh's. Steeped as the pharaohcy was in warrior tradition, males were accorded priority, although, if no suitable male was available, a female pharaoh was considered better than none at all. The eldest male son of the great royal wife thus had first call on the throne. If the great royal wife produced no sons or (in rare cases) if her sons proved unsuitable, a son of a secondary wife, a lesser son, would be designated the next pharaoh, based on his presumed ability.

Since the eldest son of the great royal wife was generally guaranteed the throne by his parentage, he could marry whomever he chose, but a "lesser" son, like Tutankhamen, had to marry the "daughter of the god," the eldest daughter of the great royal wife, his half-sister, to earn title to the throne. (The incest taboo seems universal and certainly existed in Egypt. Full brothers rarely married full sisters.[5]) In fact, whoever married this "daughter of the god" automatically became pharaoh, whether he was royal or not. In this way new dynasties began—as in the case of the Nineteenth, when Rameses I, the vizier of the previous pharaoh, married the pharaoh's daughter and assumed the throne—or old dynasties continued—as in the case of the commoner Ay who married Tutankhamen's widow to ascend to his pharaohcy. That Rameses I is counted as the first pharaoh of a new dynasty while Ay is considered part of an ongoing dynasty demonstrates how arbitrary sorting rulers into dynasties can be.

Egyptians abhorred change. Until a family had provided several generations of rulers, a new dynasty reigned insecurely. When a foreign king governed the country, as during the Hyksos era of the second Intermediate Period or during the later reign of Persian kings, people became restive, at times to the point of revolution. During the First Intermediate Period, when several aspirants claimed title to the pharaohcy, people grew despondent— even the art they produced during this time was crude. A female pharaoh, too, however pure her lineage, could unsettle the Egyptians. Despite the fact that Hatshepsut had been the "daughter

NEFERTARI, RAMESES II'S "GREAT ROYAL WIFE." *Her tomb in the Valley of the Queens was known as the Sistine Chapel of ancient Egypt.*

of the god" under one pharaoh and the great royal wife of another, her male successor set out, with popular support, to destroy all images and references to her. Yet, by the time Alexander the Great, a Greek who liberated Egypt from the domination of the Persian kings, Egyptians so hungered for a pharaoh that they embraced the fiction of this foreigner's legitimacy and crowned Alexander king.

GOVERNMENT AND ORGANIZATION

Although central to the Egyptian system, a pharaoh could not manage the country without a substantial, professional government. Something in the Egyptian character found governance congenial, almost as though taking orders and enjoying tedious record keeping were national traits. No society ever employed such a high percentage of civil servants, and no society so often and so publicly praised its government officials, rather than complaining about them. Egypt's successes, especially as demonstrated in its massive construction projects, indicates that the country generally enjoyed an efficient, effective government.

Evidence from early times, such as the Fourth Dynasty, shows son after son of a reigning monarch bearing titles of high government positions. Generally, for example, a prince was designated as the overseer of works, the chief engineer of the pharaoh's pyramid and mortuary temple. This suggests that Egypt's government originally consisted of the family of the pharaoh, although this changed as its population and power grew. By the end of the Old Kingdom and through the remainder of Egyptian history, nonroyals, nominated by the pharaoh, invariably bore the titles of government officers. From then on, royal children who did not inherit the throne generally became high priests and priestesses rather than officials in the civil government.

The evolved government consisted of four major branches. One managed the royal court and pharaoh's estates; another, the armed forces (discussed in Chapter 10); another, the religious hierarchy; and the remaining branch, managed the civil government. Each consisted of a pyramidal hierarchy (or, in the case of civil government, of two pyramids) that established a chain of authority and command and provided a structure by which a pharaoh could impose his wishes on all the citizens of his sprawling country. Government's overriding principle was that an Egyptian citizen should receive his distant pharaoh's orders from a local person whom he knew and respected. This neat structure could become confused when multiple titles were awarded to the same individual, effectively placing him in more than one branch of the government at once.

Civil Government

Civil government was headed by a *tchety*, conventionally translated "vizier," the highest civil official after the pharaoh. Two viziers, one for the north and another for the south, split the job and presided over separate central bureaucracies and governors of their respective sections of the country. The godly pharaoh stood far above practical details of management, so viziers bragged about how the least important citizen could approach them with his problems, and how they oversaw the construction of magnificent temples and pyramids. Such boasts were exaggerations. The vizier did not serve as a sole judge to adjudicate complaints—a complex legal system took care of such matters. Nor did most viziers possess the necessary architectural and construction skills to personally supervise the construction of large buildings. The truth behind the boasts is that the *tchety* held ultimate responsibility for the justice system and for securing the talents required to build whatever a pharaoh commanded. The vizier was responsible for all civil business, which he conducted through ministers, most importantly treasury, tax collection, judicial appeal and regional governors, who, in turn, managed numerous functionaries.

Headed by an official whose title translates as "overseer of the house of gold," the treasury collected crops and animals as payment-in-kind for taxes and handled their accounting and management. Beneath this minister, an overseer of granaries and an overseer of cattle supervised numerous bureaucrats who managed facilities for provisioning the army, feeding workers on national projects and maintaining surpluses against lean years.

Taxes were levied and collected by another department whose many members roamed the country assigning an individual obligation to every citizen. Levies were not based on how much an acre had produced that year, which would have encouraged farmers to hide part of the crop to lower their tax. Instead, a careful record was kept of how high the Nile rose during its annual inundation using "nilometers," stone markers set along the river's course. The height of that year's flood determined what, compared with the previous year, each farm *should* have produced regardless of what it *did* produce, and set a tax rate which generally hovered at about 10 percent[6]—not an onerous amount by modern standards. Those who did not hand over their levied amounts were beaten or imprisoned.

The treasury and tax departments were considered so important that their heads reported directly to the pharaoh, like the vizier. Both departments employed thousands of scribes to compute and record every transaction.

Regional government consisted of forty-two areas of the country called *nomes*, corresponding to our states, presided over by a local governor called a

SCRIBES COUNT THE HANDS OF WOMEN *killed in battle by the forces of Rameses II in this ancient carving.*

nomarch. Nomarchs maintained order in each territory and ensured that its assigned portion for national projects was supplied, whether in the form of taxes or labor. As the local official with ties closest to the national government, *nomarchs* exercised great authority in their territory, sometimes acting almost as local kings. Below each *nomarch* stood town mayors, village chiefs, constabularies and district councils, or *kenbets*.

Kenbets[7], appointed by the area *nomarch* from the most respected citizens in each community, functioned as Egypt's legal system, deciding most disputes, which generally concerned property. Most criminal cases and inheritance controversies also fell within their scope. Since the government did not operate through laws (no legislative body existed), *kenbets* functioned less as judges of a codified legal system than as investigative committees to uncover the truthfulness of allegations. They took depositions from those who knew the character of a person bringing suit, searched voluminous archives for old records that might bear on the case, then rendered a decision.

If the decision did not satisfy both parties, the suit could be resubmitted, but an unusual device was employed to end perennial litigation. The *kenbet* could relay the evidence to the statue of a god who would render a verdict, either by communicating to a priest or, more often, while carried on priests' shoulders by stopping in front of one of the litigants to indicate the god's favor. Usually the "divine" authority of such a verdict ended the dispute.

Kenbets used several remedies to rectify wrongs. They could order property seized and transferred to the injured party. They could inflict physical punishment such as beatings (usually a hundred blows with a stick) or mutilation (cutting off an ear or nose). Although no prisons existed in Egypt, the *kenbet* could sentence offenders to fixed periods of heavy labor in mines or quarries and could also exile serious criminals.

Since Egypt functioned with two capital cities, Memphis and Thebes, each maintained a Great *Kenbet* which served as a higher court for the lesser *kenbets* of the respective northern and southern territories. Each vizier held a seat on the Great *Kenbet* of his area, along with the top officials of the state, church and army. Capital offenses were assigned to the Great *Kenbets* alone, but, since these councils consisted of busy men of great responsibility, capital cases could not have been as frequent as in our day.

RELIGIOUS ORGANIZATION

Since only the pharaoh could directly intercede with the gods through his father Ra, one of his hereditary positions was to serve as the high priest of the land. In theory, he was the only one who could minister to the temple idols. In practice, with so many temples spread through the country, the pharaoh designated agents to act as priests on his behalf. Each temple, therefore, had its own high priest, who was appointed by the pharaoh.

As Egypt thrived, so did its priestly establishment. In addition to a principal temple for each god, important gods had subsidiary temples spread throughout the country. Furthermore, every pharaoh built a cult temple to minister to his own immortal soul. Following his lead, thousands of little chapels sprang up to preserve the memory of any dead citizen whose estate could afford the upkeep. Although no accurate estimate exists for the number of centers of worship, certainly they amounted to thousands, if not tens of thousands by the end of the New Kingdom. Not all were staffed by priests—sometimes the relatives of a deceased person maintained his small temple—but many employed full-time employees. Over time this priestly establishment came to number in the tens of thousands, drawing heavily on Egypt's national resources for clothing, food, buildings and maintenance. An estimate for the Twentieth Dynasty identified one-fifth of the population working in one way or another for a religion which controlled one-third of all the country's land.[8]

Such a large bureaucracy required extensive management and supervision. Leading the religious establishment was the overseer of the temples and prophets of all the gods, a government official who functioned not as a priest but as the civil overlord of an institution that controlled great national wealth. So entwined were Egypt's civil and religious affairs, however, that, in addition to his civil post, a vizier often held the position of overseer of the temples. Ranked directly below the overseer stood high priests—one for each god of Egypt. During the New Kingdom, however, a single god, Amun, so eclipsed the others that the status of his high priest approached that of the overseer of temples. The high priest of each god managed all the temples dedicated to his deity through a chief priest in each.

Individual temples employed their own bureaucracy.[9] Priests in general were called "god's servants"; the chief priest was designated as the "first god's servant." In the case of a large temple, like that at Karnak, a second, third or even fourth god's servant served under him. They supervised clerics divided by function into two categories. "Scroll carriers" maintained and read the sacred texts of the temple. *Wab* priests, who cared for cult objects, such as idols and their clothing and ritual instruments, were required to maintain an extreme state of purity. They had to be circumcised,[10] shave their bodies every other day from head to foot, bathe twice during the day and twice each night, wear only "clean" (non-animal) clothing—linen robes and papyrus sandals—and avoid certain foods, such as pork, fish and beans. Both groups served one-month stints of temple duty, then enjoyed three months of rest before working again. They were organized into squadrons of ten or so, and served under the command of a "god's father." All were male, but women could serve as priestesses who sang and danced for a god. In addition, every temple employed a staff of craftsmen to make linen robes and sandals for the priests, repair the temple and cook for both the idol and the staff.

All temple workers received daily allotments of food and drink. In addition, priests were paid a proportion of the products from temple lands and, in some instances, even ceded farms from temple estates. Since a priest could serve several gods, ambitious men or women could multiply their incomes substantially in the name of their religion.

The Royal Court

The pharaoh's staff constituted a major segment of society in a country whose ruler controlled immense amounts of land, officiated at innumerable official ceremonies and personally communicated with heads of foreign states. Hundreds of functionaries managed royal estates, and thousands of families worked his land. Under the supervision of a governor of the palace, another special group of officials oversaw the affairs of the king's two official residences. Each palace compound housed a troop of royal guards, a kitchen staff including serving women, musicians and dancers, groundskeepers, carpenters and other artisans, horsemen, and even zookeepers for the exotic animals most pharaohs enjoyed. A separate diplomatic staff of hundreds of emissaries and scribes conducted foreign affairs from offices in a separate structure inside or nearby the royal compound.

One special group lived inside the palace to care for pharaoh's personal needs. An overseer of royal clothes would supervise a chief bleacher, chief washer and chief rober; an overseer of wigs supervised upper and lower wig makers (rich women often wore a wig under an outer wig); a royal sandalbearer cared for the royal footwear;[11] a royal hairdresser, a royal barber, and royal bathers carried out their individual responsibilities; a team of royal doctors specializing in various ailments—with magicians for ailments beyond the ability of regular doctors—monitored the royal health. When a pharaoh marched out to preside at a temple, he was accompanied by a convoy of fan bearers, sedan carriers, servants

PHARAOH RAMESES IX OFFERS GIFTS TO AMUNHOTEP, *the High Priest of Amun during the twilight of Egypt's New Kingdom, in this Karnak temple relief.*

to clear the way, standard-bearers, bodyguards, court officials and various royal personages—an entourage that could, depending on the occasion, include as few as fifty people or as many as several hundred.

Even the royal harem had its own administration, governed by an Overseer of the Secluded who managed both the scribes and attendants who served the needs of the women, in addition to a group of doorkeepers who were responsible for their management. The doorkeepers arranged nightly appointments with the pharaoh, as he desired. Teams of musicians trained the women to entertain their king by singing to the musical accompaniment of their sisters in seclusion. Royal children were housed in a separate section of the palace apart from the adults and raised by tutors, called royal nurses, who generally were female relatives of the child's mother or of an important government official, such as the vizier.

It would be interesting to know the amount of provisions needed to sustain a royal court but, unfortunately, the only surviving information pertains to a Second Intermediate Period pharaoh whose household would amount to a fraction of New Kingdom extravagance. Even this diminished court consumed 2,000 loaves of bread and 300 large jugs of beer daily.[12]

C. 2020 B.C.E. RELIEF OF THE SCULPTOR MENTU-USER *and his wife, Hepu, seated before a large feast and requesting a thousand loaves of bread.*

Social Organization

Modern classifications of an upper, middle and lower class based on income have no parallel in ancient Egyptian society where money did not exist. As in the later feudal systems of Medieval Europe, Egyptian society was composed of three distinct classes: royalty, free people and chattel, ranked according to their autonomy. At the top stood royalty, a tiny percentage of the population who wielded all official power through the pharaoh. Underneath them lay a large group of free citizens consisting of government officials, priests, soldiers and civilians. The fact that movement was common among these four professions shows that they occupied the same tier of the social hierarchy. The sons of a free farmer sometimes entered government service, sometimes became priests, sometimes enlisted as soldiers and sometimes followed in their father's footsteps. Beneath these free citizens lay two groups with little or no freedom—slaves and serfs.

Royalty

Royal status depended on a blood relationship with the reigning pharaoh. His brothers and sisters, full aunts and full uncles and mother and father automatically belonged to this class. Rarely did unrelated commoners attain membership in this group. Exceptions include Tiya, the principal wife of Amenhotep III, whose marriage raised her to royalty, and the similarly named Tey, elevated when her husband Ay took the throne, although, in general, a pharaoh's numerous wives were considered nonroyal. One could also attain royal status by marrying the eldest daughter of pharaoh's great royal wife. In the absence of a better claimant to the throne, her husband, regardless of his parentage, became the royal heir apparent, but otherwise gained no royal status by the marriage.

Royal status conferred privileges, including the right to lifelong support by the state, but, except in the case of the pharaoh, carried no automatic power. The extended royal family, who lived together in various palaces, were not required to work, although nothing prohibited them from doing so. A pharaoh's grown sons, one of whom might ascend the throne, were likely to be awarded government positions as training for such an eventuality. This held true not only for the heir apparent, but for other male children as well, because circumstances, such as an heir's death or unsuitability, could always change the order of succession. In other cases, a pharaoh might award positions to family members as a way of manipulating institutions not entirely under his control. During the New Kingdom, for example, a pharaoh's chief wife or daughter generally became the god's wife of Amun, an appointment that gave the pharaoh direct control over that god's powerful and wealthy priests.

Free People

Free Egyptian citizens—both male and female—possessed two defining rights: they were free to travel and free to enter into contractual agreements. Although they enjoyed no other rights of modern societies, their right to make contracts permitted members of this group at least to own property and marry. Serfs and slaves were also permitted possessions, but they could not transfer them without a contract—only the free class could acquire and sell animals, property and buildings as they wished. Though most free people eked out a subsistence living, some accumulated wealth and grew into citizens of substance, and a few even earned high positions in government.

Whether rich or poor, any free person had the right to the joys of marriage. Marriage was not a religious matter in Egypt—no ceremony involving a priest took place—but simply a social convention that required an agreement, which is to say a contract, negotiated by the suitor and the family of his prospective wife. The agreement involved an exchange of objects of value on both sides. The suitor offered a sum called the "virginity gift," when appropriate, to compensate the bride for what she would lose,[13] indicating that in ancient times virginity was prized in female brides. The gift did not apply in the case of second marriages, of course, but a "gift to the bride" would be made even in that case. In return, the family of the bride-to-be offered a "gift in order to become a wife." In many cases, these two gifts were never delivered since the pair soon merged households. However, in the event of divorce, either party could later sue for the agreed gift. A third sum, called the "alimentation," consisted of a periodic subsidy from the bride's family to compensate for the additional expense of a second person in the household, and it was given with stipulations of how the wife must be treated in return. The remainder of the contract consisted of a kind of ancient prenuptial agreement, specifying what property belonged to the woman and what belonged to the man, as well as stating who would inherit what on the death of either party.

In some cases a written contract was executed before witnesses, in others only a verbal agreement took place. Either satisfied the official requirement for marriage, although, human nature being what it is, a party to celebrate the happy event generally followed. The new husband and wife presided at this affair, rather than being the guests of either set of parents.

After recovering from the merriment, the couple began married life with the presumption that their union would last until death. Of course life did not always work out so well; even in ancient times, divorces, although not common, did occur. Since neither church nor state had joined the pair, no authorization was required for their separation. All that severing involved was living apart. Yet, given marriage's contractual obligations, divorce for most couples involved a legal declaration of the dissolution of the marriage, which freed them to marry again. The original marriage contract also contained stipulations about the contractual gifts and other matters. If a husband initiated a divorce, he forfeited the entire gift to the bride, or in some cases an amount double that gift. If the wife instituted a divorce, she returned half of the gift to the bride. Regardless of who began the proceedings, the husband was obliged to continue paying the wife's alimentary money, providing full financial support until she married again. Not without its modern counterparts, this clause certainly held some marriages together that otherwise would have dissolved. Other contracted sums were generally assigned to the children.

The status of women in Egypt was incredibly advanced for the time. They held full equality under the law and could enter into contracts, own property and be brought to justice for crimes in exactly the same way as a man. They became second-class citizens in terms of jobs, however. Occupations were strictly gender linked, as they have been in most societies until recently. Men fought, ran the government and managed the farm; women cooked, sewed and managed the house.

Chattel

Little evidence indicates what percentage of the population consisted of free people. Although surely the numbers varied over time, a guess would put the percentage at something less than half of Egypt's people. The lowest rung of society was composed of slaves and serfs whose lives were completely controlled by other people. Slaves differed from serfs in that they could be individually bought and sold; serfs belonged to the land, hence changed masters only as the land changed hands. As long as they were commanded to perform legal tasks, both serfs and slaves were expected to obey their masters without question or complaint. While neither group could enter into legal marriage, a contractual arrangement that simply involved inheritance rights on its dissolution, this fact carried more technical than practical significance. Since they owned little that could be assigned to survivors in any case, serfs and slaves could enjoy most aspects of marriage, such as cooperative living and raising children. Since marriage in ancient Egypt was a social rather than religious institution, their unions closely resembled "legal" marriages in practice.

During every period of Egyptian history serfs far outnumbered slaves. Serfs originally comprised all the people of Egypt except for a tiny percentage of powerful elite that formed a hereditary caste. Since individuals remained serfs unless good fortune changed their situation, only slowly did their high proportion decline. A serf could be elevated through the intervention of a master who, in recognition of a special talent or ability, might assign the person to a managerial position on an estate—serf status was tied to occupation as well as birth. Marriage, too, was a way out of serfdom. Since free persons could not marry serfs, union with a serf required that he or she first be freed.[14] While one can imagine many parents looking askance at their child marrying a serf, others recognized the worth of a young serf as the mate for their child. In the early times of civilian armies, valor in war could also earn a serf his own land and freedom. Through one or another of these means, the percentage of serfs decreased over time, swelling the ranks of the free class until, by the height of the New Kingdom, serfs had probably declined to less than half of the population.

Slavery did not exist in the early days of Egyptian civilization. (The pyramids were not built by the slave labor shown in film epics.) Slaves originally consisted only of foreigners captured in war and increased in number during the New Kingdom as Egypt accelerated successful campaigns to foreign lands. Because the caste was hereditary, its population grew as slaves taken in battle gave birth to children in Egypt. Apparently free Egyptians could also descend to this class because of debts or perhaps as legal punishment.[15] Members of the slave class, who could be bought, sold and rented to others, formed the very bottom of the social scale.

The pharaoh before Rameses conducted an extensive military campaign into Canaan, including the upper valley of Galilee, returning with many prisoners. He began constructing a city in the delta which his son finished and named Pa Rameses. By traditional Egyptian practice, slaves would have been employed on such a large project, likely including those captured in Canaan. That Hebrews were enslaved by Egypt and forced to work constructing cities, including the one the Bible calls "Rameses," is entirely consistent with the Exodus story.

EGYPTIAN PRISONERS MAKING BRICKS, *based on a wall painting in the tomb of Theban vizier Rekhmire.*

WORK AND PLAY

EGYPTIANS LIVED IN AN ECONOMIC ENVIRONMENT COMPLETELY different from ours. Money did not exist, the idea of a workweek had no meaning and the concept of leisure time was unknown to most of the population. Surprisingly, however different the context and specifics might have been, work and play in Egypt's ancient culture closely resembled that of modern societies—at least until the nineteenth century, when machines took over the world.

WORK

Egyptians worked for food and goods rather than for money which was unknown until the Ptolemies introduced it during Egypt's final days. Since for most of Egypt's long history no currency existed for exchanging commodities at set values, essential goods were generally manufactured by the user or members of his immediate family: pots, for example, were produced by women in their homes. Commodities, such as bronze plow blades, which could not be made in the average home, were secured, not by purchase from a store, but by barter, which could be a complex procedure involving intricate negotiations. The man who made the plow blade might have enough food, pots and clothing from other barters, so something he desired would have to be bartered from a third party—a kilt exchanged for a stool, say; then the stool for a plow blade. An ancient record of one such transaction documents the trade of an ox for one fine tunic and two ordinary ones, plus ten sacks of grain and some necklace beads.[1] Needless to say, such acquisitions occurred less frequently than today and only when motivated by strong need.

FISHING SCENE, C. 1422 B.C.E., *from the tomb of the Eighteenth-Dynasty royal steward Kenamun. Fishing and hunting were often pursued as recreation rather than out of necessity.*

In an attempt to introduce order to exchanges, items were conventionally valued at amounts of copper or, for more precious objects, silver. The main measure was a weight called a *deben*, which could be divided into ten *qites*. Exchange values varied over time, but by the Late Period, when ten copper debens equaled one of silver, 95 grams of silver per silver deben had become standard.[2] These standards allowed Egyptians to assign a relative value to commodities. As a rough measure, a bushel of grain equaled one deben of copper. A small farm (perhaps an acre by our measure) could be purchased for two or three *deben*s of silver, which approximated the cost of an ox as well. A slave cost a little more. A pot of honey, an Egyptian treat, was valued at one qite of silver. Because the average Egyptian owned no silver at all and little copper, such valuations served more to indicate which exchanges were fair than to effect a transfer. These standards enabled a farmer to appraise his neighbor's land as being worth, say, about one ox, or from twenty to thirty bushels of grain.

Since most work was motivated by a need for sustenance rather than a desire for acquisitions, it followed rhythms radically different from our own. For us each day of the week has a different character. For most Americans, Monday is the first day of work, Friday is the end of a work period and Saturday begins two days of nonwork activity. Most of us sleep later on weekends, dress differently and have more control over our time than during the previous five workdays. Life marches to these seven-step patterns, punctuated by recurring holidays that serve as bonus free days along with special periods of two weeks or more for vacations of our choosing.

Nothing similar existed in ancient Egypt. Egyptians had no weekends. Most worked every day, with few exceptions. Special holy days of the year called for all the inhabitants of a given area to lay down their tools and gather at a local temple to watch a procession of idols, after which they feasted on bountiful free food supplied by the temple. The most festive of these holy days was *Opet*, when the idols of Amun, Mut and Khonsu traveled from Karnak Temple to Luxor Temple to celebrate their marriage; the Five Yearly Days, which celebrated the end of one year and hopes for a successful next year; and birthdays for each god of Egypt. For practical reasons, most of these holidays occurred when the Nile was in flood, making farming impossible in any case. During the rest of the year, one day followed another in much the same way. No regular day of rest existed until it was introduced much later by the Jews in Palestine and borrowed by later Christians. Indeed, names for individual days of the week did not exist in the language, nor did that seven-day grouping we call a week. The character of work periods was instead determined by what nature demanded—weeding, repairing canals, plowing or harvesting. No calendar told a farmer how to schedule his time when he woke each morning.

Calendar

The year was divided into three seasons, marking nature's rhythms, each consisting of four thirty-day months. "Inundation" began the year around our September, when the Nile overflowed and flooded the farmland. "Emergence," which referred to the reappearance of the land from the receding water, was planting time, and was followed by "harvest." Each season called for work appropriate to environmental circumstances. During inundation, when the waterlogged land could not be worked, the farmer repaired his tools and house. Emergence began with reconstructing the canals that brought essential Nile water to the fields, after which came plowing, planting, then tending the crops as they grew. During harvest, farmers reaped and processed the crops before storage. Of course, three seasons of four thirty-day months added up to only 360 days, which left five days unaccounted for. This yearly five days provided Egyptians with the closest they ever got to a sustained holiday: no one worked during the long new year's celebration.

THIS C. 600 B.C.E. FLASK *may have held a liquid used in a ceremony to mark the beginning of the new agricultural year in late summer.*

Despite being nameless, each day was marked in calendars as representing specific theological events thought to have occurred on that particular day. Thus, the first day of the second month of emergence was considered the day Ra had lifted up the sky, whereas the twenty-sixth day of the first month of inundation marked the time Sekhmet's ferocious eyes first caught sight of her human prey. These mythical events lent every day a quality, marking it as auspicious, if some fortunate event had occurred, menacing, if the contrary, or neutral. Egyptians took these matters seriously, planning important events to coincide with auspicious days and taking extra care on menacing ones (see, for example, the list on page 98 of the days of the second month of the season of emergence with their lucky and unlucky characters).

As to the intervals of a day, Egyptians invented the hour—the same twenty-four equal day divisions we use today. These intervals were measured either by marks down the side of a candle or by lines on a bowl that showed the water remaining after steady dripping. Although appointments could be set and kept by such devices, the average farmer needed no more indication of time than the position of the sun or the moon, and none of his countrymen understood divisions finer than an hour. The word for minute—let alone the ultra precision of a second—did not even exist in the language.

Farmers

Farmers, the vast majority of the population, repeated the same pattern year after year, but with greater regularity than elsewhere in the world where rainstorms, snow or swings of temperature made agriculture less predictable. Each time the Nile receded, Egyptian farmers returned to the fields to plow after having spent the previous month readying their tools. Plowing was relatively easy in the still-moist ground. If a farmer had cattle, two would pull while he leaned his weight on the plow to ensure deep furrows, while a son guided the team in a straight line; otherwise, he would enlist two men to take the place of the cattle. After the furrows were dug, the farmer followed with a mattock to break up the large clumps of dirt lifted by the plow. Then it was time for the women to scatter the seeds from wicker baskets, slung by a cord over their shoulders, into the furrows.

A PLOWING FARMER *from the tomb of Egyptian artisan Sennedjem.*

Later, encouraged by strewn grass or straw, a herd of sheep would be driven onto the land to bury the seed with their hooves, allowing it to germinate hidden from hungry birds and rodents.

Next came a season of nurture to ensure bountiful crops. Dirt dikes and canals needed continual repair to assure a constant water flow to every young shoot. Farmers alternated work in their fields with regular stints at the Nile, raising bucket after bucket of river water up the bank to spill into the system of canals used by neighboring farms. The *shadoof,* a cantilevered pole, made this work easier than walking every bucket up the bank, but no less monotonous. When not participating in his community water chore, a farmer had weeds to clear, rats to fend off and birds to shoo—the reason the family cat often accompanied his master to work.

Egyptian Calendar: Emergence, Month 2

Day 1
Very Favorable

The gods and goddesses are in festival. The day of Ptah's lifting the heavens of Ra with his hands.
Make a holiday

Day 2
Very Favorable

The day the gods receive Ra. The hearts of the Two Lands are festive.

Day 3
Very Adverse

The day of the going forth of Seth and his confederates on the eastern horizon, and of the navigation of Maat to the place of the gods.
Do not go out of your house on any road today.

Day 4
Very Favorable

Show your heart to your local gods. Propitiate your spirits. Exalt your crew on this day.

Day 5
Very Favorable

If you see anything on this day, it will be good.

Day 6
Very Adverse

The day of the raising of the djed-pillar of Osiris. The gods are sad and their faces downcast when they remember Osiris.

Day 7
Very Favorable

Make invocation offerings in your house to the spirits. Make abet-*offerings to the gods and they will be accepted on this day.*

Day 8
Very Favorable

The day the gods and goddesses are in festival.
Make a holiday in Latopolis.

Day 9 *Very Favorable*	The day the god enters to distribute the ration of all the gods of Ker-aba. *Anything you see on this day will be good.*
Day 10 *Very Adverse*	The day of the going forth of the Udjat-eye for singing in Heliopolis. The day of elevating the goddess of the sanctuary of Mnevis. Ra raises Maat again and again to Atum.
Day 11 *Very Favorable*	The day of the feast of Neith, of taking the writing material that is in her house and of the going forth of Sobek to guide her majesty. *You will see good from her hands.*
Day 12 *Very Favorable*	*Anything you see on this day will be good.*
Day 13 *Very Adverse*	The day of the proceeding of Sekhmet to Latopolis. Her great executioners pass by the offering of Latopolis on this day. *Do not go out of your house on any road today.*
Day 14 *Mostly Favorable*	The day of seeing the rebel and killing him by Seth at the prow of the great barque. *Do not go out at dawn on this day.*

Day 15	The gods go forth for him in heaven. His two hands hold the *ankh* and was-scepter which he offers to the nose of Khenty-Irety at the time of his reckoning.
Day 16	The day of the awakening of Isis by the majesty of Ra . . . when the son Horus saves his father. He has eaten Seth and his confederates.
Day 17 *Very Favorable*	The day of keeping those things of the wabet of Osiris which have been placed in the hands of Anubis.
Day 18 *Very Adverse*	The day of the going forth of the seven executioners. Their fingers are searching for the Akhet-eye in the towns of Iyet and Latopolis.
Day 19 *Mostly Adverse*	The day of the mourning of the god. *Do not go out alone in daytime.*
Day 20 *Very Adverse*	The day of the proceeding of the goddesses of heaven southward to the road
Day 21	The day of the birth of cattle. They go to the place where the meadows are in the neighborhood of the foremost god.
Day 22 *Very Favorable*	*Anything you see on this day will be good.*

Day 23 *Very Favorable*	*Anything you see on this day will be good.*
Day 24 *Very Adverse*	The gods are descending into the river. *Anyone who approaches the river today will not live. Do not sail a boat on this day.*
Day 25 *Very Favorable*	*Anything you see on this day will be good.*
Day 26	The day of the going forth of Min to Coptos. He is guided to it, boasting of his beauty. Isis sees that his face is beautiful.
Day 27	The day of the feast of Sokar in Rostau before that of Onnophris (a form of Osiris) in Abydos.
Day 28 *Very Favorable*	Onnophris is pleased and the spirits are joyful. The dead are also festive.
Day 29 *Very Adverse*	The day of the instigation of fighting, of the creation of rebellion, and of making an uproar among the children of Geb. *Do not do anything on this day.*
Day 30 *Very Adverse*	House of Ra, House of Osiris, House of Horus. *Do not talk with anyone on this day.*

As soon as the grain ripened, about three months later, local officials appeared to measure the field to set its taxes. Only then did the whole family arrive to harvest the crop before it spoiled or was eaten by animals. Some cut the grain heads with a short sickle held in one hand while the other hand held the grain steady; others gathered the loose heads into piles, tied them with lengths of straw, then loaded them onto donkeys for transport to the local threshing area. The long wheat stems were left standing in the field for later harvesting as straw for the livestock.

At the threshing area, the whole community assembled to separate usable seeds from unusable stems and chaff. First oxen were driven round and round to break the seeds free while the men turned the mixture over to ensure every seed received a hoof. Afterward, the same pitchforks carried the straw away, leaving only the finer grain and its hulls (chaff) on the threshing floor. Using wooden scoops, the men lifted this mixture above their heads, letting it spill back to the floor so the wind could blow the lighter chaff away. In the end, only the seeds remained, and these were distributed to each family in proportion to its production. As the year closed, a short New Year's hiatus signaled that it was time, once again, to start repairing the tools—and to begin another year just like the one before.

Scribes

Those who worked at jobs less controlled by nature followed rhythms set by their masters or by supply-and-demand principles. Government workers were allowed to rest every tenth day. Craftspeople worked according to demand.

Scribes, the largest group of workers after farmers, included cadres of thousands of bureaucrats, private individuals hired to handle accounts and correspondence for large estates, and freelancers. Because no public school system existed, the average Egyptian could neither read nor write. The sons of scribes, higher officials and occasional precocious farm children attended local temples for instruction in letters. Except for separate classes convened for royal or otherwise socially prominent girls, all scholars were male. Each set out in the morning carrying a small basket of bread and beer from home and returned again in the late afternoon.

Beginning instruction consisted of copying hieroglyphic signs over and over until they were committed to memory. Because papyrus was too expensive for this repetitive task, thin slabs of erasable limestone or wood boards with replaceable gesso surfaces were used instead. After learning his ABCs (or, in this case, his vultures, feet and baskets), a worthy child graduated to papyrus and longer classic texts—generally consisting of moral platitudes. These skills were not easily mastered. In addition to twenty single-syllable picture signs, over one hundred two-syllable (*pr*, *wr*, etc.) and an equal number of three-syllable signs (*nfr*, etc.) had to be committed to memory, along with almost the same number of "determinatives"— endings indicating whether a word's meaning had to do with an activity, an animal, an abstract thought and so

STATUE OF A SEATED SCRIBE. *No public school system existed in ancient Egypt, and instruction in letters was reserved mostly for sons of scribes and higher officials.*

on. With the language, which included a grammar and three tenses, mastered, a student had learned only one of the three forms of Egyptian writing. In addition to hieroglyphs—the picture symbols we most often associate with Egyptian writing—a more cursive form called hieratic was employed for handwriting, and a more abbreviated version called demotic was used for quicker notes.

When all three symbol systems had been committed to memory, a pupil who showed aptitude could move to advanced courses in mathematics and basic building practices, both of which were taught through practical examples rather than abstraction rules. Problems such as computing the number of bricks needed for a wall of a certain dimension, the amount of provisions a specified number of troops needed for an expedition of given duration or the number of men required for moving an obelisk of a given size prepared graduates for high civil positions in the army or on government construction projects, although most students progressed no further than mastering the reading and writing appropriate for more mundane occupations.

Such repetitive instruction surely bored most children. Letters abound from fathers who, looking toward the rewards of a good job following their son's graduation, urge them to persist, criticizing those who play hooky in local bars and brothels. Since a number of dated and corrected student exercises survive, it seems that assignments were a principal teaching tool. Instead of grades providing motivation for good work, one father reminded his son that "a youngster's ear is in his back; he only listens to the man who beats him."[3]

Despite the difficult course of instruction, some students graduated to don the dress of the scribe's trade—a long skirt, rather than the normal short kilt. They carried foot-long scribal palettes—rectangles of wood with two depressions in one end and a slot in the other. The slot held writing brushes; the depressions served as pots for mixing black and red ink. Black was used for the body of a text, and red indicated chapter headings or an especially important phrase. As a scribe, a young man enjoyed opportunities for advancement. Certain orders of priests required scribal skills, as did the quartermaster corps of the army and a host of government jobs above the lowest level. The vast majority of scribes, however, filled the ranks of clerks or simple accountants for the duration of their professional lives.

Craftsmen

Those who made objects, whether utilitarian or artistic, earned no great status in Egyptian society, however wonderful their creations might seem to us today. Lists of offerings to various temples refer to furniture and statues in the same citations as grain, beer and cattle. A clearly prejudiced scribe, comparing his life with that of craftsmen, wrote:

I have never seen a sculptor sent on an embassy, nor a bronze founder leading a mission: but I have seen the smith working in the furnace mouth. His fingers are like a crocodile's claws; he stinks worse than fish roe.[4]

To be sure, life was hard for such workers. Since only the most basic tools were available to them and producing finely made goods required infinite patience. But in his description, the scribe exaggerates the miseries of the work and ignores the genuine benefits craftsmen enjoyed. They could take pride in their work and in the knowledge they possessed to create it, as one sculptor noted proudly on the walls of his tomb:

I am an artist who excels in my art, a man above the common herd in knowledge. I know the proper attitude for a statue . . . I know how a woman holds herself . . . the way a man poises himself to strike with the harpoon, the look in an eye at its moment, the bewildered stare of a man roused from sleep . . . the tilt of a runner's body. I know the secret of making inlays that fire cannot melt or water dissolve.[5]

Self-esteem was important because of the lack of public recognition accorded to artists and craftsmen: artists, let alone furniture makers or builders, never signed their works. Only a score of artists' names are known from all the eras of Egypt's history, and then only from the discovery of their own tombs or the excavation of their homes, except in the singular instance of one tomb painting of a banquet scene in which the owner included portraits of his painter and sculptor to thank them for their work.[6]

In addition to painstaking labor, knowledge of materials was essential for each craft. No directions on papyri explained how to make things because that information was transferred from master to apprentice as part of an oral tradition. In this way, knowledge of a craft was passed—usually by father to son—from generation to generation.

Craftsmen enjoyed little independence. The jeweler needed metal and stones for his creations and the carpenter needed various woods; however, gold, silver and semiprecious stones, along with most desired woods, were all royal monopolies. To obtain the supplies they needed, most craftsmen worked for estates that manufactured an array of goods, or a temple or, if fortunate, the royal workshop—larger organizations that could secure the raw materials required.[7] While the estate carpenter could obtain his chisel from the estate smithy more easily than he could on his own, he was also subject to rigid supervision and told what to produce. A goldsmith, for example, was given raw ore only after it had been carefully weighed; the completed gold object was weighed again to ensure that no precious metal had been stolen during the process. Under the vigilant eye of an overseer, a covey of scribes recorded every object and judged its suitability. The wonder is that lovely objects were produced in such abundance, for innovation and aesthetics had little place in this bureaucratic process.

At least the arrangement gave the craftsman security—regular pay in the form of food and drink and, in most cases, shelter. Because leaving one employer to find work with another was almost impossible, craftsmen depended on the good will of their patron. The bounty of their reward varied with his generosity, whether he was a nobleman, a chief priest or the pharaoh. Luckily for the craftsman, patrons believed that the treatment of their workers would be known to the gods and affect their own reception in the next world, In messages meant for divine eyes, tomb after tomb records how generously owners dealt with underlings.

BRONZE STATUE OF ISIS *with gold and electrum inlay, c. 600 B.C.E. Despite the level of skill required to create such exquisite figures, craftsmen were not publicly recognized in Egyptian society.*

Businesspeople

A small portion of the populace earned their living as independent businesspeople, working on their own by bartering for needed materials without the intervention of a patron. Because the number of such independent workers is difficult to estimate—no general census was taken in ancient Egypt and this group would not be included in lists of temple or estate employees—we can only refer to scenes depicting what look like modern Middle Eastern marketplaces filled with single individuals offering various goods for sale. It may be that every village of some size contained a number of independent workers selling in a central location. Still, given that wealthy patrons were supplied by their own workshops and nonwealthy clients had little disposable surplus to barter, living must have been precarious for such people. It is even probable that the majority of those shown in market scenes, rather than being individual businesspeople, had been sent by large estates to dispose of their own surpluses.

International trade was also under government control, and all brokers of commerce between countries were state employees. (Travel outside the borders of Egypt was all but unheard of for ordinary citizens.) The reason for the monopoly was that supplies of certain foreign commodities, such as copper, tin and tall timber, was so necessary to the Egyptian economy that their acquisition could not be left to private initiative. Moreover, the greater the government control of foreign trade, the more it could be used, backed by the might of the Egyptian army, as an instrument of politics to favor friendly foreign governments and punish others.

Miners and Quarrymen

By any accounting, the worst occupations in Egypt were those of quarry and mine workers. The work was so exhausting and the conditions were so dusty, dank and dangerous, that mine stints were sometimes used as jail sentences for serious crimes.

Until sandstone (which can bear greater stress) came into vogue in the New Kingdom, limestone was the material of choice for large construction projects. Quarries for both these soft stones were plentiful in Egypt, but freeing the blocks of either material involved dusty, dirty work using copper or bronze chisels and picks which, blow upon blow, chipped away the stone. Work proceeded from the top layer down, since swinging a pick downward was less fatiguing than swinging upward. Luckier workers toiled in open pits; the less fortunate worked underground. For a subterranean stoneworker, extracting the first blocks required crawling in spaces just large enough to wriggle through. His body covered in stone dust, he labored in a dark and eerie world peopled by shadows made by his flickering oil lamp, constantly at risk of being crushed by rocks or falling prey to endemic lung disease.

Yet the work of the quarryman was easy compared to the work of those who mined precious gold and turquoise, following seams wherever they led through holes deep in the ground. Time was not taken to enlarge mine shafts with timber supports, so the miners were forced to crawl through spaces that seldom allowed room to stand, swinging picks all day on their stomachs in order to chip precious gifts free from hard rock. As employees of a government monopoly, working for food and drink, they were not allowed even the smallest grain of gold or minuscule turquoise gem for themselves.

Herders

Tens of thousands of cattle, goats and sheep were the responsibility of herdsmen who roamed the plains of Egypt caring for their charges, while other herdsmen settled on farm estates with smaller herds. Both carried long staves to enforce their commands, although the real affection they felt for their herds is illustrated by the names they bestowed on their animals: "Beauty," "Golden" and "Brilliant."[8]

A herdsman lived with his herd, guiding them to fresh grazing areas, defending them against hyena and crocodile predators, carrying the sick and injured on his back. When a cow gave birth, he was at her side, cooing affectionately and, when necessary, easing the calf from her womb; when a stream had to be forded, he shouldered those calves too small to walk safely across. Just as today, cattle were rounded up, lassoed and branded; of course, in Egypt, what was burned on the cattle's right shoulder was a hieroglyphic sign.

Marshmen

Egyptians called their Delta *Mehit*—papyrus marsh. Although sufficient dry land existed in this area for tens of thousands of cattle to graze, almost a third of it remained under water throughout the year, providing work and shelter for an unusual group of people. Marshmen hunted, fished or gathered papyrus, and, in consideration of their moist work conditions, wore either no clothing at all or tied a simple wrap of cloth around the waist and through their legs.

Papyrus—the material on which all official writing was done—constituted a necessary commodity in Egypt. A natural marsh grass, as tall as ten feet high, all stem except for a halo of tendrils at the top, papyrus grew abundantly in the Delta environment. Its harvest provided not only a living for marshmen, but the material for their boats and homes as well. Thanks to the pockets of air inside its cellular stem, cut papyrus served as a fine material for boats, which were made by lashing together enough lengths to create a kind of punt which could be poled through the still, shallow water. When the same papyrus was stood upright, laced together and plastered with mud, it provided material for a simple shelter for the marshman and his family.

Each day a marshman punted through natural stands of papyrus, cutting stems below the waterline, then stacking them onto his boat. These bundles would be delivered to papermakers who sliced the stems lengthwise into thin strips, then cut them into foot-long lengths before placing them in layers, first side to side horizontally, then side to side vertically. When beaten with a wooden mallet, the two thicknesses compressed to paper-thin dimensions while exuding a sap that acted as a natural glue when dried. The end result was a sheet of paper-like writing material called papyrus—the origin of our word "paper"—that was trimmed and smoothed with a polishing stone before use. Sheets could be glued to make continuous scrolls of any length desired, which in some cases measured more than a hundred feet long.

Marshmen, who also caught fish by spearing them in the shallow Delta waters and trapped birds in large nets in the same marshes, enjoyed a degree of unsupervised independence unusual in highly structured Egypt.

PLAY

Long hours of incessant work allowed little playtime for farm workers; others enjoyed only a few free days granted by their employers from time to time. Most play, therefore, involved children, independent marshmen or people rich enough to have estates with overseers. Yet abundant evidence points to the playful spirits of all Egyptians, even those without the leisure for pure play. Whenever workers are shown in tomb scenes, they are described in hieroglyphs as encouraging one another, bantering with fellow workers and singing.

Recreation

Since tomb walls served as pictorial records of what the deceased wanted to recreate in his next life, they tell us what the owner enjoyed in this life as well. Most common are scenes of banquets, hunting and fishing. At least the class of people who could afford decorated tombs found some of their fondest pleasures in sport.

Much like today, fishing and hunting were pursued more for the pleasure of the catch than for the food. Marshes provided a favorite arena for the activity. Often couples are portrayed enjoying the outing together, both simply and practically dressed—probably a relief from the formal attire usually worn by this class. Some scenes show a husband drawing a bead on a duck with his bow while his faithful wife holds the next missile ready. Others reproduce a couple posed in the same attitudes but substitute a curved throwing stick as the weapon, and yet others show the husband poised to hurl his harpoon at underwater prey, also under the admiring gaze of his wife.

Desert hunting provided the thrill of the chase. Egyptians, mounted in chariots, usually in groups of three or four to corral their prey, pursued speedy game such as rabbits, antelope or gazelles with bows or spears. Even the most dangerous animals—fierce lions and leopards—were hunted in a desert more verdant than it is today. Sometimes a tied cow was used as bait, and hunting dogs, swifter over short distances than chariots, were employed as well. Indeed, Egyptians are the first people on record, though not necessarily the first in fact, to domesticate the dog, a greyhound-like species known today as the saluki.

More certain and surprising is the fact that they first domesticated cats and used them as hunting animals in the marshes.

Children practiced with bows, spears and throwing sticks by the hour to gain enough proficiency to hit live targets, and adults honed their skills regularly as well. Bullfighting was the one known Egyptian spectator sport. The Egyptian version pitted bull against bull rather than man against beast, but referees with short sticks watched, ready to step in to prevent fatal injury to either animal. Besides sports, other Egyptian amusements included sailing for its own sake with no objective other than to enjoy the cool breeze of the Nile. Music provided another favored entertainment. Festive scenes on tomb walls almost always depict an orchestra, generally with dancers swaying to its rhythms. Old Kingdom bands consisted of harp, drums, oboe and flute, with a variety of mandolins and lyres; a double flute was added by the New Kingdom. While a type of straight bugle existed, its shrill tones only issued commands for troops and never figured in musical ensembles.

Harps, ranging from half the size of a man, and played kneeling, to taller than man-sized and played standing, consisted of four to seven cat-gut strings in the smaller versions and as many as ten to twenty-two in the larger. All were tied to an oversized sounding board which used stretched leather to amplify the sound. Blind harpists, probably because their handicap gave them better memories for the lyrics they sang, are often depicted. Flutes or, more correctly, reed pipes, were blown from their ends rather than their sides as with the modern flute. Surviving examples include instruments with three to fourteen holes; another common type joined two pipes together, probably producing a semblance of harmony. Mandolins, thin oblong sounding-boxes with six to eight strings attached to a long arm, were held vertically like guitars; a pick was used to strum the instrument.

Percussion instruments were many and varied. Drums consisted of a sort of tom-tom several feet long, slung over the shoulder with a cord and played with drumsticks. Used not only to set a beat for a band, this style of drum was employed by the military to give Egyptian troops their marching cadences. Other drums were shallow in depth and struck with the hand. Both the tambourine and the

MURAL OF A BLIND HARPIST *from the tomb of Nakht, an Eighteenth-Dynasty astronomer, priest and scribe.*

forerunner of castanets, a pair of five-inch sticks clicked rhythmically in one hand, were also popular. A special percussion instrument called a sistrum was made of metal in the shape of the head of the cow goddess Hathor, patron of music. Her horns were elongated so several wires on which metal disks were loosely strung could be attached crosswise, producing a metallic rattle sound when shaken.

Dancers' rhythmic clapping added more percussive sounds to a performance. Only women, most often naked or with only a sash around their waist, danced at banquets. They are often depicted bending backwards in gymnastic-like contortions as their long hair, tied at the ends with weights that swayed to the music, touched the ground. One scene shows part of a troop of dancers, their hair pulled high to simulate the tall, white pharaonic crown, posing in the familiar attitude of a pharaoh smiting his enemies while others in the group acted the role of victims. Given the dancers' slim bodies and noticeable breasts, this dance must surely have been performed for comic effect. In a solemn dance performed for funerary processions, dancers with caps hiding their hair slid their right feet forward, with arms, palms up forming a circle over their heads, then slid their left feet ahead while their right arms moved to a forty-five degree angle and the left descended behind the body. Step by slow step the dancers made their way to the tomb, followed by singers, mourners, friends, relatives and servants.

No notation to record Egyptian music existed, but lyrics were written out and some have been found. Their bittersweet tales generally encourage enjoying the moment because of life's fleeting nature. One New Kingdom song advised:

Men's bodies have returned to the earth since the beginning of time
And their place is taken by fresh generations.
As long as Ra rises each morning
And Atum sinks to rest in Manou,
So long will men beget and women conceive
And through their nostrils they will breathe;
But one day each one that is born must go to his appointed place.
Make a happy day, Oh priest . . .
Pass thy day in happiness . . .
Think on the day when thou must fare to the land where all men are as one.
Never a man hath taken his possessions with him to that land,
And none can thence return.[9]
Another, of similar sentiment, counseled,
Follow thy heart and thy happiness as long as thou art on earth.
Consume not thy heart until there cometh for thee that day
When man begs for mercy,
Unless the god whose heart beats no longer hears them who call upon
    him.[10]

Although both these songs were inscribed in tombs, their philosophy was also commonly embraced by the living. In the Late Period, most festive banquets ended with a fake mummy in a small coffin paraded around the diners and making, in a more graphic manner, a similar point about human mortality.

Games

Games existed in great variety, from sedate board types to more physical ones, with most of the latter being played by children. They loved their version of tug-of-war in which one team's captain grasped the wrists of the other captain while, behind, each team formed a human chain to try to pull them apart. "Your arm is much stronger than his! Don't give in to him!" one team urged its captain on a tomb wall from 4,000 years ago. Another favorite game resembled the "buck-buck" game played by modern-day Boy Scouts. A standing group of six to eight boys formed a line by linking their arms over their shoulders. The object of the game was for the other members of their team to leap on top—not an easy feat—and settle on all fours. Then the other team had its turn. One scene illustrating this game included the score: two children succeeded. Another game consisted of seating two children back-to-back with their arms grasping the ankles of their outstretched legs. The object was for a third child to jump over this human obstacle, a challenge complicated by the obstacle's attempts to trip the jumpers. Although the seated children kept their eyes closed, the jumper was required to yell a warning as he ran toward them. Also popular was the universal "odds and evens" in which two players shot out as many fingers as they wished after yelling either odd or even; a count of the combined fingers determined the winner.

Wrestling, beloved of both men and boys in ancient Egypt, achieved a great degree of complexity and required long training. Tombs of Middle Kingdom nobility in modern Beni Hassan show hundreds of vignettes of paired wrestlers—with only a ribbon around their waists—illustrating as many different holds and throws, from half-Nelsons to hip-rolls. A match began, as in our own day, with two opponents coming at one another in a semi-crouch, reaching for a first hold.

NEFERTARI PLAYS SENET *in this relief from her spectacular burial chamber.*

Marshmen and other boating people substituted a kind of joust for wrestling in which, as spectators rooted for their favorite, the crew of one small punt tried to knock the other crew in the water with long poles. Other games taught military skills, as one in which contestants wielded short sticks simulating swords or battle axes and used small boards fixed to one lower arm to ward off an opponent's blows. Others involved aiming arrows and spears at targets. Given the Nile's proximity, swimming, of course, was a favorite pastime for all children.

Girls and young women enjoyed their own varieties of games. Many involved balls carved from wood or made by sewing leather around a packed wad of straw. Juggling two or three balls was popular, as was a simple game of catch. To make tossing a ball more interesting, one girl rode piggyback on another and threw the ball to a similarly mounted rider, attempting to keep three balls moving at once. Perhaps the first girl to drop the ball became the "horse" in the next round. In another, more gymnastic, exercise, two participants stood back-to-back with outstretched arms while two others grasped their arms and leaned back almost horizontally with their feet resting against each other. The entire ensemble then spun around as often as they could until overcome by dizziness.

More sedate activities included four board games known from examples found in tombs—an indication of how much they must have been enjoyed. The oldest, called *mehen*, consisted of a serpent etched on a board whose body, divided into segments, coiled to the center. Pieces representing three lions and three lionesses were found in a drawer in the board along with a red and a white ball. Since no instructions were included, its rules are unknown, but most likely it was an antecedent of such modern games as Chutes and Ladders, in which a piece moves from square to square, some with rewards, others with penalties, and the objective is to reach the end before one's opponent. How moves were decided is a question, since dice did not exist. Other board games did come with either ivory or wood wands, each about eight inches long, some with round ends, others with fox-like heads. One side of the wand was curved, the other flat and inscribed with three bands of lines. The way in which the wands fell when they were thrown probably decided the move.[11]

SENET BOARD, C. 1200 B.C.E. *In this popular game, players threw sticks to determine their moves across the 30-square board.*

Equally old was a game of many squares and multiple pieces that looks remarkably like our checkers. The top and bottom of a game box from the early New Kingdom gives us information about two other board games.[12] One board layout, called *senet*, consisted of three rows of ten squares each. The other, called *tjau* ("robbers"), consisted of three rows of four squares at one end of the board from which eight more squares formed a line toward the other end. This "tail" row was bordered by a hound facing a lion above and a lion facing two gazelles below. Six dome-shaped ivory game pieces were found inside the box, along with six spool-shaped pieces, three pairs of game wands and a pair of knucklebones. How these games were played remains unknown, but they appear to be games of position much like Go or Parcheesi.

Toys

Children have always played with dolls, and Egyptian children were no exception. Some of these beloved playthings were stuffed with cloth; others were carved from ivory or wood. One unusual type was made from a carved piece of wood, thick or even bulbous at the bottom, decreasing to a tiny top with shoulders and arms barely indicated. Because of their shape, excavators call them "paddle-dolls." They are often found with bead-hair covering the "head." More familiar were dolls, sometimes with movable arms, accurately carved from wood. Models in wood or clay of cats, dogs, donkeys, mongooses, hedgehogs and pigs show Egyptian children's love of animals. War toys, such as a two-inch-high painted wood chariot, existed as well. For babies, there were rattles, either simple pottery bulbs with handles or more engaging models of animals with pebbles inside, which soothed infants as they do today.

Mechanical toys, operated by strings, are sometimes found. One catlike wood animal has a mouth that opens and closes with the pull of a string. A toy crocodile performs the same motions. Another toy consists of a man bent over an inclined board while holding something in his hands—either rubbing clothes on a washboard or kneading bread. Whatever the object, he moves it up and down the board whenever a string is pulled. A "dancing dwarves" toy consists of three dwarves in a line who spin when activated by a string.

5

FOOD

THE VARIETY AND READY AVAILABILITY OF FOOD IN AMERICA today would amaze ancient people. The fact that meat can be enjoyed on a regular basis even by lower economic groups, and that expensive dishes, such as steak and lobster, have been tasted by the family who cleans the mansion, as well as its owner, is truly a modern phenomenon. During the European Middle Ages most peasants had never tasted meat—as was also the case for poor farmers in Eastern Europe and Spain as late as the beginning of the twentieth century. The farther back in time we go, the greater the disparity between the dining habits of the wealthy and those of the poor, in addition to the meager choices available to both.

Between Egypt's agricultural bounty and her power to command the resources of neighboring countries, she was truly an anomaly of the ancient world: literally thousands of years would pass before anyone would again eat as well and enjoy such variety as the ancient Egyptian. Considering the country's huge population by the standards of the time—as much as three million at the apex of the New Kingdom—this fact becomes all the more striking. Despite so many mouths to feed and lacking any mechanized farm equipment, its economy produced sufficient excess that Rameses the Great could donate half a million cattle to various temples over his sixty-seven-year reign, in addition to gifts of other food in proportionate amounts.

Rich and poor did not set exactly the same tables. Most farmers dined infrequently on meat and never tasted expensive imports. A cow in ancient Egypt cost the equivalent of an entire year's income for a craftsman or the annual harvest of a small farmer.[1] The average citizen would not waste such a precious

PAINTED LIMESTONE STATUETTE *of woman making beer, an invention of the ancient Egyptians.*

commodity on dinner. On the other hand, a goat—valued at only a sixteenth of a cow—might be an appropriate menu choice for a special occasion, such as a wedding or a birth, even for a poor person. Everyday protein was obtained from fish or other nonanimal sources.

Just as we use the phrase "meat and potatoes" to describe a basic meal, ancient Egyptians referred to the staples of their diet as "bread and beer." One list of troop provisions specified twenty bread rolls per soldier per day; the number of jugs of beer were not mentioned.[2] Since bread and beer were manufactured from grain, the greatest source of energy and nutrients for the Egyptian lower classes came from cereal products.

Egypt's two indigenous grains, barley and emmer wheat, both grown in flat fields, flourished in the country's hot climate and, once the canals that supplied them with water had been constructed, required little care. When ripe, the top of the plants were harvested using a crescent-shaped scythe with a row of sharp flint triangles embedded in the wood and held in place by dried resin. The cut heads were gathered, spread on a community threshing area, then trodden by cows, goats, donkeys or even pigs to free the grain from the stalks and split open the hulls. The stalks were removed, then the mass was winnowed—thrown several times in the air. The heavier grains fell back to the threshing floor, while the lighter "chaff" (hulls) blew away.

After collection, the grain was stored in beehive-shaped silos until needed. Then, several handfuls were placed on a stone quern with a gently curved surface for milling. A stone shaped like our rolling pin with a curve to match the curvature of the grinding surface was rolled back and forth, grinding the grain into flour, which was caught in a container at one end of the quern. In the early days, this was women's work, but it evolved into an industry capable of producing great quantities, with men milling the grain in huge cylindrical pestles which they stood alongside, working mortars fixed to the end of poles. The flour produced was made into dough by adding water then kneaded and leavened with a pinch of day-old dough that had naturally bred yeast. After it rose, the dough was shaped for baking.

Bread came in a multitude of forms from crescent, round, oval, pyramidal, disk and hexagonal shapes, to exotic shapes of women, animals and birds for special ceremonies or magical use. These could be baked in a variety of ways. Sometimes tall ovens were used; other times a flat stone heated by a fire beneath it acted as a sort of griddle for flat bread. There were also conical stoves, similar to Indian tandoori ovens, on whose inner surface dough was placed for fast grilling, or heated pottery molds. Additives, such as honey, anise or cumin, were sometimes used to flavor the basic wheat and barley breads.

So important was their bread to ancient Egyptians that they gave it up during times of mourning,[3] a custom similar to the Christian period of Lent, a meaningful sacrifice only because of the food's importance. Otherwise bread figured in every meal—from a farmer's breakfast of bread and perhaps milk to the most elegant feast set by a mighty pharaoh. Both commoner and king ate toasted bread, enjoyed it as a stuffing with roasted animals and fowl and partook at the end of the meal of sweet cakes made by adding honey to the bread. In their use of grains, the main difference between farmers and the upper class was that the latter washed his meal down with wine, the former with beer.

Beer, produced from the earliest days of Egypt, is generally considered to be an Egyptian invention.[4] Although beer's chemistry is complex, simple, natural procedures produced acceptable versions. Grain and malt in solution produce alcohol; carbonation caused by the fermenting action of the yeast is a by-product. When ancient Egyptians exposed moistened, unmilled grain to the air in warm conditions, it germinated and, after crushing, became malt. By baking bread of coarse flour lightly enough to prevent the heat from destroying the yeast, then crumbling the loaves into water and adding some of the malt for flavor, they produced—after allowing time for the yeast in the bread to ferment the mixture and straining it through a sieve—beer of about 7 percent alcohol.[5] Both barley and wheat beers were brewed in this manner, sometimes with such additives as date juice for a sweetener or red dye for special holidays.

Beer contained nutrients and, thanks to the sanitizing action of the alcohol, was safer to drink than still water which could harbor any number of harmful microbes. It was also, of course, intoxicating if drunk to excess. Abundant tomb scenes depict the results of overindulgence (though wine was the more likely culprit in these upper-class tombs), but sober people deplored the condition. A scribe named Ani described its effects and warned against visiting a house where liquors were served.

> Boast not that you can drink . . . a jug of beer. Thou speakest, and an unintelligible utterance issueth from thy mouth. If thou fallest down and thy limbs break there is no one to hold out a hand to thee. Thy companions in drink stand up and say "Away with that sot." If there cometh one to seek thee in order to question thee, thou art found lying on the ground and thou art like a child.[6]

Bread and beer did not exhaust the Egyptians' uses of grain: it was also stewed to produce gruel, baked as groats to accompany the main course of a meal, and even used as a religious symbol. Mummies sometimes wore a necklace braided from wheat leaves, and often tombs contained full-sized beds spread with mud in which barley had been planted in an outline of the god Osiris. When it sprouted, even in the dark tomb, it symbolized both the regeneration of the god as well as the hopes of the deceased for his own rebirth.

Other than grain, the poorer classes depended mainly on fish, supplemented by wild fowl for their protein, both of which cost only the time required to catch them. Fish abounded in both the Nile and in Egypt's one true lake, located in an area called today the Fayum. Ancient records note that the tax on a single year's catch from this lake would amount to $1 million today.[7] Only a small percentage of saltwater fish were consumed; the majority came from fresh water.

Once a year, as the Nile's floodwaters receded from the land, fish became trapped in the mud and could be gathered by hand in great numbers, but for the rest of the year Egyptians employed a variety of fishing methods. For sport, fish were speared or hooked, but seines were employed for larger catches, as well as smaller nets, thrown, set in place or even lashed between two boats as a trawl. Catfish of various species were popular for their flavor as well as a kind of local fish called Nile perch, which could attain sizes above 100 pounds.

THE DIVERSE EGYPTIAN DIET, *which included fish, fowl, and varieties of sweet fruit, is depicted in this relief from the tomb of Menna, an ancient scribe.*

Because Egypt's warm climate caused rapid spoilage, fish generally were salted, pickled or split open and sundried until used. Recipes included simple roasting and boiling or stuffing with bread and spices. Fish roe counted as a delicacy, as did newly hatched fry, cultivated for the purpose in artificial ponds. Fishcakes made from shredded flesh also constituted a treat. One recipe from Ptolemaic times called for a marinade of oil, onion, pepper, coriander and other herbs spread over a large fish as it baked,[8] a recipe which could please any modernday fish lover. The Nile also yielded turtles, clams and even crocodiles. Crocodiles could be caught on hooks, trapped in nets or speared. Some tomb paintings record brave lads in the act of crocodile wrestling.

Thanks to a large population of birds native to Egypt's marshes, fowl provided variation in the diet of both rich and poor. Since Egypt lay on the main migratory route between Europe and lower Africa, hundreds of thousands of fowl, tired and easy to catch, alighted each season in Egypt both before and after their long flight across the Mediterranean. Egyptians showed their passion for birds by creating twenty-four separate hieroglyphic signs for various species, with many more represented by signs in combination. Ducks, geese, pigeons and doves were regularly consumed along with countless smaller species. The upper classes hunted fowl as a sport either with a bow and tiny-tipped arrows or with special throwing sticks in the form of a slight "s" shape. Nets were employed for food gathering; large ones were either thrown or set off with the pull of a string, and individually sized traps were tripped by prey. Egypt was also renowned for inventing bird "incubators," which allowed both pigeons and doves to be raised in cotes where, in addition to housing eggs and the birds themselves, their dung could be gathered for fertilizer. Chickens found their way to Egypt from western Asia around the time of the New Kingdom but were far from common during much of ancient times.[9] Ancient Egyptians had to make do with pigeon, goose or duck eggs for their breakfasts.

Vegetables form a large part of the diet of most farming countries, and Egypt was no exception. Its farmers grew onions and garlic, which they used extensively, along with radishes, lettuce, celery, leeks, parsley, several kinds of squash, cucumbers and various beans, including fava beans, chick peas, lentils, peas and, possibly, lima beans.[10] Aquatic plants also found their way to the table. Egyptians were fond of the lotus plant for its perfume and attractive large flower, but they also ate its root and the beans of a related species that tasted like nuts. Papyrus, a water weed in the swampy Egyptian environment, which provided material for writing, was also gnawed for the sweet sap in its stem.

A special place in the Egyptian diet was reserved for sweet fruit. Figs were enjoyed for both their fruit and juice, which could also be fermented into a fig wine. Abundant grape vines yielded grapes, wine and, when sundried, raisins. Melons were harvested, including the special summer treat of watermelon. Of course, plentiful date palms provided their sweet fruit, fresh or dried. In fact, the hieroglyphic symbol for dates also signified sweetness in general, as in a "sweet person" or "sweet act," while the sign for "one year" was a stripped palm rib, since these trees grew one new frond each month. Another species of palm, the dom palm, supplied a tasty nut that could be eaten raw or ground into flour. More exotic fruits included jujubes, pomegranates and perseas, with juniper beans and almonds imported as exotic foods for the wealthy. A few unclear references suggest that apples may have existed although they formed no great part of the diet.[11] The olive, though not sweet, was a common cultivated fruit enjoyed both for itself and for its oil. Chocolate pudding was simulated by grinding carob beans into milk which then jelled.

There was nothing bland about the Egyptian diet. The availability and variety of spices used in Egyptian cuisine of the period would impress any modern cook. The liquorish taste of anise found constant use, along with the "sweet" flavor of mint. Cumin was much used, especially as a coating for fish, but dill, marjoram, rosemary, thyme and sage each added its distinct taste and perfume. Mustard plants yielded their seeds, although they were not ground with vinegar into the mustard mixture we use today, and safflower existed as well. Celery seeds were commonly used for seasoning. Of course, salt brought out the flavors of whatever it was sprinkled on, but pepper was not yet cultivated in Egypt. For the wealthy, two imports added exotic flavors—cinnamon and coriander.[12]

Although the average Egyptian could not afford meat regularly, he consumed milk in greater quantities than was common in most cultures. The lactose intolerance of many Asians and Semites did not seem to affect the Egyptians who, until they were weaned at three, drank milk as their only food and continued to consume it throughout their lives. Cows, goats and even asses supplied substitutes after a mother's milk had ceased. No evidence of butter or cheese exists, although it seems likely that cheese, which easily could have accidentally occurred as a byproduct of old milk, was available.

Additional dishes appeared on the tables of the well-to-do. The wealthy considered beer the beverage of working people and preferred the smooth taste of wine for themselves. Grapes—either as low pruned bushes or as trellised vines— grew abundantly, especially in the Delta region famed for its vintages.

Demonstrating the extent to which Egyptians favored this drink are the numerous tomb paintings that depict the harvesting and pressing of grapes to extract their juice. Egyptians used the age-old method of trampling grapes with bare feet in vats large enough to hold from four to six people, a process which, unlike heavy presses, does not add the bitter, acidic flavor of crushed stems. To prevent falling into the grape mixture, workmen grasped ropes tied to a beam above the vat. Sometimes they were encouraged in their work by children beating a rhythm with sticks.

As the juice began to flow, it ran into a container set below a spout near the bottom of the vat, although some liquid would remain even after vigorous dancing on the grapes. The residue, called must, was shoveled into a cylindrical cloth bag up to four or five feet in length. Sticks attached to each end of the bag were vigorously twisted by several men to squeeze the last drop of juice through the cloth fibers. To prevent the torque of the twisting motion from bunching up the sack, a boy sometimes stretched horizontally from one stick to the other—hands on one, feet on the other—holding them apart. Alternatively, one end of the sack was fixed to a pole so only the other end turned.

Since grapes carry natural yeasts on their skin, fermentation was instigated simply by setting the juice in a warm environment—no difficulty in steamy Egypt. The juice was poured into pottery jars that stood about two feet tall, in which the conversion of grape sugar to alcohol took place. After fermentation, the opening was sealed with a conical stopper of mud and straw and left to dry hard in the sun. If any sugar remained, however, continued fermentation would generate a gas that would burst a sealed container. To eliminate the problem, a small hole drilled in the stopper or the neck of the jar was left uncovered until it could be safely sealed. The mud stopper was stamped with vintage information that

THE HARVESTING OF GRAPES, *which were fermented to produce wine—a favorite libation in ancient Egypt—is illustrated on the tomb walls of the royal scribe, Userhet.*

included the vineyard that had produced it, the year of production and the quality of the contents, which ranged from "good" to "very good" to "very, very good." Sometimes the name of the producer was also included, as we do today with fine wines.

The tomb of Tutankhamen gives further evidence of the Egyptian appreciation of wine: included among the great treasures found at this famous burial site were twenty-six amphorae of wine. Jar labels indicate their origin to be from the Delta region, which boasted the finest vineyards in Egypt. The fact that only four of the two dozen had contents labeled "sweet" indicates that Tut preferred his wine dry. Twelve jars differed from the others in having long necks incorporating long handles. Since these were Syrian style jars, it may be that the wine inside was imported, but because jars were commonly reused, we cannot know for certain whether Tut drank domestic or imported blends. Vintages were indicated by citing the year of a pharaoh's reign without mentioning which pharaoh. One jar bore the vintage "year thirty-one," although Tut is known to have ruled only nine years. Either this wine was a rare old vintage from the time of his grandfather (Tut's father reigned only seventeen years) or it was in a reused jar with its old label still affixed.[13]

The unanswered question about Egyptian wine is whether it was red or white. Abundant scenes show the color of the grapes which range from dark purple to light rose, but grapes of any skin color yield the same white juice. What determines the color of the wine is whether the juice ferments in its skins, which produces red versions. What type Egyptians made is not known, although later Greek writers remarked on the dark color of Egyptian wine.

Other kinds of wine were produced in smaller amounts from the juice of figs, perhaps of dates, and certainly of pomegranates. Grape juice was also drunk as an unfermented syrup by boiling the juice down to a very sweet drink. Since wine turns to vinegar when exposed to the air, Egyptian knowledge of this acidic liquid, by accident if not by design, was unavoidable because the clay containers in which wine was stored admitted air through their pores—in fact, wine jars found in tombs today all contain nothing but dried residue. Whether Egyptians used vinegar in cooking or in salads is not known.

Unlike poorer classes, the well-to-do dined regularly on meat; however, even the richest did not eat meat every day, as indicated by a list of food delivered to a minor pharaoh who received bread and beer daily, but not meat.[14] Vast herds of cattle of several species roamed the grassy Delta to satisfy the carnivorous appetites of those who could afford them. Temple and tomb scenes show one species of long-legged cow with wide-spreading, lyre-shaped horns, perhaps akin to the early longhorned cattle of Texas. Other scenes depict a squatter, shorter-horned species. In color both types ranged from brown to red to dappled. Perhaps the tall type was raised primarily for its meat; the shorter, for milk. Miniature models show cattle stables housing from four to six cattle in adobe enclosures with a manger built into one wall and stacked bales of hay. Miniature workmen in these models hand-feed the cows to fatten them before butchering.[15] Demonstrating their fondness for beef, tomb owners commissioned butchering scenes for their tomb walls, all showing a steer on its back with its four legs trussed together. First the legs were hacked off, then the head was removed with long knives and, finally, the body was cut into various chops and hung to bleed out and cure.

> Herodotus records the preparation of a cow sacrifice:
> [T]hey take the paunch of the animal out entire, leaving the intestines and fat inside the body; they then cut off the legs, the ends of the loins, the shoulders, and the neck; and having so done, they fill the body of the steer with clean bread, honey, raisins, figs, frankincense, myrrh, and other aromatics. Thus filled, they burn the body, pouring over it great quantities of oil.[16]

He then tells how priests and temple attendants feasted on the meat when it was done. Altogether the recipe sounds delicious, including the oiling of the skin to keep it moist and tender. We may assume that what was good enough for the temple staff was enjoyed by the wealthy at their banquets as well.

Pigs were plentiful in Egypt, although their use as food is controversial. These animals were associated with the evil god Seth, the mortal enemy of Horus embodied by the pharaoh. For this reason, many of the Greeks who visited Egypt during its later days believed that Egyptians did not eat pork. Yet it is known that Seth was worshipped by some Egyptians; indeed, some pharaohs were named Seti after this god. Either the Egyptians worshipped Horus to whom the pig was anathema, or they worshipped Seth who favored the pig. In either case, the Greeks reasoned, religious strictures would prevent the killing of pigs and consumption of pork. Still other commentators claim that Egyptians shared the Hebrew belief that pork was unclean, therefore unhealthy, even suggesting that the Hebrews may have acquired their aversion to pork during their stay in Egypt.

What were all the pigs doing in Egypt then, if they were not eaten? Since the parasite in pork that causes trichinosis is so tiny that the connection between undercooked pork and disease was only discovered in the nineteenth century, it is unlikely that either the ancient Egyptians or Hebrews would have known about its health dangers. As to the reports of the Greeks, they were based on a failure to understand the

CATTLE KEPT IN ADOBE ENCLOSURES *were hand-fed and fattened by workers before being slaughtered. Their meat was a delicacy reserved for wealthy Egyptians.*

Egyptian religion or what it meant to associate an animal with a god. Egyptians saw no contradiction in revering both Horus and Seth, for each was a powerful god, despite the fact that these two divinities might have warred against each other. The fact that Egyptians identified a certain animal with a god did not stop them from enjoying a meal of the beast. For example, one special steer was singled out to become the emblem of the god Apis and pampered all its life, then mummified after death. In addition, pharaohs referred to themselves as the "Strong of Bull So-and-So." Yet Egyptians relished beef, regardless of the fact that they worshipped one member of the species and viewed their godly pharaohs as sharing bovine attributes.

So it was with pork; Egyptians of most classes loved it. The only truth to the Greek reports is that priests, who followed severe dietary strictures, avoided touching a pig, let alone eating one. Since the Greeks reported herds of hundreds of pigs and described how they were fattened, they should have known as much. If further proof was needed, numerous scenes in tombs, going back to the Old Kingdom, show processions of people carrying food. Pigs figure prominently. Indeed, the Roman author Athenaeus, who lived for a time in Egypt, recorded one way the Egyptians ate pork that may be the earliest reference to a sandwich.

> [E]ach diner is served with a loaf of pure wheat bread molded flat, upon which lies another loaf which they call oven-bread; also a piece of swine's flesh.[17]

Both goats and sheep, called "small cattle," were eaten by the Egyptians, despite the fact that rams were associated with the god Amun and worshipped in various temples. Sheep of two varieties existed. The most common species grew a pair of horns that curled around almost in a circle. A different species had straight horns that spread several feet wide and was portrayed as the head of the ancient ram-god Khnum. However, this second species is seldom depicted as an animal, so it may have become extinct early in historic times. Sheep were certainly domesticated in the earliest days of Egypt, and they roamed in large herds throughout the country; one record refers to a flock of 5,800.[18] These utilitarian animals supplied wool, in addition to their milk and meat. Goats also existed in great numbers. One record lists a herd of either 9,136 animals or 31,256, depending on the interpretation of a difficult passage. Since pictured goats all have short hair, Egyptians must have used these animals for milk and meat, but not for wool.

In addition to these meats available in regular supply, wild animals provided food on a more irregular basis. Ancient paintings show that many species of animal roamed what is now a desert adjoining the cultivated land, supported by a climate moister than today's arid one. Gazelle, antelope, ibex, hartebeest, oryx, addax, wild donkeys and deer were avidly pursued by hunters. In early days, before horses were imported into Egypt, hunts consisted of groups of men either driving their prey into a netted area or a smaller number of men hunting with dogs. Egyptians were possibly the first people to domesticate the dog from a wild species that resembles the modern saluki hound. They followed a pack of these rangy dogs and finished off with bows and arrows whatever prey the dogs hamstrung. Lone hunters sought smaller game, such as rabbits or hedgehogs.

When the horse and chariot came to Egypt after the Second Intermediate Period, dangerous game became part of the quarry, including lions and leopards. In addition, speedy ostriches, fierce wild cattle, and even mammoth elephants, fell to Egyptian sportsmen. Hyenas, too, are shown both hunted and trussed by ropes, and hand-fed in a pen. Their flesh is bitter and they have never been known to be raised for hunting or domesticated as pets, so it is difficult to imagine the use Egyptians made of them. Nor were they ever sacrificed by the Egyptians.

Egyptians also kept working animals. Oxen pulled carts and, occasionally, helped haul heavy stones, although humans performed most of that labor. Donkeys carried smaller loads, including riders, and helped thresh grain. There were pets as well. In addition to dogs, Egyptians loved cats, which they were the first to domesticate from a similarly-sized wild feline. Monkeys provided amusements for both children and adults, and most homes kept birds for their songs.

The end of a meal called for something sweet. Pure sugar, which we obtain from sugar beets or sugar cane, did not exist in ancient Egypt, but honey did. Egyptians learned to cultivate bees and even how to use smoke to drug them so the honey could be collected without paying the price of stings. Some writers contend that honey was a royal prerogative based on the fact that an ancient royal title for the pharaoh was *bity*, "He of the Bee."[19] This theory is contradicted by the ease and negligible cost of producing large supplies of the sweet nectar that would naturally be desired by many, as well as by the difficulty of enforcing such a restriction in the case of wild bees. Additional sweetness came from fruits and their juices. Sweet pastries and cakes existed as well. One recipe comes from the tomb of Rekhmire, a vizier during the New Kingdom, who must have relished a particular cake. By inscribing the recipe on the wall of his tomb he assured himself pieces of it for eternity. First, "tiger nuts" (tubers of cyprus grass which grew wild in the marshes) were ground into flour. The flour then was mixed with honey and baked.[20] Where one recipe survives, there must have been others.

When Egyptians prepared for death they covered their tomb walls with scenes of whatever they enjoyed most during life, believing that the gods, seeing these pictures, would provide more of the same in the next life. The most common of all scenes are meals. Most show only a husband and wife eating while they gaze at each other, but many show festive banquets, replete with guests. Egyptians loved to eat and adored feasting with their friends. What they loved in life, they wanted to take with them to the next world, so food is often found mixed with other objects in tombs. Ducks, geese and various grains have been identified.

A typical, lavish banquet consisted of a group sitting on the floor or at individual round tables. Often they reposed on low chairs or stools under which lay a basin for washing their hands, sometimes with a pet cat or monkey beside it. Men and women ate together, both dressed in flowing linen gowns that reached the floor. The women held lotus flowers in one hand for the perfume and wore a perfume cone on their head made of a fatty substance that released a pleasing aroma as heat from the head slowly melted it during the course of the evening. Heaps of food completely covered the small tables. There were breads of several shapes and varieties, whole roasted, trussed fowl and joints of meat, several kinds of vegetables and assorted fruit. The mountains of food seem impossibly high as depicted and each item is shown whole and individual, none on a plate or in a bowl. This is because the owner of the tomb wanted no ambiguity about the food he desired for eternity, so each bit is depicted unequivocally, if not realistically.

At an actual banquet, rather than a pile of food, various courses would have been served one after another in containers. Plates were not used, but ceramic

LADIES AT A BANQUET *wear perfume cones and share mandragora fruits in this
c. 1400 B.C.E. relief.*

bowls or, more likely at such formal affairs, blue glazed and painted faience dishes
would have held the food. Cups of similar material stood ready for wine and were
continually refilled from large pitchers carried by circulating servant girls. Other
servant girls whisked away each bowl from a finished course, replacing it with the
next. Supplemented with a knife for cutting mouth-sized morsels, the primary eating
utensil was the eater's hand, which explained the water pitcher below each chair.

As dish after dish arrived at the table and cups were replenished, an orchestra
of lute, harp and drum accompanied one or more singers. Professional dancing
women, naked except for a slim waist sash, moved energetically to the music,
their activity emphasized by round weights at the ends of their long hair. With

so much to eat and especially to drink, accidents were expected. Paintings show servant girls holding basins beneath the mouths of celebrants who have eaten or drunk too much. Except for that, the party sounds like fun even today.

The Egyptian diet proved ample and reasonably healthy for most of the population. A calculation of the daily food intake in Ptolemaic times, which was not the most bountiful era, arrived at 3,780 daily calories for the average adult from grain alone.[21] Considering that the American average for all food hovers around 2,000 calories today, this statistic seems remarkable. The only reason Egyptians were not all obese is that their occupations generally involved hard, physical labor which burns calories. Their situation resembled American farmers before mechanization, who ate more at breakfast without weight gain than the average person today consumes in two days. Actually, the Egyptian diet was healthier than a simple calorie calculation implies. Their calories did not come from sugars, greasy gravies or fried foods, but entirely from natural products. Herodotus ranked Egyptians as the healthiest people in the world (after the Libyans). Since he lacked an understanding of nutrition, this merely tells us that Egyptians presented more vigorous, trim figures than his Greeks. From the thousands of statues and paintings of Egyptians that survive, it does seem that every man stood slim and well muscled, every woman slender and gently curved. They portray creatures of perfect eating habits.

Remembering that only a rare person would choose to have himself portrayed as other than perfect, however, such likenesses must be taken with a dose of skepticism. After all, these paintings and statues generally depict people in the prime of their life, despite the fact that they existed in tombs which generally held old bodies. Surely there were old Egyptians and obese Egyptians, not to mention diseased Egyptians. Occasionally such imperfections are depicted, even in the same tomb that elsewhere presents the owner as an Adonis or a Venus. The purpose of Egyptian funerary depiction was more to show how the deceased wanted to look in the next world than how he looked in this one. Nevertheless, the rare statues showing age, double chins, rolls of belly fat and dwarfism clearly prove that not everyone attained perfection. It seems that most Egyptians presented more vigor and trimness in their appearance than their contemporaries, as eyewitnesses attest, but with exceptions and without immunity from the inexorable ravages of age. Credit for their general good appearance goes to exercise and diet.

The greatest problem with this diet was its effect on the teeth, evident in severe wearing and signs of dental abscesses in mummy after mummy. Making bread from grain swept off the ground introduced quantities of sand in the final loaf, an abrasive that would wear away granite, let alone the dentine of teeth. A diet of such bread eventually ground the teeth away, exposing their roots to decay. On the other hand, normal cavities were rare because of the absence of pure sugar.

Egyptian Food

Meat: beef, lamb, pork, goat, gazelle, antelope, ibex, hartebeest, oryx, addax, wild donkey, deer, rabbit, hedgehog, ostrich, duck, goose, pigeon, dove, smaller birds

Vegetables: onions, garlic, radishes, peppers, lettuce, celery, leeks, parsley, peas, squash, cucumbers, fava beans, chick peas, lentils, lima beans(?), papyrus, lotus root and nuts

Fruit: figs, grapes and raisins, melons, dates, dom nuts, jujube, pomegranates, persea, carob, juniper beans, almonds, olive, apples(?)

Spices: salt, anise, mint, cumin, dill, marjoram, rosemary, thyme, sage, mustard seeds, celery seeds, safflower, cinnamon, coriander

6

CLOTHES AND OTHER ADORNMENTS

WHAT DID AN EGYPTIAN MAN WEAR UNDER HIS KILT OR AN Egyptian woman under her dress? Probably nothing. Garments designed for modesty would have to wait for people more obsessed with sex than the ancient Egyptians who were practical to the point of working naked in hot, swampy terrain. Yet they loved clothes. A New Kingdom architect's tomb contained seventeen sleeveless tunics, twenty-six shirts and fifty triangular loincloths to assure his fashionable appearance in the Next World.[1] The loincloths, simple linen triangles with strings at two corners, were worn by draping the point down the back and tying the strings around the waist before pulling the point through the legs to tuck in the string at the front. Most likely no additional layers covered them, since similar loincloths are pictured as the sole attire of other workers.

Of course, loincloths represented the low end of the Egyptian wardrobe. When attired for formal occasions, Egyptians could out-dress anyone with lovely, elegant gowns worn by both genders—the original unisex clothing. White— the whiter the better—was the color of choice in most eras; color was added by numerous accessories. Dresses fit close to the body to reveal any imperfections of figure, which may be why Egyptians maintained the slim shapes depicted in their portraits. Heads were adorned, and cosmetics generously painted the faces of both women and men. As in every other culture, differences in style proclaimed differences in social status.

A ROYAL COUPLE DISPLAYS THE HEIGHT OF EGYPTIAN FASHION *in this c. 1335 B.C.E. relief: flowing, pleated white linen, colorful sashes and ornate, beaded collars.*

Materials

Fine linen remained the most used fabric throughout all the eras of ancient Egypt. Because it "breathes," linen worked well in the warm Egyptian climate where insulation was seldom needed, and it could be loosely woven into a gauze that allowed air to circulate around the skin. In addition to being cool, it was strong and glowed with an attractive sheen. Cotton did not arrive in Egypt until Roman times. Wool clothing existed, but since it was forbidden in temples[2] and tombs and since most surviving clothing comes from burials, actual articles of wool material are rare.

Egyptians cultivated thousands of acres of waving flax, the plant that yields linen. Through trial and error they learned that harvesting the crop at different stages of ripeness resulted in different kinds of fiber. When the flax stem was green, its soft fiber could be spun into the finest thread; when yellow, stronger fiber would hold pleats well; when brown, tough fiber could be woven into ropes and mats. The fibers inside the stem, however, did not form easily into thread, for they were surrounded by pectin, a stiff, woody core that required several stages of liberation.

The entire plant was first pulled up by the root and taken to a home or small factory where the work of producing thread took place. After drying, the stems were vigorously "rippled," pulled through a comb-like device that sliced them into long ribbons which were soaked for two weeks in vats of water to dissolve the unusable surrounding pectin. Even after soaking, some bits of the pectin would still adhere to the fibers which were first dried, then beaten with wood mallets before being scraped over a sharp, lipped tool. Then the fibers, freed of unwanted material, had to be combed straight. Single fibers were attached end to end by being twisted to form twin strands that could be rolled into balls and placed in containers until spun into thread. Some of these holding containers amounted to little machines. One consisted of a heavy limestone bowl nine inches in diameter—large enough to hold two balls of the rolled fiber—with a pair of loops at the bottom through which the fiber ran. This device maintained tension on the fiber while holding the balls in their container.[3] Another device used a hole in the lid to guide the fiber under the tension provided by the lid's weight.

Spinning, which straightened and strengthened the fibers, meant exactly what the word says. Egyptian spindles consisted of a wooden shaft, four inches or more in length, to which a whorl—a two-to-four inch disk—was attached nearer the top than the bottom. The fiber was tied to a groove at the top of the shaft (later to a hook), then the spindle was rolled vigorously down the spinner's thigh which set it spinning, stretching the fiber by its weight while twisting it for strength. This produced thread of a consistent diameter. Generally, Egyptian thread was two-ply: the ends of two fibers spun once were attached to the spindle and twisted together. Single Egyptian threads were spun counter-clockwise, the natural rotation of flax, while added plies were spun in the opposite direction to prevent the unwinding of individual threads. As thread was produced it was wound into a figure-eight skein on pegs attached to the wall or the ground.

Plain white linen was preferred during most Egyptian eras; for added whiteness, fabric would be exposed to the intense Saharan sun to bleach it. Egyptians of the Eighteenth Dynasty, however, favored colored fabrics, and women during all eras who could not afford fine linen colored their fabric to disguise its cheapness. Of course, colored fabric required colored threads. Egyptians produced blue, black, brown, red and yellow threads and some, such as green, were created by double dyeing with separate colors (blue and yellow).[4] Colored thread made patterned fabrics possible in addition to solid colors, and, alternatively, white fabric could always be hand painted with figures and hieroglyphs.

After the thread had been produced, it could be woven. The original Egyptian looms, dating from prehistoric times, were horizontal—simply two wood beams anchored to the floor by short pegs. Working such a loom required kneeling, and the length of the fabric that could be woven was limited by a weaver's reach. By the New Kingdom, vertical looms—consisting of two beams anchored to the ends of a tall, upright wooden frame—had come into wide use. These looms could be worked while sitting or standing to produce longer lengths of cloth with less discomfort for the weaver and allowed such techniques as tapestry weaves (where the thread is wrapped around the loom back) to be developed.

ANCIENT EGYPTIANS USED BOTH HORIZONTAL *and vertical looms to weave fabrics up to seven and a half feet wide.*

Whatever type of loom was used, weaving followed the same principles. Rows of threads were looped around the length of the beams at the top and bottom, forming long warp rows. A crossing thread (the weft) was passed over then under successive warp threads, beginning at the bottom of the loom and working up to the top. Rather than laboriously running the thread under and over each warp thread individually, Egyptians invented a time-saving method.[5] Alternating warp threads were attached by loops of string to a wooden stick (known today as a heddle rod) as long as the width of the loom and resting on the remaining warp threads, creating a space between each set. This permitted the crossing weft thread to be attached to the end of a dowel that was thrown through this valley in one motion, completing a row of the fabric with a single pass. For the next pass, which had to reverse the over and under of the previous row, a second rod, attached to the remaining warp threads, raised them above the others. A wide paddle (a weaving sword) could now be shoved between the two warp sets to force a space. Then the weft rod was thrown back across, creating the second row of the cloth. In this manner, the weft passed over and under different warp threads every two rows, forming a tightly woven fabric.

Cloth could be woven finely indeed. An example from as early as the Second Dynasty of 160 warp threads and 140 weft threads per square inch[6] would have required both extremely fine thread and the use of a "beater stick," a narrow wood strip that extended the width of the fabric. After passing such a strip through the valley after a weft row had been laid down, the weaver beat it vigorously against that row, pressing it close against previous rows.

Fabrics up to seven and a half feet in width have been found, showing that looms at least that wide were in use. Single pieces of fabric up to seventy-five feet in length have been recovered from tombs, for which the warp threads must not have been cut to the length of the loom but merely held in place, probably by weights. Once a loom-full of weft rows had been completed, the piece was moved down to bring fresh warp threads onto the loom for continued weaving. Side fringe along the fabric was created by leaving loops of weft thread loose at the edge of each row instead of pulling them tight; end fringe by leaving lengths of warp thread. Both were common on Egyptian cloth. More elaborate kinds of fabrics were also produced. Examples of toweling, where little loops of weft are pulled loose between the warp threads, date as far back as the Middle Kingdom. Beautiful embroidery of colored thread sewn into figures and patterns on finished cloth were found in the tombs of two Eighteenth-Dynasty pharaohs, Tuthmosis IV and Tutankhamen. Needles of bone, copper and bronze were used for sewing, aided by stone thimbles with a dimple on top to catch the needle.[7] Tapestry, found among the clothing in the same two royal tombs, is created when patterns formed of different colored thread show on both sides of the fabric: rather than weaving each color under and over alternating warp threads, it was simply looped around the warp threads to be covered. The resulting slits between each patch of color and the adjoining area were sewn together after the weaving was complete.

Despite Egyptians' love of linen, it took second place to wool on chilly winter nights. Excavated in Egypt from as far back as prehistoric times, wool was used primarily by those who could not afford more costly linen but also by the well-to-do as capes and stoles to fend off cold. Spinning wool was a more complex operation because the hairs of sheep were much shorter than the several-feet- long flax fibers. A few hairs at a time had to be twisted using a spindle, then more added at the top, but staggered, to permit a new hair to interlace with others already spun. Once produced, however, wool thread was woven in the same way as linen.

Sheep, goats and cattle also provided skins for clothing and other uses. Rawhide became thongs for attaching metal to wood for tools and weapons, and, before the introduction of nails and glue, for attaching one piece of wood to another in carpentry. Leather not only formed the reins of chariots, the quivers of arrows, the braces bowmen wore to protect their forearms against the snap of the bowstring, but also headbands, belts, bags, dog collars, chair and stool seats, covering for boxes, material to write on and tents. One remarkable use of leather was the cut-out kilt. This kilt was made by carefully slicing a hide to form a web of interlocked strands, sometimes as narrow as a string or even a thread, with one area left solid at the seat and another for the waistband. From pictures of wheat harvests it seems that these delicate garments were commonly worn during such work. Such a kilt would be both cool and modest. Egyptians also learned to appliqué leather, tan it, dye it and paint on it, resulting in some lovely work. Because gazelle hide was favored for its softness and color, scenes of gazelle herds in pens that were once interpreted as attempts at domesticating this wild animal might be better considered portrayals of penned leather stock.

Clothing manufacture constituted a cottage industry in which, after women had spun, woven and sewn enough clothing for their families, they bartered any surplus for supplies. Tomb paintings and miniature models also depict men sewing and weaving in workshops with two or more looms, as would be the case on a large estate with many people to dress, at a temple with its groups of priests or, especially, at the royal court.

Kinds of Apparel

The simplest, most common clothing for males was the Egyptian kilt, a rectangular piece of fabric that was wrapped tightly around the waist then tied in the front with cords or belted. It extended from the waist to just above the knee. One end was wrapped over the other, but the front of the fabric, where the ends crossed, was still loose enough to permit the legs to move in a normal stride. Sometimes the bottom end of the overlapping part of the fabric was cut away in a pleasing curve, or the fabric could be cut into an arc to produce a curved slit in front rather than overlapping all the way down. A special addition for this revealing front was

THIS C. 1325 B.C.E. LIMESTONE FRAGMENT *displays the pleated kilt of a New Kingdom scribe. Kilt variations that featured a protruding, stiff, inverted "v" section of fabric would have interfered with labor and, hence, were worn only by scribes and other high-ranking officials.*

first added by a pharaoh but worked its way down the governmental hierarchy over time: a tapering ribbed flap fell from the waist to show beneath the parted front curve of the kilt. Alternatively, one end of a wide sash could descend down the front of the kilt. Kilt fabric was also pleated to form regular vertical lines, another reason for favoring linen, but leather examples, both solid and cut into net, are known. Beginning in the New Kingdom, kilts grew long enough to reach mid-calf, becoming male skirts. The fabric was usually cut very full to form numerous gathered folds, although it still clung close enough to the body to reveal its outlines.

Males, from pharaohs to farmers, wore simple kilts—as often as not with bare chests—when working, resting or fighting. To dress up a little, or to fend off a late afternoon chill, a shirt—either a short-sleeved jersey or a shoulder-strapped band around the chest—was added. A stole of fabric might also be thrown over the shoulders to cross the chest. One peculiar kilt variation featured a stiffly starched front that stood out a foot or more in an inverted "v." Of course this projection would have interfered with physical labor, which was the whole point: to demonstrate that the wearer was an overseer or a scribe who never needed to sweat. A similar principle led overseers and government officials to don the long skirt style—demonstrably less practical for vigorous work than its shorter relative. Kilts did, however, even show up at formal evening occasions, but these were covered by an ankle-length overskirt of diaphanous linen and topped by a shirt.

The most common woman's attire was a sheath held up by shoulder straps, a long, narrow dress that began at the ankles and rose to just under the breasts. Often a band of contrasting material bordered the top, or the top was sashed. This almost bare-breasted version sometimes substituted wider straps that covered the breasts more completely. A longer version enveloped the whole body, like a tunic, leaving sleeveless armholes and a slightly scooped neck. Still another version added short sleeves to a tied keyhole neck. In every case, however, the apparel followed the slim shape of the body and reached down the leg to the ankles. These democratic dresses were worn both by the lady of the house and by her female servants.

At banquets, however, the lady of the house would never be mistaken for a servant, although she might be confused with the man of the house, for both males and females wore the same sort of fine dress, something very like the saris still worn throughout India. The fabric consisted of nothing but a rectangle, four times as long as its width, with the manner of draping creating the garment. One corner of the rectangle was tucked into a waist cord at the side, and the whole fabric was wrapped completely around the waist once. Next, pleats were formed by tucking the fabric judiciously into the waist cord. The fabric was wrapped around the back again before returning to the front where it was tossed first under the far shoulder then over the other shoulder from behind. With the free end now falling down the front, it was tossed over the shoulder it had previously gone under, brought back under the other arm and finally tied in the front to the fabric's other end, the one previously tucked into the waist cord.[8] The effect could be lovely indeed. Overall, it appeared that a shawl had been tied around the hips over an underskirt, while another shawl with a peak training down the back had been thrown over the shoulders, covering one arm to the elbow but leaving the other arm half bare. Attention would be drawn to the waist where all the wrapping came together at the tied ends of the fabric, from which lovely folds fell to the ankles.

Variations of draping produced different looks. Instead of going under the far arm from the front, the fabric could be thrown over that arm from the front, then over the other shoulder from the back, to tie at the waist. This produced a garment that covered both arms equally to the elbow with less emphasis on the waist. Another variation sent the fabric under the near arm from the front and over the opposite shoulder from the rear, leaving half the chest bare.

In addition to sheath and sari-like apparel, a third kind of dress, mainly but not solely for women, used two separate rectangles of fabric. One piece was about seven feet long, the other two thirds that length; both were twice as long as their widths. Together they formed a skirt-and-shawl ensemble. The larger piece was gathered at the waist to form the skirt, and the shorter piece was thrown around the back of the shoulders while the ends were gathered together and tied at mid-chest. Less closely following the outline of the figure, this outfit often consisted of material so finely woven that the body's outline could be seen through it. A common variation enlarged the shawl into a cape. In the case of this larger second piece, the skirt too would be longer and fuller, and, rather than gathering such a large skirt at the waist, its top would be grasped at each side to form ends that could be knotted beneath the breasts. This created folds outlining the hips and waist. The cape was pulled over the shoulders and tied together with the skirt, which thereby covered both arms to the elbows and formed what looked like a single garment. Both these variations later became characteristic attire for women in other nations. The most usual ancient Greek dress for women consisted of the Egyptian skirt and shawl worn over an undertunic for Greece's cooler climate; classical Roman women commonly wore the Egyptian skirt and cape variation, again over a tunic.

A fourth style of dress consisted of a full length envelope of fabric, more suited to men than women. A five-foot-high by seven- or eight-foot-wide rectangle was sewn together along the short ends, forming a doubled piece of cloth. The top was sewn straight across. A scoop was then cut in the top center for the head, and slits were made at the top of both sides for the arms. This left the only large opening at the bottom, so the dress would be pulled down over the head until the head and arms stuck through their appropriate holes. It formed a very full robe, similar to a choir gown of today, but it was seldom worn in this simple manner. It was usually pulled to the body by slitting the sides so the front half could be pulled to the back and pinned at the waist, while the back half was drawn around to the front and secured with a sash. The sash was wide enough to drape the back from the waist to the bottom of the buttocks and long enough to wrap twice around the body, tie in the front and still leave an end long enough to fall to the top of the feet. When a woman wore this type of dress, the back unsewn half was hand gathered into ends that could be tied at the waist; the front half simply fell in multiple folds. As a variation, instead of tying the back together, a sash narrower than the male version could circle the body just below the breasts and secure the back flap across the hips.

Despite their abundant folds and turns of fabric, Egyptians often dressed up what was already elaborate by adding colorful waist sashes whose ends dangled in the front to mid-thigh. The sash could be a simple ornamental cord, strands of colorful beads or a solid piece of patterned fabric. Its ends might be further embellished with religious symbols, such as the cow face of the goddess Hathor, or by secular motifs, such as lotus flowers. Sometimes the simple strapped tunic worn by most women was elevated by a web of bead netting worn as an overdress. At other times, beads or buttons (never used to close openings) were sewn to the dress in patterns.

Of course pharaohs as well as certain government officials wore special attire to indicate their rank. In addition to distinctive crowns, a bull's tail descending from the waist in the back of a kilt could be worn only by the king. Originally, the pharaoh alone was permitted to sling a leopard skin—complete with its head— over his shoulder, but that emblem was later adopted by his highest official and finally by high priests. All priests wore distinctive garb: a simple robe of white linen that fell full to the ground, clearly distinguished from the form-fitting clothing of the laity. This outfit was adopted by high officials as well, who often held priestly status in addition to their government positions. Children wore nothing at all until they were old enough to walk under their own guidance, then both sexes wore a simple kilt until eight years old or so when they donned the same apparel as the adult of their sex.

No outfit would be complete without shoes or, in the Egyptian case, sandals. Their design was so practical that they are still worn today throughout most of the world. To a foot-shaped sole, a thong was attached where the big toe and its neighbor come together. Another strip was anchored to the sole's sides about two-thirds of the way back. The wearer slipped his foot into the sandal, inching along until the front thong worked its way between his toes and the rear strip gripped the foot in front of the ankles. Such sandals, made of either rushes or leather, were produced in quantity for both genders. Those made of rushes were frequently padded for comfort. Sometimes a third strip joined the toe strap to the ankle strap which fixed their positions and made stepping into the sandal easier. The ankle strap could also be widened so it would not cut the flesh. Occasionally another crossing strap was added between the front of the sandal and the ankle strap to form an almost-shoe; a heel strap might be sewn on as well.

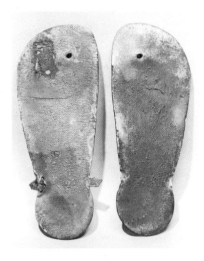

LEATHER THONG SANDALS *worn by Egyptians often included an ankle strap and a padded sole to ensure comfort.*

Jewelry

Colorful accents for the Egyptian's white attire took the form of abundant jewelry for both sexes. Necklaces, bracelets, armbands, anklebands, earrings and finger rings, worn generously by both men and women, solved that problem. So enamored were the Egyptians of their jewelry that even colorful dresses were dressed up by heaps of baubles, which increased in amount and complexity as the centuries passed.

AN ELABORATE PECTORAL ADORNMENT, *inlayed with lapis lazuli and glass paste, from the tomb of Tutankhamen. This neck adornment portrays the winged scarab underneath a sun disk, flanked by two ankhs and eyes of Horus.*

Although earrings were unknown to Egyptians until they saw them on the Hyksos during the Second Intermediate Period, it was love at first sight, and both women and men wore them from then on. Two types were common: rings or studs—each was attached through a hole in the earlobe. Even statues sculpted without earrings generally portrayed this hole. The ring style was usually made of metal; gold was common. Ranging from thin wires to hollow tubes three-quarters of an inch in diameter, these circles left a gap for insertion. In some cases, gold foil covered a baser metal to lend a gold look. Earrings were also carved from shell, bone, carnelian and red jasper, or molded of faience, and might be inlaid with turquoise or lapis lazuli. Ear studs were mushroom shaped with only the flat end showing through the front of the ear so the stem could hold them in place through the lobe. Faience examples are common, although gold, either solid or as gilt, is also known. Examples from Tutankhamen's tomb show that intricate pendants might be hung from them as well. An unusual type of earring consisted of metal coils with several twists that dangled from the ear. Ear plugs also surface from time to time, and female mummies sometimes exhibit the dangling lobe holes caused by such large insertions.[9]

When it came to jewelry for their necks, Egyptians threw subtlety to the wind. They wore anything from chokers, to single-strand necklaces, to multiple strands, to pectorals, to pendants and broad collars up to ten inches wide. Besides their decorative function, necklaces served amuletic and status purposes. Both sheet gold in the shape of flies—military symbols for Egyptians—strung on bead strands and heavy gold circle chains were awards for special service to the country and proudly worn by the recipient. Amulets in the shape of one god or another comprised the numerous rows of necklaces. A string of hippopotamus charms, symbolizing the pregnant hippopotamus goddess Tawert, for example, might be worn by a pregnant woman to call for protection from this goddess of childbirth. Metal, faience or stone shaped like oyster shells ensured health, as did figures of the dwarf god Bes. Cowrie shells, either the real thing or carved facsimiles, warded off the evil eye. Young children often wore a fish amulet as protection against drowning. Indeed, fifty or more different emblems protected against as many misfortunes.

The most characteristic Egyptian neckpiece was the broad collar. This consisted of multiple strands of beads, tubes or amuletic figures which terminated in solid ends anchoring the strands. Ties emanated from the end pieces to knot around the back of the neck, forming a collar that covered much of the chest and extended over the shoulders. Because the collar could be weighty, a counterpoise generally trailed down the back to balance and hold the piece in place.

Smaller chokers formed of several bead strands tied tightly around the neck enjoyed great popularity with women in the Old Kingdom, although they fell from favor thereafter, to be replaced by looser neckwear. A single strand dangling an amulet or colorful stone was popular during the earliest times. Gradually, elements were added until the strand was covered, and several strands of different lengths could be worn at once to create the necklace of one's desire. Pendants, a single amulet hanging at the end of a cord, evolved from the New Kingdom on into pectorals to decorate the mid-chest. Pendants could be rectangular plaques telling a little story, say a scarab holding the sun in its front legs, flanked by two kneeling, worshipping gods beneath a cornice suggesting a temple, or they could be massive breastplates shaped like a falcon, a vulture or a ba-bird, the symbol of the soul. Some of the finest jewelers' work in gold and inlays was invested in such pieces which, not infrequently, hung beneath a broad collar.

Nor were the limbs forgotten. Beginning in the New Kingdom, broad bands circled the biceps above bracelets ringing the wrist. Such bracelets consisted of flexible strands of beads or, more common later, rigid bands. Whether they were of rows of beads, carnelian or other stones, or bands of bronze or gold, perhaps with inlays, they added flashes of color. Originally, bead strands were simply tied to the arm, but later the ends were fixed to clasps that snapped together. The other, rigid, type was hinged on two sides, one of which was held by a pin that could be drawn out to remove the band. Ankles as well were circled by bands of similar construction.

Not one but multiple finger rings—made of stone, faience or metal—added to the decorative scheme. If of faience or stone, they would be pierced through and attached to a metal ring or encased in a bezel. The idea behind both methods was to allow the center piece to turn over, revealing its back. The most popular ring shape was the sacred scarab beetle, which symbolized existence to the Egyptians. Thus, the wearer's name might be inscribed on the base to symbolically wish the owner long life. Alternatively, a god or the pharaoh (a living god) might be inscribed on the base with a request that he or she preserve the wearer. Since hard stones were difficult to carve, the most commonly used material was soft steatite, a grayish white stone glazed in lovely blue or green. Rings were also frequently made of faience which, although easily molded into complex shapes, broke if struck. It may be that these fragile rings were party favors, such as wedding gifts from a newly married couple to their guests.

The waist was also adorned: a woman's girded by draped strings of beads or amulets; a man's cinched by a close fitting belt. Needless to say, a wealthy man or woman fully encased in finery could bear several pounds of jewelry.

HAIR AND HEADDRESSES

Even with every other part of the body adorned, hair was not forgotten. Not satisfied with the lovely black color of their hair, Egyptians devised complex cuts, wigs, ribbons, fillets and diadems to dress their hair up to the standards of the rest of their attire.

There were several hairdos for men. Workmen wore short hair left in bangs across the forehead, then shaped to the head halfway down the neck. This produced a rounded look. Early depictions also show tight curls, but straight hair is portrayed as a norm later. In an alternative cut for men, the back was clipped straight across, and the hair was pushed behind the ears, framing the head and lengthening the face. This could be combined with a ladder cut to create three or four horizontal rows. This square cut grew more complicated in the New Kingdom, when the back fell to shoulder length, sometimes including tight curls, or perhaps plaits, that ran the length of the hair. About the same time, a new cut came into vogue, angling from the nape of the neck to a longer front that spilled to just below the shoulder.

Women always wore their hair longer than men—at least to their shoulders, but generally trailing a foot or more down their backs. Bangs and a center part were popular, in both cases with the hair lining the face over the ears, instead of behind the ears as a man would wear it. The ends were cut in a straight line. As with men, fancy ladder cuts creating horizontal rows were often seen, but curling in tight spirals, or perhaps thin plaits, was also common through all eras.

Children before the age of puberty wore a distinctive cut. All the hair of male children was shaved on one side and in back leaving only one long side lock reaching below the shoulder. Female children cut their hair to a mid-neck length except for the same side lock that fell below the shoulder—the Egyptian sign of childhood. These side locks were sometimes braided into three or so large strands twisted together.

Serious hair decoration called for complex wigs, though, strangely, Egyptians did not try to fool anyone into thinking the wigs were their own hair. Statues often show a line of natural hair peeking out below a wig. Since owners of statues had the last word about how they were portrayed, they must have been proud of their wigs, suggesting that these were expensive, prized articles. Wigs were composed of human hair which, in the case of a long wig, would represent as much as a decade's worth of growth from someone's head.

One unusual early female wig, shown on the Third Dynasty statue of princess Nofret, consisted of a big head of bobbed hair cut straight all around and standing out a good three inches when it reached the bottom of the neck. In general, longer wigs extending at least to the shoulders were most common. One version consisted of thirty or more long, dangling coils of hair emanating from a central part and tied at the end. A variation separated the coils into two lappets, each tied with ribbon to form a large mass framing each side of the face. Long hair arranged into ten or so ladder-cut rows counted as a second type; a third type combined the first two: rows of coils laddered into layers. Two wigs could also be worn together, for example, a shorter wavy wig over a longer coiled wig. Male wigs followed

WIGS CONSISTING OF LONG COILS *or ladder-cut rows, often adorned with golden diadems inlayed with precious stones, were common in ancient Egypt.*

female styles except that they were shorter—shoulder length or a little more—and usually lacked the center part. Beeswax seems to have been the substance that kept the cuts and curls in place, both on wigs and natural hair. Patting an Egyptian head would have felt like rubbing a large, warm crayon.

Facial hair was all removed, with two exceptions. During the early Old Kingdom, numerous statues of men show thin mustaches seldom seen after that time. Pharaohs always wore beards on ceremonial occasions, but private citizens never did. Statues and paintings of pharaohs, however, invariably show lines running from the beard to the ears, clearly indicating the ties of an artificial beard. Presumably the beard recalled an early pharaoh who sported an actual growth, but the tradition persisted long after the style had gone out of general favor. The fake beards consisted of two varieties: one was woven coarsely to show horizontal rows; two tresses were braided together in the other. Both versions consisted of five inches or more of beard that tipped forward at the end.

Hair and wigs were adorned in various ways. A simple ribbon around the head, often tied in a bow, sometimes with long ends trailing down the back, retained favor throughout all eras. This developed into a plain fillet, or circle, of leather or gold. The Middle Kingdom achieved a height of artistic excellence in hair ornamentation. One example, belonging to a princess named Khnumet, was an airy, openwork gold diadem of tiny flowers on almost invisible wires interspersed with six Maltese crosses, all accented by touches of lapis lazuli, turquoise and carnelian. The dainty flowers would have seemed to float through her hair. Simpler, but no less elegant, was a sheet-gold diadem of Princess Sithathoriunet that was ornamented with inlayed rosettes. A gold cobra rose from the front, two tall gold plumes rose in the back and two pairs of gold "ribbons" trailed behind. Worn with this confection were hundreds of quarter-inch gold tubes that lined her long curled hair to complete an all over golden look. Men also indulged in diadems, as proven by a gold circlet from Tutankhamen's tomb with a rearing inlayed cobra in front flanked by a vulture head. Gold ribbons trail behind while ribbons on each side of the head end in rearing cobras. Probably the height of fantasy headgear was a Middle Kingdom example consisting of a gold plate worn on the top of the head. From it hung twenty-five long rows of overlapping rosettes, originally inlaid with carnelian, turquoise and glass. Placed over the hair (or wig), it sent stream after stream of glittering rosettes cascading past the shoulders.

Despite Egypt's fiery sun, hats were rare. Except for pharaoh's crowns, only simple kerchiefs for men are ever depicted. Two primeval royal hats, one representing the original northern kingdom, the other the south, served as crowns throughout Egypt's history. The crown of the south, known as the White Crown for its color, consisted of a tall cone with a ball-like protuberance at the end. The Red Crown of the north flared to a flat top about seven inches high, but the back swept up in a narrow projection a foot above the rest. Where the flat top joined the rear projection, a wire-like appendage angled forward to coil in a front spiral about as high as the rear piece. Since even a pharaoh could not take his crowns with him to the next world, no examples of either type have been found, leading to speculation about their

WEARING A COMBINED CROWN, *pharaoh Ptolemy VIII stands between the goddesses Wadjet (left), who wears the crown of the northern kingdom, and Nekhbet (right), who wears the crown of the southern kingdom.*

material and construction. Only statues and paintings give any indication of their appearance and often show a combined crown incorporating both. Pharaohs during the Old Kingdom, however, are generally portrayed in a special kerchief, called the *nemes*, worn by the famous Sphinx as well. Paintings and statues indicate that it consisted of two parts. First a gold circlet with the royal cobra rising from the front was placed on the head. Then a kerchief was held over the head and its front part was tucked into the front of the circlet. When the remainder of the kerchief dropped, it fell naturally into creases on either side of the face and spilled down the back past the shoulders. The two ends were pulled over the shoulders and sometimes cut into lappets. In a longer version, the back was gathered and wrapped in a sheath of the same fabric as the rest of the kerchief to form a column. The kerchief material generally was striped.

With the advent of the New Kingdom a fourth crown eclipsed the previous three. Called the Blue Crown, or, less accurately, the War Crown, it consisted of a kind of helmet. Its round back section joined in a line with a round front of slightly smaller diameter. The front part was divided by a ridge into two halves. A gold cobra and band lined the helmet front and another gold band lined the back. Circles or pits dotted the headdress. Its material is not known, although dyed, embossed leather is a possibility. At the same time a special crown came into vogue for the chief royal wife. More a headdress than a crown, it consisted of a gold vulture lying on top of the head. The vulture's head reared above the wearer's face while its wings elegantly cradled her head.

COSMETICS

Brightly made-up Egyptian males would have shocked us with the quantity and brightness of their "face paint," and the women were not outdone. Eyes of both sexes were surrounded by a thick line that trailed out to the temple, causing the eyes to stand out brightly. Originally the favored color was green, thought to have health-giving properties, but black grew more common after the Eighteenth Dynasty. The composition of both colors is known: ground malachite, in the case of the green version; ground galena, in the case of the black. These were mixed into a paste, probably with the addition of some fat,[10] and stored in cosmetic jars until used. Small sticks of wood, bone or ivory were dipped into the jars and used as applicators for drawing the lines.

Women reddened their lips with a brush dipped in a paste of red ochre and fat. Although not certain, it seems from the bright red on the lips of some male statues that men followed this fashion as well. Rouge consisted of red ocher again, probably with fat to make it adhere, and was applied with a pad. It is likely that henna, used today in Egypt to color the palms of hands and soles of feet red, was employed by the ancient Egyptians to dye their nails.

Makeup must also be removed in some way. Since Egyptian cosmetics

A SMALL COSMETIC VESSEL (C. 1500 B.C.E.) *belonging to King Thutmose I's daughter, Meretnubt, displays a frieze of heraldic birds flanking a cartouche below a ring of lotuses.*

were composed of fat that would not wash off with water, Egyptians concocted a cleansing cream. Powdered limestone mixed with vegetable oils gently abraded away the makeup.

Lovely cases held stone or faience cosmetic jars in individual compartments. Such cases usually included space for that essential cosmetic aid, the mirror, which in Egypt always followed the same shape. The reflecting part consisted of a highly polished metal circle slightly flattened at top and bottom. A tang inserted into a holding handle, often of wood, sometimes of metal, ivory, faience or even stone, usually modeling an object, such as a papyrus column. The Egyptian word for mirror literally translates as "see-face," which states its purpose well.

Considering that Egyptian cosmetics used fat as their base, they must have quickly turned rancid, hence requiring something to mask the odor. Perfume formed an essential component of every lady's beauty collection; it was added to cosmetics and used on its own. Egyptian versions, however, differed from modern perfumes whose alcohol bases aid the dispersion of the scent. Egyptians never learned to distill alcohol. Their method was to soak some fragrant material in fat or oil which would absorb some of the odor, then wring out the fragrant oil through a cloth, much as they did with the must of grapes. The fragrant oil could then be applied to the body.[11] Analyses of ancient remains suggest that iris roots formed the fragrance of one perfume and balsam another, but other additives included cinnamon, cardamom, myrrh, honey, even wine and the flowers of the henna bush, sometimes in complex mixtures.

In addition to smearing perfume on various body parts, women employed a special perfuming device at banquets and parties. A cone of fat impregnated with perfume was placed on their heads which, when melted slowly by body heat, released its aroma throughout the evening. In addition, incense would burn throughout a party to freshen the air. One famed incense was frankincense, a resin that seeps through the trunks of special trees that grow only in southern Arabia and Somalia. The search for frankincense explains continued expeditions to Punt, as the Egyptians called Somaliland. A quantity was recovered from Tutankhamen's tomb that still gave off a pleasant odor when burned 3,000 years later.[12] The other famous incense was myrrh, which served as a perfume as well. A resin, like frankincense, it grew only in the same areas. Both produced fragrant fumes at parties, and both sanctified idols in temples.

Before dressing and applying cosmetics, a question arose about unwanted hair, a problem solved as in our day by razors and tweezers. These appliances originally were made of copper until harder bronze became the metal of choice when its secret arrived in Egypt after the Middle Kingdom. Razors resembled a modern surgical scalpel; tweezers were formed exactly the same way as our own. For the sake of the face, a whetstone to hone the razor's edge was a necessary accessory. Some leather and some wooden cases survive as the original Dopp kits for carrying all three hair removal instruments. Of course, with the Egyptians' intense interest in hair, combs abounded. Rows of long teeth were carved from wood or ivory to create a comb that differs from the modern version only in that it was held vertically to achieve greater pulling power than our horizontal types.

ARCHITECTURE

ALTHOUGH PYRAMIDS AND TEMPLES FROM ANCIENT EGYPT STILL impress us thousands of years after they were built, all that remains of the homes where people were born, grew to adulthood and died are occasional low mounds of mud outlines. Temples and tombs endure because Egyptians made a sharp distinction between their religious architecture, constructed of permanent stone for eternity, and all other buildings, even palaces and fortresses, which were built of less durable adobe.

NONRELIGIOUS BUILDINGS

Ancient Egyptians had to contend with enormous temperature swings. At noon on a summer day, in this country surrounded by desert, the temperature could reach 120°F; nevertheless, because the Sahara does not hold its heat, temperatures could fall into the upper thirties on winter nights. In addition to sheltering people from both heat and cold, residential architects had to provide some sort of sanitary devices as well as storage facilities for preserving food. Because rainfall was infrequent and slight enough, plentiful sun-baked mud (adobe) served adequately for the main construction material, as it has in the American southwest.

Homes

Thousands of years before air-conditioning or central heating was invented, Egypt developed a solution to its temperature extremes by evolving a housing plan that remained viable from its creation in the time of the Old Kingdom to the end of its history. The basic Egyptian house for all but the very poor consisted

THE GREAT SPHINX AND PYRAMID OF CHEPHREN (KHAFRE) *at Giza are Fourth-Dynasty masterpieces of Egyptian architecture.*

of a high rectangular enclosure wall with an entry door at the narrow end that faced north, if possible, to take advantage of the prevailing breeze. Inside, the compound was divided into three facilities. Just past the entry door lay a garden with a central pool of cool water that also irrigated trees and shrubs planted around it. Next came a roofed area raised on columns open at the front to catch breezes and provide shade for family and guests, after which came apartments for the owner and immediate family, walled and roofed for privacy and to seal out nighttime cold. These three elements—an open courtyard, a columned portico and private apartments—made up the architectural plan of all Egyptian houses, however large or small they might be and however many times these elements might be multiplied to incorporate additional three-part shelters for servants and, in a palace, for a harem.

Refinements to this basic structure could include stairs leading to a roof terrace where poles supported an awning—shade for family or guests—to catch breezes not felt at ground level. Some of these terraces incorporated ingenious scoops which trapped daytime breezes and circulated them through vents to the apartments below. To minimize the heat, windows in inner rooms were placed high to let the hottest air exit as it rose. Windows were small in area—light was not desired when the sun shone so hot and bright—and unglazed, merely slatted with wood to keep birds out. Bedrooms incorporated raised alcoves for sleeping and adobe benches along one or more walls for sitting and supporting objects; niches in the walls held small oil lamps. Closets had not yet been invented. Bathrooms, which adjoined the bedrooms of more expensive houses, consisted of a latrine wall enclosed on three sides for privacy, with a channel running to the outside of the enclosure. A screened area beside this section held wooden stools with holes in their seats above a bowl. Poor farmers simply used outside areas near their houses for sanitary purposes.

Farm houses included an area behind the private apartments that held stables for animals along with silos to protect grain from predators, thus adding a fourth division for farmers to the three-part Egyptian house. The silos were domed structures of adobe brick that stood six feet high with a door halfway up for access to the grain inside and a trapdoor in the roof for filling the silo. A modest house would have four or more such granaries. Larger dwellings might also include a separate slaughterhouse where cows and other animals were butchered and their meat was hung to cure. By the time of the New Kingdom, cellars were added, providing additional spaces for storage and for work such as weaving and baking that could be performed in cool, subterranean conditions.

As in modern urban areas, housing in crowded cities grew upward rather than spreading outward: thriving Thebes and Memphis consisted of homes that typically rose three or even four stories above a narrow base and employed common walls to form row houses with granaries erected on rooftops. Houses formed orderly grids along roads or alleys that fed into main thoroughfares which crossed in the center of the city (the hieroglyph for a city is two roads crossing in the center of a circle: ⊗).

In size, Egyptian homes were comparable to those of our time. While a mansion could be as large as 25,000 square feet and contain thirty rooms or more, more modest homes used about 2,000 square feet for their six to twelve rooms. The poorest class, however, lived in shelters of less than 1,000 square feet and four rooms.[1] Complex mansions began with a huge open court and grand portico, after which came servants' quarters. Apartments for the owner were positioned in the center of the compound with harem quarters adjoining. Each quarter had its own open court, pool and a separate portico, in addition to living apartments, so each section of the compound reproduced the standard three-part plan. Private passages led to each separate quarter so that an owner would never have to walk through the servants' rooms at the front to reach his living compound. A kitchen, granaries and offices—all separate structures—lay to the rear.

The main construction material for all housing, for both the rich and the poor, was adobe, a word that derives from the original Egyptian name which was similarly pronounced. Made from inexhaustible Nile mud, mixed with sand or straw for bonding and to prevent shrinking as it dried, the moist mixture was placed in rectangular wood frames, about nine by four and one-half by three inches[2] (larger for government buildings), to form bricks. The frame was lifted away to allow the mud to bake hard in the sun. The

DEIR EL-MEDINA, THE WORKERS VILLAGE, *housed the masons, painters, and sculptors who created the many tombs on the West Bank. Single-story mud-brick dwellings consisted of four to five rooms, on average.*

enclosing walls of the compound and supporting and dividing walls of the residence were all constructed of adobe bricks, including the stairs to the roof terrace. Roofs, however, were made from logs—generally the wood of date palms—laid in a row and covered with smaller slats running in the opposite direction, all of which would be plastered with Nile mud to prevent water seepage. The plastered logs became the terrace, although they remained visible below as the top rooms' ceilings. Columns for the portico were also wood— either a single substantial palm trunk or a bundle of slimmer sycamore trunks bound together. In both cases the top would be carved into a stylized capital that depicted either palm fronds or lotus buds. Doors were wooden planks, attached, not at the side wall by hinges, but at the bottom with a metal spike which turned in a hole in a block of stone; a metal post anchored the top to a wood door beam. Doors were sealed with bolts, made of metal or wood, that slid into clasps.

Thanks to infrequent rain, the life span of adobe was adequate for residential housing. To counter the occasional sprinkle, roofs sloped slightly to produce a natural runoff of water into drain spouts attached to the lowest corners. Likewise, windows and doors often carried wooden hoods to force dripping water away from those openings, and the walls forming the compound enclosure were rounded on top, since flat tops would have held water and soon decomposed.[3] In poor homes, floors were made of packed earth; in more elegant ones, floors consisted of adobe bricks plastered over, like all the walls of the house proper. Interior walls were painted with a white background on which bright painted designs or scenes from religion or nature provided the home's main decoration.

Furniture was scanty, even for the rich, consisting of chairs, often set on a dais, low stools, beds, boxes for clothing and jewelry and small, portable oil lamps. Tables, generally round, were sized for individuals rather than families. Beds, also small, were simple wooden frames on legs with twine lashing for a mattress and a separate curved headrest which supported the head at the neck. Ovens—consisting of baked clay drums, one-and-one-half feet wide at the base and equally tall, but narrowing to half that diameter to force the heat to the top—were located away from the residence area. They were plastered over with Nile mud for insulation except for a hole near the bottom which provided draft and permitted the fire to be stoked. More costly homes included a built-in fireplace, located in the outer court, shielded on three sides by walls to keep its heat away from the family. Most homes incorporated a small shrine in the portico for prayers and offerings to the family's favorite god, since Egyptians rarely attended temple services.

Ancient Egyptian residential architecture contributed to a genteel living style. A family could sit beside their pool, taking in the beauty of shrubs and low sycamores, or be joined by friends in the shade of the columned portico for talk or food. Conversation and eating finished, they could retire to the privacy of their own rooms. Owners often painted good luck wishes around the compound's main entrance, such as, "May Amun-Ra, Lord of the Thrones of the Two Lands, give life, prosperity, health, joy, favor and love," or, "Mayest thou enter into this house, being healthy."[4] What more could be asked of any home?

Palaces

Kings lived in style with hosts of retainers. Unlike modern countries with royal heads of state, Egypt did not maintain a national palace into which succeeding rulers moved. Although palaces covered acres of land, they too were constructed of adobe to last only a generation or so, allowing the next pharaoh to build a new residence to his own specifications. Each ruler constructed not just one new residence but several for the different places he needed to reside—the twin capitals of Thebes and Memphis at the very least. Unfortunately, none of these grand palaces has survived, so what we know of them is based on tomb pictures and on the few floors and crumbling walls that today comprise the remains of the two best preserved examples. These belonged to a father and his son, Amenhotep III and the heretical pharaoh Akhenaten, built during the Eighteenth Dynasty, the apex of Egypt's wealth and power.

Akhenaten's palace may well have been the grandest ever constructed in Egypt.[5] A hundred-foot-wide thoroughfare, the Royal Road, divided the palace proper from the royal residences, joined by a bridge over the road. This bridging of structures was an innovation in Egypt, perhaps modified from Assyrian buildings that also spanned thoroughfares. On the east side of the road lay the formal palace, called the House of Rejoicing of the Aten, including the state reception rooms, some government offices and servants' quarters; on the west stood the residence area for the pharaoh, his immediate family and personal retainers.

The private residence of the king on the west side ran for 100 yards beside the Royal Road and stretched back for at least 150 yards more. Servants' quarters (or, perhaps, residences for royal guards) were discretely passed on the right before entering a square garden, 150 feet on a side, that occupied the northern side of the compound. South of the garden lay the private apartments of the royal family inside their own walled structure. Its three areas consisted of personal servants' quarters filling the west half, a separate structure in its southeastern corner of six rooms plus bathroom, presumably for the six daughters of the king, and the pharaoh's private rooms. Separated from the children's area by a court and a wall, a large columned hall divided the king's suite of two rooms on one side, with a bathroom and latrine, from an open area with an altar on the other side. Additional courtyards and rooms for family recreation filled the middle part of these private apartments. The rest of the compound, its easternmost third, consisted of magazines for storing food and an artificial pond in the northeastern corner 40 feet in diameter. A family of eight could live most comfortably in this 145,000-square-foot home.

Across the bridge, on the other side of the Royal Road, stood the formal, state palace of the pharaoh, a huge structure that stretched for at least 700, if not 1,000, feet along the Royal Road and ran back from it for at least 600 feet more. It comprised several distinct areas: a palace, a festival hall, servants' quarters and vast suites of rooms, generally considered harems,[6] lining the Royal Road.

The only entrance from the road led into a pair of courtyards back to back, dividing what early excavators considered the harem into two roughly equal parts. The northern half centered around a sunken garden with a pond, flanked both east and west by rows of fifteen rooms. North and south of the sunken garden stretched more halls and still more rooms. One hall in the north section contained a floor sublimely painted with scenes of a fish-filled pool surrounded by marsh grasses and fowl. At least fifty rooms in the southern half bordered four large courtyards, making this structure seem far too large for harem purposes, especially for a king with only two known wives in addition to his queen, Nefertiti. An absence of bathrooms confirms the point. More likely this vast complex of suites, north and south, consisted of offices for various high and middle grade government officials. If so, they worked in grand surroundings, though some labored in mere cubicles.

Deeper into the compound, behind the "harem" lining the Royal Road, lay servants' quarters to the north and the palace proper to the south. The servants' quarters, which covered an area at least 30,000 feet square, consisted of roomy suites composed of a bedroom, bath and living room bordering a courtyard. Although never completely excavated, such servants' suites would probably number fifty or more.

The state palace, south of the servants' quarters and west of the harem, consisted simply of eight grand courtyards and one august hall. Uncharacteristic of Egyptian palaces, this part was constructed of stone. One hall, the farthest north, which ran the entire 500-foot length of the building, incorporated a magnificent dais on the long, 45-by-30-foot wall, with a roof supported by twelve massive columns fronted by a ramp for access. Larger-than-life-sized statues of the king and his queen lined the three innermost sides. Presumably this space was used for huge gatherings to hear the king speak from the dais. A door behind the dais led through a long transverse hall of columns where representations of trussed ducks hung on the column sides and carved foliage decorated their tops, above a floor of pure alabaster. This hall opened into a central courtyard with ramps from the three other sides for chariots to ride into any of seven additional courtyards. Each courtyard averaged 100 feet on a side, but only the central one contained carved stele—two dozen of them—with scenes of the royal family at worship. Porticos flanked the eastern companion of the central courtyard, leading to the Window of Appearances, where the pharaoh and his family would present themselves to citizens below and distribute gold rewards for special service.

South from the state palace stood another, separate, square structure, 300 feet on each side. In this huge hall, square pillars were used to support a ceiling gaily painted to look like vines against a yellow background; its walls were tiled in plant patterns in accordance with the nature religion of Akhenaten. At the far end of this hall two narrow rooms bordered a sunken area. It may be that this structure served as the coronation hall for Smenkare, who briefly succeeded Akhenaten before Tutankhamen.

Although some functions of the many of parts of Akhenaten's palace are not understood today, enough remains to impress with its size and grandeur. The two massive compounds combined accommodations for servants, probably offices for government offices, private rooms for the king and his family and awesome spaces for public events.

Although not quite as large as the palace of his son, Amenhotep III's palace at Malkata across the river from Thebes is more easily understood.[7] Inside a 1,000-by-1,500-foot compound, lined with passageways for patrolling guards, lay a variety of separate structures. The pharaoh's apartments faced the Nile behind gardens which ran the length of the south face of the enclosure. Interior walls of these living quarters were painted with ornamental designs, along with scenes of hunting, flora, fauna, ladies of the court and the pharaoh. Beside it stood the harem, a separate building one fourth the size of the king's quarters, with a separate structure behind it serving as the royal kitchen. Also along the south face, next to the palace, stood a building to house the palace guard. In the center of the compound, on the east side of the palace proper, another distinct structure held offices, as well as housing for servants and the workmen who maintained the compound. This building was 600 feet long by about 150 feet wide. Entrance to the whole compound, for all but the highest personages, was through the northwest corner where the official rooms—grand audience hall, throne room and so on—were situated. Behind these, trailing south, a hall of columns 150 feet long and lined with offices for high officials led to the private apartments of the pharaoh. Far to the rear of the enclosure (north) stood a grand 500-foot-square festival hall, where the anniversaries of Amenhotep's coronation were celebrated. Just outside lay an artificial lake, two miles around, for private outings on the royal barge.

After this Eighteenth Dynasty magnificence, palaces changed. By the Twentieth Dynasty the palace of Rameses III at Medinet Habu, although probably not his main residence, was no larger than the accommodations Amenhotep III provided for his royal guards. Rameses III's palace was surrounded by truly massive defensive walls, suggesting that this pharaoh feared powerful enemies. Egypt's fortunes had begun to decline.

Offices

Extensive buildings must have existed to accommodate the thousands of government officials who managed the country, but such utilitarian structures were not the sort of thing anyone preserved. One of the few examples whose plan could be reconstructed from residual remains was the office of the main tax collector in Akhenaten's city of Akhetaten. It consisted of a rectangular walled 120-by-190-foot structure which included special provisions for storing and protecting grain and animals, the forms in which taxes were paid. For security, a gatekeeper lived beside the two entrances to serve as a watchman. A large area beyond the entrance was walled to hold horses and donkeys; another was divided into magazines for storing tons of grain. After being accepted and recorded here, the animals and grain would have been shipped to larger facilities for permanent storage. The gatekeeper's family lived in a typical large house toward the rear of the compound, and their servants resided in separate quarters along the back enclosure wall. Fully half of the area inside the compound remained open to facilitate the comings and goings of taxpayers with their goods.

This example of a "home office" was not typical of government buildings which generally consisted of walls surrounding smaller cubicles where government functionaries labored—the records office in Akhenaten's city of Akhetaten consisted of a rectangle almost 300 feet long by 50 feet wide, inside of which over forty rooms averaged 10 feet by 20 feet. Workers commuted to these offices from their homes.

Fortresses

Egyptian military architecture ranged from simple towers to fortified cities. The Egyptian outpost in Kush, called Semna, which combined a walled town and a fortress, serves as a typical example.

Built in the New Kingdom on Middle Kingdom foundations, Semna represented centuries of experience with military architecture. Egyptians had often warred against fortified cities throughout the Middle East, experiencing at first hand those devices that made capture difficult. Most of the countries Egypt attacked had built and rebuilt their forts after numerous captures, correcting mistakes and improving defenses. They had to defend against only a limited repertoire of assault methods—arrows and javelins hurled at defenders, attempts to scale walls with ladders, sometimes digging under or through walls or using battering rams to break through fortress gates. Since both attacking Egyptians and defending Hittites or others learned the same lessons, fortresses throughout the Middle East came to resemble each other, looking exactly like Medieval fortresses from Western Europe, which faced the same kinds of attacks.

In the Semna example, one side of the fort followed the Nile for about 340 feet; the other three sides created a square shape for the fort except that a hill at the northwestern corner forced that wall inward, making the fort outline suggest a fat "L." Made of adobe bricks anchored together by reed mats every few courses, the fortress walls were thirty feet thick to give them strength to withstand battering rams. Narrow parapets, crenellated on the side facing outward to protect archers from enemy missiles as they fired their arrows, ran along the top of the walls. A five-foot-deep by fifteen-foot-wide dry moat surrounded the wall on all sides except the one along the river to delay an army hoping to scale the fort, while exacting a price through weapons fired from atop the walls. Two landward entrances to the fort were guarded by flanking high towers allowing archers to take aim on three sides at anyone trying to enter. Here a bridge spanned the moat, since there had to be a way for friends to get inside. More towers projected from the wall at regular intervals so an enemy attacking at any place could be fired on from three sides. At the Nile side stairs ran from the wall to the river, protected from missiles by a heavy stone roof, to allow supplies to reach the fort even while besieged or, if necessary, to allow the defenders to escape. Inside the fortress two main streets crossed at the center where a temple stood. Homes for civilians lined the streets, separated from a military zone consisting of large barracks for the troops, a command headquarters and magazines for supplies enough to withstand a siege. Access to the parapets was provided by ramps and stairs. A system of drains running outside the fort disposed of waste and rainwater.

Other Egyptian forts included narrow, winding alleys inside the main gates to concentrate any attackers who tried to make their way through, so that archers could pick their targets with little chance of missing. In general, most of the modern principles of military architecture had been worked out by the Egyptians of the New Kingdom, if not before.

TEMPLES AND TOMBS

Even though buildings for the immortal gods or for a mortal Egyptian's eternal life were constructed of permanent stone, they owed much to the design of the Egyptian house.

Temples

Temples were called the "House of the God So-and-So" because they were viewed as residences for a god. Indeed, anyone familiar with the three elements of an Egyptian house will recognize the same parts in every temple. First, inside a rectangular enclosing wall, came a large courtyard, open to the sky, followed by a broad colonnaded court, roofed but open at the front. Behind stood a collection of small walled rooms with ceilings where the statue(s) of the god(s) resided. Conventionally these parts are called the forecourt (or peristyle court), hypostyle hall and the holy-of-holies.

The greatest difference between temples and houses, in addition to the use of stone for temples, was that the floor of each succeeding area rose as their ceilings progressively lowered. Passing through a temple brought the believer into successively more intimate and darker environments, as access became more restricted. Only priests could enter the holy-of-holies, for example. One other difference between a temple and a house was found at the front (although later copied in palaces). Here, one of the architectural signatures of Egypt formed the temple entrance—a pair of pylons. These gently sloped, instead of perfectly vertical, walls rose from twenty feet to over a hundred feet on either side of an entrance door. Long poles, fitted into niches in the pylons, gaily flew banners from their tops. Such flagpoles were the hieroglyphic symbol for divinity.

EIGHT TOWERING PILLARS OF RAMESES II, *represented as the god Osiris, flank the hypostyle hall of the Great Temple at Abu Simbel in this painting by Scottish artist David Roberts (1796–1864).*

Other temple-related buildings, such as priests' houses, magazines for storing food, bakeries and amulet factories, surrounded the temples, making them hives of activity rather than solemn edifices. All these parts were encompassed by a brick enclosure wall that defined the temple precinct, to which an alley formed by two rows of small sphinxes or other statues led the way.

The Twentieth-Dynasty mortuary temple of Rameses III, named "United with Eternity," across the Nile from Luxor, serves as a clear example of a developed temple.[8] It consisted of a walled rectangle 500 feet long by almost 100 feet wide—large enough to house a modern football field with plenty of room around it. A great pylon gateway at the eastern end served as the temple entrance. One-hundred-foot-tall flagpoles were fixed to this pylon, which stretched 210 feet wide at its base and rose 75 feet in the air and anchored a massive door in the center, 33 feet high by 12 feet wide. Inside were two successive open

courtyards rather than the usual single court. The first, 125 feet deep, was bordered by columns on its north and south sides supporting a partial roof to create covered ambulatories on those two sides. A ramp at its west end led to a second pylon, through which stood a second open courtyard as large as the first but seeming smaller because its covered ambulatory ran around all four sides. A ramp at its western end led to the roofed temple proper. First came a large hypostyle hall, 60 feet deep by the 93-foot width of the temple. Its central nave rose on eight massive columns almost 30 feet high supporting a ceiling higher than the smaller (22 feet tall) columns to either side, thus allowing for stone windows in the gap where the roof from the lower columns met the taller ones. On its northern side stood four chapels, including one for Rameses III himself. A "treasury" for storing temple equipment occupied the south side of the hypostyle hall beside a small chapel for the pharaoh's namesake, Rameses the Great. Beyond this first hypostyle hall stood a second, 25 feet deep, that reached as high as the lower parts of the first hypostyle hall. Entry to a sanctuary for Ra-Horackhty ran from its northern side, and an entry to a sanctuary for Rameses III ran from its southern side. Behind this second hypostyle hall lay a third almost identical to the second except for being lined with statues of the gods *maat* and Toth bearing faces of Rameses III. At the end of this final hypostyle hall stood a sanctuary (15 feet square) for Amun, the main god of the temple, flanked by sanctuaries for his consort, Mut, and their son, Khonsu. A number of small rooms behind and beside these sanctuaries served as temple storage.

Since temples endured, sometimes for hundreds of years, succeeding pharaohs added embellishments, complicating their basic plans. The extreme case is Karnak Temple which grew, thanks to additions made by twenty or more pharaohs, until it occupied an area of 600 acres and consisted of seven separate temple complexes, the most important of which were the complex for Amun, the one for his wife, Mut, and a third for their son, Khonsu. The main temple for Amun was approached through a corridor of statues of recumbent rams

RAMESES III'S MORTUARY TEMPLE AT MEDINET HABU, *aerial view. A 75-foot-tall pylon served as the entrance to two successive open courtyards, followed by the roofed temple proper. The floor dimensions of the structure exceed the size of a football field.*

(the animal associated with Amun), followed by not one but six sets of pylons. Behind the first (130 feet high), probably built in Ptolemaic times, lay an almost 300-foot square forecourt, uncharacteristically lined down the center with a row of 60-foot paired columns that supported a roof. One-third of an entire temple built by Rameses III intruded into the right rear of this courtyard then continued outside. In the front left of the courtyard, three chapels erected by Seti II served as way stations for the sacred barques that carried temple idols in processions.

The second pylon, built by Horemheb and Rameses I, was fronted by two colossal statues of Rameses the Great. Beyond lay the grandest hypostyle hall in Egypt, extending 170 feet in depth by 340 feet in width. Its central nave rose nearly 80 feet on twelve massive pairs of columns, each almost twelve feet in diameter; its lower sides consisted of a forest of sixty columns, each rising 46 feet tall. A small court after the third pylon (added by Amenhotep III) provided access from the right to a processional way that led to the temple of Mut, 300 yards away. The court also contained two pairs of obelisks (built by Tuthmosis I and Tuthmosis III). The fourth pylon (added by Tuthmosis I) prefaced another hypostyle hall whose roof was removed by Hatshepsut so she could erect two 90-foot obelisks. The roof was later restored by Tuthmosis III who bricked in her obelisks to hide them.

Then began the most holy section of the temple where no one other than priests and the pharaoh could enter, a warren of structures that became more crowded over the centuries as pharaoh after pharaoh added his personal homage to Amun. The fifth pylon (added by Tuthmosis I) was followed after a narrow columned hall by a sixth small pylon (built by Tuthmosis III). Beyond, and all enclosed, lay the most holy sanctuary. First came two columned rooms where offerings were prepared, then, in the center, the reason for all this building: the shrine of Amun-Ra.

There was more. Behind the sanctuary stood another entire temple built by Tuthmosis III to celebrate his military successes. Even farther back, Akhenaten had built a temple for his god, the Aten. Outside the main temple, to the left, stood a small temple to Ptah and a large temple to Montu, the original god of Thebes. Beside the main temple, on the right, reposed an artificial lake 250 feet by 400 feet.

Measured either by its area or the mass of its stone, Karnak Temple is the largest religious structure ever built. The fact that it first rose in the Middle

A TRIUMPHAL ARCH *stands in front of the imposing 60-foot-high pylon of the Temple of Khonsu at the Karnak Temple Complex.*

Kingdom and endured until the end of Egypt's independence, a span of more than a thousand years, helps explain its size. Almost every pharaoh throughout that time paid for the successes he enjoyed or the ones he wished for by heaping bounty on this one temple complex. According to one accounting, more than 90,000 priests were associated with this temple, although it must be understood that many of these managed and worked on the vast temple estates throughout the country and did not reside at Karnak.

The fluttering banners in front of the temples provided a festive atmosphere. Their tall masts, sometimes more than 130 feet high (the first pylon at Karnak) soared above the pylons. Since no Egyptian timber grew that tall, masts of the famed cedar from Lebanon had to be imported for this purpose, then clad in a sheet of metal, most often electrum (an amalgam of silver and gold). The poles were attached to the pylon by metal cleats near the top, while anchored at the bottom in a metal box fixed to both the pylon and the ground. Pylons were constructed of either stone or adobe bricks, and they were hollow inside to leave space for stairs to the top. Pairs of doors, as tall as forty feet, fit between the pylons. Temple columns were always made of stone, formed of drums stacked on top of each other until they reached the required height. They rested on a stone base slightly wider than the column, and the column top was carved to represent palm fronds, lotus buds or, less commonly, a papyrus cluster. Unusual types of columns included fluted examples with a simple rectangular top (forerunners of the Greek Doric style), or human shaped, in the form of a pharaoh or of the god Osiris.

Stone walls in and around the temples provided fine surfaces for carving, and they were adorned with images of gods. Temple walls were also covered with scenes of pharaohs smiting their enemies, which led early excavators to doubt that these were religious buildings, not realizing that Egyptians believed their victories in battle were ordained by the gods and evidence of their gods' might. Shrines in the holy-of-holies often included altar-shaped stone structures in the center or front. These were not for sacrifices, which Egyptians seldom performed, but for resting sacred litters until the god's statue was placed on board. Idols were generally made from metal—bronze, silver or gold. Temples almost always bordered water—the Nile or a canal—for easy transport by boat of the massive quantities of stone used in their construction. Unlike religions such as Islam, in which temple orientation is important and prescribed, Egyptian temples pointed in a variety of directions.

In addition to the three-part temples described, Rameses the Great built a unique structure at Abu Simbel. This temple was carved into a stone mountain, so the outside served as the forecourt, and the hypostyle hall and holy-of-holies stood behind each other inside the cavern.

Two other kinds of temple were erected during special eras, both associated with the worship of the sun. The Sun Temples of the Fifth Dynasty were mere rectangular open courtyards with a large platform at the far end on which a squat obelisk, called a benben, stood. According to one theory, the pyramidal top of the *benben* symbolized rays emanating from the sun. It seems that obelisks, whether the benben sort or the more familiar slender shafts, were all associated with the sun.

The other unusual temple formed part of the religious revolution of Akhenaten that celebrated the visible sun, the Aten. Enough remains of the Great Aten temple in Amarna to indicate its general design.[9] An eight-foot-thick enclosure wall,

THESE ALABASTER BASINS WITHIN THE GREAT SLAUGHTERHOUSE *at the Sun Temple of Niuserre in Abu Gurab may have been used to contain the blood of animals sacrificed to the sun god.*

measuring 2,350 feet long by 900 feet wide, surrounded the temple. The formal entrance, along the short end facing the Nile, was surrounded by the usual pylons, but in this case it was not as wide and was decorated with more poles and banners (five on either side) than usual. Another entrance on the long north face included a ramp for animals. Inside, worshippers faced a separate, large stone structure, the Gem Pa Aten (Finding the Aten), fronted by its own pair of pylons. To the left stood a separate portico of stone colonnades, and to the right was a field of 920 limestone offering tables laid out in a dense rectangle running away from the entrance. The Gem Pa Aten, which stretched back for 600 feet, consisted of a covered portico, open in the center, leading to six successive open halls, each lined with hundreds of offering tables. The two final halls contained a high altar and surrounding chapels, each with an altar or offering tables.

Behind the Gem Pa Aten came a vast field (1,000 feet by 850 feet) densely covered with brick offering tables. An empty area at its end provided space for slaughtering hundreds of animals. The final quarter of the temple contained a sanctuary surrounded by its own wall with an entrance through pylons, leading into a wide court that introduced another entire temple surrounded by more walls. This temple inside a temple contained more courts filled with offering tables, surrounded by small chapels with separate offering tables.

The idea behind this unusual temple was to provide a consecrated place for offerings to the sun god, making this temple different in several ways. Instead of a dark, mysterious place, it was open and bright. Instead of small numbers of professional priests, this temple invited all believers inside. Rather than serving as the home of an idol, it provided facilities for making offerings, which could be done in private chapels, inside an open building or in a vast court outside. Where a believer made his offerings depended on his rank, but all practiced their ritual under the open sky so the sun could look down on its gifts. Animals were sacrificed, as the area for slaughter inside the enclosure shows, as was bread. Egyptologists found vast quantities of molds for bread outside the temple walls.

Tombs

In the beginning, before the pharaohs, Egyptians simply buried their dead in pits in the sand. When jackals and tomb robbers ravaged such pits, Egyptians learned that sand did not protect the body or the goods buried with it. Because preservation of the body was essential for an afterlife, more substantial protection had to be invented. Wood coffins were tried, which kept the animals away but not the human thieves. The next step was to encase the grave inside a solid structure. The first containers, called *mastabas*, the Arabic word for the benches they resembled, were simple adobe rectangles whose walls angled toward the center. Inside, compartments held the owner's goods, while the body lay in a simple pit below ground, covered with logs on which sand was piled to represent either the heaped sand burials of distant ancestors or else the primeval mound of creation. Everyone who could afford the cost of such a tomb, from wealthy government officials up to pharaohs, built a mastaba for himself.

As pharaohs increased their power, they created a special kind of tomb, beginning in about 2700 B.C.E., when a pharaoh named Zoser added another, smaller, mastaba on top of a first one, then another and another until six were stacked in a 200-foot-high facsimile of a wedding cake. Called the Step Pyramid, this new kind of tomb set pharaohs in pursuit of more and more imposing burial places. The next breakthrough came with the first king of the next dynasty. The pharaoh Sneferu stacked eight mastabas on top of each other 300 feet in the air, then filled the steps with dressed stone to form smooth, slanting sides. This was the first true pyramid. The sides, however, formed an angle too steep for its soft limestone cover, making the structure unstable, so the pyramid was abandoned before the burial chamber inside was completed.

SNEFERU'S PYRAMID AT MEIDUM, *the first attempt at a pyramid with smooth, slanting sides, consisted of eight mastabas stacked on top of each other. The structure's steep angle precipitated its collapse.*

Sneferu continued his experiments with a second pyramid whose sides climbed at the sharp angle of 54 degrees. The angle abruptly changed to 43 degrees about half way to the top, however, marking the point at which cracks developed inside the burial chamber and at the pyramid base so the weight of the building had to be reduced. Despite the lower than planned height of this Bent Pyramid, it was a truly massive building that stood 310 feet tall from a base 620 feet on each side, with a volume three times Zoser's Step Pyramid. Because his second attempt proved unstable, Sneferu built a third, even larger pyramid with the new 43-degree slope that ascended 343 feet from a base 722 feet on each side. This structure counts as the earliest true pyramid that survives intact today.[10] Together, Sneferu's two completed pyramids incorporate more tons of stone than the famous Great Pyramid.

Sneferu's son, Khufu, capped the Pyramid Age with the largest tomb ever built. Although today it has lost 40 feet from its top, it originally rose 481 feet in the air, on a base 756 feet square, rising at a 51-degree angle. Inside, a magnificent passageway leads a third of the way up the pyramid to a granite chamber 34 feet by 17 feet by 19 feet high, in which a polished granite sarcophagus held the mortal remains of this pharaoh. Complex devices, such as passageways that led to dead ends and massive stone plugs that sealed the true route to the burial, sadly proved to no avail. The pyramid was picked clean in ancient times.

This was only the first of three startling pyramids built at Giza. Khufu's eldest son, in a short reign of eight years, began a pyramid he did not live to finish, but his half brother Khafra took up the pyramid challenge again at Giza with a massive effort beside his father's Great Pyramid. Since it stands on higher ground, Khafra's pyramid rises even higher than its neighbor, although it originally stood 10 feet shorter. Its gleaming casing of white limestone, transported by boats from quarries across the Nile, still covers the top. The mass of the limestone blocks that form the interior were cut from the surrounding Giza site. Probably in the course of freeing all the stone for the Great Pyramid, quarrymen struck a seam of harder rock which, as the more easily worked stone was quarried around it, emerged as a small hill. Khafra had this rock outcrop carved in the shape of a 200-foot-long recumbent lion bearing his own face—the famous Sphinx.

Khafra's son, Menkara, raised the last of the famous Giza pyramids. Much smaller than its neighbors at an original 218 feet in height, it is distinguished by a lovely casing of hard red granite transported from Aswan, 500 miles to the south. The casing covers only the bottom quarter of the pyramid, however, for Menkara died unexpectedly after a reign of twenty-eight years, leaving his pyramid and mortuary temple incomplete.

Pyramids continued to be built through the Middle Kingdom, although they were made from softer adobe with only a veneer of stone. Whether stone or adobe, all the pyramids were robbed. Something new had to be designed to prevent thieves from tampering with the body. During this time, government officials in the middle of Egypt began excavating grand tombs inside stone hills. The idea spread south, and the southern pharaohs, who began the New Kingdom, continued the practice with their tombs excavated first in the hills and then deep under the ground of the Valley of the Kings. If a mass of stone could not protect their bodies, perhaps a secret hiding place would do the job. So that thieves would not pick up the scent, mortuary temples where offerings and prayers were made to the departed pharaoh were separated from the tomb proper, sometimes by miles. The subterranean tombs were referred to as *per djet*, the eternal house, following something like the three-part plan of a house for the living, although modified for a very different use.

An outside entrance was first plastered then covered with dirt and rocks to hide its location after the body was safely placed inside. Inside, a short hall led to a pair of wooden doors opening to a corridor that descended for a hundred feet or so. A square pit, twenty feet deep or more, was dug in this corridor, not as a device to foil robbers, but to catch the water from occasional thunderstorms so it would not flow farther. At the end of this corridor came the first room, called *stja neter* (way of the god).[11] Doors sealed this chamber from a larger "waiting room" (*wesekhet iseq*), whose walls were covered with religious texts and pictures to ensure resurrection in the next world. Here, the opening of the mouth ceremony was performed on the dead body to enliven it magically. Through another door stood the great columned room of the tomb, the *per nebu* (house of gold), in the center of which, surrounded by veiled shrines, lay the sarcophagus for the deceased. Doors closed off a small room where *ushabtis* (worker statues) were stored, ready to answer the call of the gods to work in the next world so the tomb owner need not lift a finger. The final room, through the last pair of doors, called the *per hedj en pa neferu* (treasury of the beautiful things), held clothing, jewelry and furniture for the departed one. The series of rooms resembled the open beginning of a house (the waiting room), followed by the columned second part (house of gold), then the smaller, sealed apartment at the rear (the treasury of beautiful things).

Over time, additions complicated the basic design. The corridor to the tomb might bend and turn, sometimes including stairs. Rooms for more and more personal possessions were added to the sarcophagus room, or behind the treasury or even leading off the entry corridor. The original single columned hall might be multiplied into two or three. In a few cases, simplification reduced the tomb proper to a single large room with an alcove. Devices to foil robbers included huge stones blocking the corridors, corridors that led to dead ends and secret rooms whose entrances were sealed, plastered and painted to look like the rest of a solid wall.

For decoration, the limestone walls of a tomb were smoothed then covered with a thin coat of plaster. In the beginning of the New Kingdom, this plaster was painted white, but by the Nineteenth Dynasty yellow had come into favor. In any case, the corridors of a pharaoh's tomb were covered with painted scenes, usually maps of the route to the next world, indicating all the obstacles and ferocious beasts to be encountered along the way. The walls and columns of the larger "gold hall" contained scenes of the pharaoh and his wife beside various gods, but the ceiling sometimes represented the heavens with painted stars.

Wealthy nonroyals dug subterranean tombs as well, although they differed in certain respects from those for royalty. Instead of being separated from the tomb by a distance, their mortuary chapels sat directly above. Behind a first room and columned hall above ground, a corridor ran below to a shrine for a statue of the deceased.[12] Scenes that adorned the tomb walls of the non-royal presented secular rather than religious themes. Typically the owner is shown, surrounded by his family, enjoying a feast, hunting marsh fowl or overseeing workers in his fields—

A SMALL PYRAMID *sits atop the subterranean tomb of a worker at Deir el-Medina.*

any event he fondly remembered and wished to repeat for eternity. Inscriptions told the gods of his accomplishments so that he could earn the respect in the next world that he had enjoyed in this one. A final difference appeared in a series of tombs for artisans and builders at Deir el Medina near Thebes. Above each of their chapels sat a small pyramid, previously the prerogative only of royalty.

8

ARTS AND CRAFTS

EGYPTIAN ARTISTS WOULD BE SURPRISED THAT WE CONSIDER their work art. Craftsmen toiled in anonymity, signed none of their works and attained no fame during their lifetimes. Their society recognized no difference between fine art forms, such as painting and sculpting, and "lesser arts," such as pottery or cabinetry. Practitioners of any of these skills were regarded as simple workers on a level with, say, carpenters.

Art was produced cooperatively in workshops, in a kind of assembly line. One worker chiseled a statue's arm, another smoothed the curve of its cheek, while still another etched the line of a toenail—all working at the same time on one statue. In the case of a painted wall, one crew filled in a single color, followed by the next crew with a second color, and so forth, until a last crew added the fine details. With rare exceptions, no artist could point to anything and boast, "I made that myself." Art was a team project supervised by an overseer responsible—much as a modern-day general contractor schedules workers and monitors production—for the quality of the work, but certainly not the level of creativity.

Because recognition of an individual artist's work was unheard of and regard for creative endeavors was low, artists felt no pressure to innovate. Even for the few recognized for their superior work, it was their craftsmanship rather than their imagination that earned them praise and rewards. When Egyptians found a style of portraiture they liked, all their artists repeated it over and over, creating an art of canons—set proportions, gestures and subjects—which they refined for thousands of years. Long practice on the same restricted themes made them experts at their craft. What could be more pleasing, for example, than

DETAIL OF A FISHING SCENE *from the tomb of Menna, a royal scribe of the Eighteenth Dynasty.*

the enigmatic smile beaming from the Sphinx and many another statue made throughout Egypt's history? Egyptian art allows us to trace a lovely expression, a gesture or a figure grouping from its inception through its proliferation at various social levels. An innovation originally designed to please a pharaoh was soon copied for the enjoyment of ordinary citizens—much as designer clothes today are knocked off for the masses. What began as one artist's unique accomplishment soon became the province of all.[1]

Egyptian artists developed their methods with different goals in mind from those of artists who work today. Statues, carvings or paintings, first and foremost, were created for utilitarian purposes, rather than to generate enjoyment for the viewer or to excite his admiration. Some of the finest art, in fact, lay in tombs intended to be sealed for eternity from the eyes of any living person. Since most Egyptian creations were commissioned by individual citizens to serve their needs in the afterlife, artists were forced to maintain a certain realism in their work. A statue for a tomb owner might be more handsome, lean and muscular than the subject was in life, but it had to resemble that person.

Scenes in his tomb that depicted feasting, hunting and so on had to portray those activities clearly to the gods on judgment day. (Egyptians fashioned animals with particular care, as well, because of their reverence for the god represented by each creature.) The need for accuracy and realism, however, did not destroy the beauty of Egyptian art: the more pleasing the portrayals, the better its utilitarian purpose was served.

Sculpture and painting in particular were commissioned for reasons that do not exist in modern societies. In ancient Egypt only a pharaoh commissioned art for a purpose we would find familiar—to enhance a building or monument and thereby gain admiration for the donor. Commoners commissioned artwork to ensure the afterlife they desired. Their religion instructed that a portrait statue of the deceased, his "double," be placed inside the tomb to receive the food offerings required for his next life. Commoners also had scenes painted on the walls of their tombs for a different, although still religious, purpose—to show the gods what they enjoyed so that similar pleasures would be available to them throughout eternity.

Sculpture

Sculpture, the preeminent Egyptian art form along with architecture, evolved from humble origins. Before 3000 B.C.E., crude animal figures, of which only a few survive, were carved clumsily in soft stone or barely molded from clay. Then, just before the dawn of the First Dynasty, a remarkable series of royal palettes and mace heads, vigorously carved in low relief, appeared. For the first time, figures of people and various animals, especially a large bull, were represented with sinews and muscles in the act of moving. The skills required to achieve such depictions were not discovered suddenly but evolved from centuries of stone carving. Egyptians had mastered the hardest granite and dolerite by the fourth millennium, shaping it to a desired form as if it were pliable clay. Some pieces were clearly modeled on clay vessels; even the tied string that sealed the lid was reproduced in stone. Another, in fragile schist, copied every reed of a woven basket. Vases and cosmetic jars—from half an inch to several feet in height—were produced from every available kind of stone in sophisticated styles and proportions which demonstrate that stonework served as the basis for Egyptians' sculpting techniques.

Sculpture in the round, however, did not achieve real competence[2] until the Third Dynasty. The first known masterpiece, a seated, life-sized limestone statue of the pharaoh Zoser, posed magisterially on his throne in a ceremonial robe, his head covered with the *nemes* kerchief and his chin adorned with a fine beard, was carved for his Step Pyramid enclosure. Offerings were made to this statue from outside—behind a wall pierced with two holes at the level of the statue's eyes, symbolically allowing it to observe the gifts being presented. The statue retains great dignity even today, despite the fact that its eyes, doubtless carved of valuable rock crystal, were gouged out in ancient times.

Aptly, ancient Egyptians revealed their attitude toward sculpture by calling its makers "enliveners."[3] To the Egyptians, Zoser's statue symbolized the important religious concept that a statue could function in the place of the individual portrayed. Offerings left for the pharaoh's statue would, magically, serve him, even though he had left his tomb to travel to the next world. The pharaoh had provided future dynasties with a model that could be emulated by any commoner with the means to do so.

In the Fourth Dynasty, literally hundreds of almost-perfect statues in the round demonstrate that tomb portrait statues had become commonplace within the higher levels of society. Notable among many others, a pair of life-sized, seated limestone statues of prince Rahotep and his wife Nofert, although heavy in the legs and trunk, present sensitive facial portraits. Rahotep sports a narrow mustache above a determined mouth; Nofert wears a serene expression despite a fat wig that allows a bit of her own hair to show below. Both look out through translucent rock crystal eyes that seem eerily real. While the limestone of such statues is relatively easily worked, the hard granite used for the larger-than-life statues of the pharaoh Khafra, the builder of the second Giza pyramid, is not. Khafra is represented with a well-modeled torso, again on too-massive legs, and a sensitive face, framed by a wonderful device: a falcon cradles Khafra's head with its outstretched wings, underlining the point that here is a man with power behind him. From the same Giza plateau come scores of bodiless sculpted limestone heads, called "reserve heads," as lifelike and individual as could possibly be.

Excellent bas reliefs also became common during this exceptional era. The least tomb hieroglyph counts as a minor masterpiece, and wall scenes are tours de force. Competent artists were sufficiently abundant by this time that mere courtiers and government officials could embellish their tombs with outstanding, rather than merely adequate, carving. Monumental statuary, embodied by the colossal Sphinx, appeared for the first time as free-standing work—as in the case of the two-foot-tall head of the Fifth Dynasty pharaoh Userkaf, which is all that remains of a more-than-twice life-sized seated statue. The first metal sculpture was produced in the Sixth Dynasty. Inscriptions record an earlier copper statue of a Second Dynasty king, but a corroded, striding, larger-than-life (almost six feet tall, as reconstructed) Pepi I and his two-foot-tall son are the oldest metal statues yet found in Egypt. Since copper does not flow readily into molds, these pieces were formed of copper sheets nailed to a wooden core. Finer work lay ahead, when the more easily cast bronze arrived in Egypt during the Middle Kingdom.

The collapse of central authority during the First Intermediate Period disrupted the training of artists and resulted in crude work throughout most of that era, but with the return of a stable central government in the Middle Kingdom came a resurgence of interest in art. Strikingly, pharaohs' statues began to portray faces with lines of age and expressions of concern, as opposed to the idealized portrayals of the Old Kingdom: for the first time real people look back at the viewer. A previous delicacy of expression was replaced by a better sense of proportion and composition, as exemplified by statues of seated scribes, knees held to their chests, in a posture which appropriately earned them the name "block statues," while the nuances of older bas reliefs gave way to more elegant, simpler forms. In a continued democratizing trend, more citizens began to commission fine artists to produce work for their tombs, including charming wood and clay models—produced by the hundreds in sizes ranging from less than a foot to over two feet tall—of servants bearing offerings, soldiers arrayed for battle, houses and workers engaged in various occupations, such as cattle feeding, or bread and beer making. These models were placed in tombs to enable the gods to recognize what pleasures the deceased looked forward to in the next world.

As fine artwork continued to proliferate during the New Kingdom, pictures replaced these tomb models at the same time that monumental statuary attained superhuman scale. When Egypt conquered the "vile Asiatics" to establish the New Kingdom, the mighty conquests of its divine pharaohs were underscored by wall carvings depicting the pharaoh as ten or twenty times the size of ordinary people. Egypt's augmented position in the world demanded more impressive artistic symbols.

Exemplifying this trend, obelisks, imposing gifts from pharaohs to adorn temples, emerged as a new art form. Consisting of one massive piece of solid rock—unlike the stone bricks of our national obelisk, the Washington

PAINTED WOODEN FUNERARY FIGURINE *of a female mummy, dated c. 1567–1085 B.C.E.*

Monument—the granite spires of the Egyptians passed 100 feet in height and approached 400 tons in weight. Lines of hieroglyphs covered all four faces; and the point, sheathed in electrum, an alloy of gold and silver, shined like the sun. The hieroglyphs, of course, all describe how wonderful the pharaoh was to donate such a mighty monument.

Not all New Kingdom statuary aimed for the colossal or monumental. Although the buildings of the female pharaoh Hatshepsut were designed to awe, her triangular face carved on wall reliefs and statuary conveyed a benign dignity, the concern of the mighty ruler for her subjects. After Hatshepsut's "feminine" statuary, Amenhotep III's pair of 60-foot-tall, 350-ton megalithic seated statues so impressed ancient Greek visitors that they called them the Colossi of Memnon. Outdoing all his predecessors, Rameses the Great erected a 65-foot-tall, 1,000-ton statue at his funerary temple, and followed it with a rock-cut temple at Abu Simbel whose four gigantic images of the pharaoh were designed to erase all thought of conquest by any enemy approaching Egypt from the south. Altogether, New Kingdom Egypt produced more monumental sculpture than any other people at any time, anywhere.

Increased contact with art styles of other countries during this period influenced Egyptians to portray clothing and coiffures more sensuously. Lines in painting, bas relief and sculpture became more fluid, a style which culminated in an artistic revolution under the reign of the heretical monotheist Akhenaten. Images of the pharaoh and his family produced during this period portray them with grotesque jaws jutting to sharp points, craniums elongating into bulbs, necks lengthening impossibly, and chests of both men and women showing evident breasts before sloping to wasp waists then swelling again into elephant thighs that decrease to slender ankles. It was also the first time royalty were ever portrayed in intimate vignettes: Akhenaten kisses a child in his lap; his wife Nefertiti holds another daughter who tugs at her earring, for example. Traditional generalized scenes of Egyptian art were replaced by eternalized moments in time—slices of life—as if the pharaoh were an ordinary mortal. This revolutionary change in the principles of artistic depiction lasted only for the lifetime of this one king.

When Rameses became pharaoh, his love of the colossal resulted in an unequaled spate of building, which severely strained the resources of the country. Religious wall carvings began to show an obvious haste in execution, as the loving care previously lavished on them gave way to a debased style that sacrificed elegance for dramatic effect. But out of this arose a new technique—sunk relief—which was faster to carve, eliminating the need to chisel away the entire background surface, and, in the stark Egyptian sunlight, emphasized outlines by causing them to create deep shadows.

Sometime after Rameses' death, when the court moved north to the Delta, pharaohs' tombs ceased being built in the Theban Valley of the Kings. Although royal burials continued in the Delta, its high water table destroyed much art of the Late Period. What survives, mostly in the form of statuary, demonstrates the Egyptians' continued facility for carving all types of stone but without their earlier fine aesthetic.

As fine art became democratized, its quality declined—a trend exemplified particularly by Egyptian bronze statues. Bronze was brought to Egypt in the Middle Kingdom primarily for weapons, but gradually it became a favored medium for statues as well. The material, particularly well suited to casting, flowed into a mold's every crevice to produce replicas exact to the thinnest line, and the cheapness of the material allowed everyone to purchase bronze statues of his favorite god(s). Egyptians learned to cast bronze statues using the lost-wax method. First they carved a figure in wax, then coated the wax with moist clay. After firing, the wax melted and ran out a hole left for the purpose, while the clay skin hardened into pottery. When molten bronze was poured through the same hole that had allowed the wax to escape, it solidified into an exact replica of the original wax image. Early single-piece ceramic molds, shattered to release their bronze statues, had evolved by the New Kingdom into reusable molds, formed of separate halves, which could be used to produce countless replicas. During the remaining thousand years of Egypt's existence, hundreds of thousands of bronze statues of various gods were produced. Generally they stand less than a foot high, but decrease in size to as small as an inch or so, with the same themes repeated so often that excavated examples bore even museum curators. Much finer are specially commissioned bronzes, sometimes inlayed with gold or with components in semiprecious stone, created for wealthy patrons.

The appearance of Egyptian statuary differs markedly today from its initial state. Originally wood or soft stone statues were covered with a thin coat of gesso—a plaster-like material composed of chalk and glue that dried to a smooth, white coating—and provided a perfect surface for painting. The figures we see now, most of which retain only faint traces of their previous colors, would have been so brightly painted, given the primary hues favored in the Egyptian palette, that we would find them garish by modern standards. Even hard stones that took a smooth polish were fair game for highlights of paint or gilt. While eyes and lips might be colored appropriately, jewels, belts and head wear provided opportunities for serious embellishment.[4]

PAINTING

Egyptian painting began as a medium separate from sculpture, but the two came together in temple and tomb reliefs that required both subtle three-dimensional modeling and a brightly painted finish.

THIS DECORATIVE PLAQUE REPRESENTING THE NILE GOD HAPY *was cast in a copper alloy via the Egyptian lost-wax method, c. 680 B.C.E. The democratization of art over time led to the proliferation of deity figurines in cheap materials, such as bronze.*

Early drawing, elementary stick figures scratched on rocks in about 7000 B.C.E., depicted people, animals and birds. By 4000 B.C.E., drawings with the same stick figures, but now with boats, began to appear on pottery vessels. Sometime before 3000 B.C.E., the oldest Egyptian mural had been installed in a house in southern Hieraconpolis; enigmatically, it portrayed several groups of men engaged in land-and-sea battles.

Given paint's fragile nature, it is remarkable that a masterpiece of color as old as the early Fourth Dynasty has survived. Nevertheless, beside the pyramid of Meidum, deep inside the tomb of a courtier named Itet, stands a damaged wall painting of his sons netting birds in a marsh. Miraculously, a row of two ganders and a female goose have survived intact, their sure lines and strong color preserved, with every feather still in place and as fresh as the day they were painted. Nothing else as wonderful survives from this dynasty, but the Fifth Dynasty, a period in which permanent stone bricks replaced adobe in the tombs of nonroyals, provides hundreds of wonderfully painted bas reliefs in numerous tombs at Saqqara and elsewhere.

A representation of the tomb owner, either seated as a statue before a table heaped with food, or carved in high relief striding from the rear wall toward the main room, provides the focal point of each tomb. Most striking, however, are the painted processions of servants bearing produce from the owner's farms portrayed on adjacent walls. In the finest examples, every animal has been drawn with such precision as to be a minor masterpiece. Other walls show crop harvests, wine making, cattle herding, stone vessel carving and hunting. One outstanding example, the tomb of Ti at Saqqara, depicts a marsh as an infinite row of tall reeds, creating a background of vertical lines that emphasizes the shapes of the wild fowl and fish in the foreground. Another wall shows a carefully drawn herd crossing a stream with submerged sections of their legs indicated by paint alone, while the portion of their bodies remaining above water is depicted in carved relief.

Such scenes teach us a great deal about how ancient Egyptians lived. These snapshots from life that began in the Fourth and Fifth dynasties culminated in hundreds of intricate pictures in Theban tombs during the New Kingdom. Although

ARTISANS USED A STICKY TEMPERA *mixture to illustrate stories like this one, which features flutists and dancers, on tomb walls.*

less finely carved—not every sinew and feather is detailed—New Kingdom tomb art is the first to tell a story solely with paint, eliminating altogether the narrative hieroglyphs traditionally carved around a scene. These New Kingdom works portray whatever the dearly departed wanted to remember and experience again in the next world: the joys of family life, including dining with his loved ones, the pleasures of the hunt for either fowl or animals and information about the person's everyday life; how beer, wine, bread, fabric and boats were made or how beef was prepared; what his day on the farm consisted of, such as overseeing reaping, threshing or surveying; and references to any official honors he had received during his life. These tomb paintings all provide a fascinating record of life from long ago and, at times, outstanding examples of a painter's skill.

The tomb of Ramose, an Eighteenth-Dynasty mayor of Thebes, stands as a superior example of classic Egyptian painting. Despite consisting only of black outlines, both Ramose and, most engagingly, his wife look out with classically beautiful faces that profoundly touch the viewer. A row of mourners illustrated in full color on another wall express their grief as they tear their hair and wail. Greater detail is evident in the tomb of Rekmire, a vizier under Tuthmosis III, with its scenes of craftsmen at work, officials collecting taxes and foreign dignitaries being received at court, in addition to such expected scenes as a hunt and a banquet.

Surprisingly, one servant girl pictured in this tomb, who is pouring a libation at the banquet, stands three-quarters rear toward the viewer, a pose seldom seen in Egyptian art. Closer inspection shows her to be performing an impossible feat. Although her legs are not crossed, the foot farthest from the viewer overlaps the closer foot. Such strange depictions illustrate what unique principles form the basis for Egyptian art. Unlike later Greek art and that of other cultures that follow its traditions, Egyptian art never attempted to record a moment in time, never contrived to fit three-dimensional figures into the two dimensions available to a painter, never attempted to fool the viewer into thinking the real thing lay before him. The aim of Egyptian artists was simply to record an event for eternity, not capture a fleeting moment; to present a situation unambiguously, not show how it looked from a single point of view. Egyptians usually portrayed generic rather than specific situations because they wanted an object or gesture to be understood and identifiable. Superimposition, with nearer objects covering what lay behind them, was assiduously avoided to prevent any misinterpretation of an obscured object. Perspective, portraying objects more distant from the viewer as smaller than those closer to him, never entered the realm of Egyptian art. A building would be shown from the front and from the top all in the same composite view because, if only one side were depicted, the rest of the building would be hidden and therefore, by Egyptian standards, nonexistent.

People were almost always shown in exactly the same attitude: from the side, but with shoulders turned toward the viewer so both arms could be seen, and in a striding position so both legs and feet would appear. When it was important to show the person actually doing something, say, carrying a bundle or cutting down a tree, the shoulders still had to turn and both arms still appear in their entirety, a principle which sometimes resulted in comical distortions. More peculiar, even the outside of a foot was drawn as if seen from the inside so that the arch, an essential feature, would be visible. Painted figures are generally depicted with two identical hands—either two left or two right, but seldom one of each. The rare exceptions to this canon always pertain to people considered unimportant, such as the rear view of a servant girl noted above. Animals too were carefully delimited to show their most salient features, although, being less important than humans, they were sometimes permitted to romp and turn more "realistically."

Early on Egyptians established a canon for representing human proportions. The body was divided into eighteen equal squares, from the soles of the feet to the top of the forehead.[5] If the drawing or statue were full-sized, each square would be one "span," that is, the width of a palm. Two squares measured off the face and neck, ten covered the bottom of the feet to the waistband of a tunic, achieving a long-leg look, shoulders spread six squares wide, and so on. Children were generally represented as much smaller than life; even adult children came up only to their father's knee. In royal portraits, the pharaoh might be many times the size of his wife, who stood at about the height of a five-year-old—the same height as enemies and even friendly troops in battle scenes that included the king. The obvious principle was that size corresponded to social importance.

Perhaps because of their desire to present the essential features of real things accurately, Egyptian artists found it difficult to fantasize. Their attempts to portray the mythical creatures who populated the next world produced unimaginative results: they simply combined one known object with another— the body of a man, say, with the head of a snake or even a knife.

Despite an entirely different intention and a traditional lack of imagination, Egyptian artists often conveyed a feeling that still touches us today, an especially surprising fact given the limited materials available to them. Egyptians employed a palette of only a few, mainly pure, colors. Black, white, blue, red, yellow and brown came directly from a bowl; green, pink, orange and gray were mixed from two of those basic colors. Almost no other colors appear, except gilding with gold. That these colors were produced primarily from natural minerals accounts for the vividness that wall paintings retain thousands of years later. Brown, red and yellow came from different oxides of iron, white from powdered chalk or gypsum, and blue from frit: finely ground blue glass. Black, however, since it was derived from soot, sometimes turned brown or reddish over the centuries.

What was mixed with all these powders to make them flow onto a wall and adhere? These were certainly not oil paints—discovered only during our Renaissance—nor watercolors, but a kind of tempera: the carrying medium was a sticky substance that dried hard in air. Although chemical analysis still leaves doubt about whether the medium was glue, gum from the acacia tree or albumen (egg whites),[6] we have good evidence about how a wall was prepared and the steps involved in painting it.

First, the stone wall was rubbed smooth with blocks of sandstone. If the wall was cracked or pitted, it was initially evened out with a coating of straw and mud. A final thin coating of gesso—powdered gypsum mixed with a glue—provided a smooth canvas that held paint well. Workers then stretched strings coated with powdered red ochre and snapped them against the wall, like a modern-day chalk line, to produce a grid that ensured properly proportional figures in adherence to Egyptian principles of art. Then a team of master draftsmen drew the outlines of figures and scenes in red. If the walls were to be raised in bas relief, carvers next cut away the background so the figures stood out about a quarter inch or so; masters then cut details into the figure outlines. The painters came next, filling in the figures with solid colors. Finally, a master painter went over the work and corrected any mistakes with black outlines. In many cases, a final coating of protective material was applied over the color to seal out dampness. In some instances, beeswax was used; other times, a varnish consisting of an unidentified tree resin.[7] Large brushes made of date palm ribs beaten to separate the fibers into bristles were used to paint backgrounds. Smaller brushes with diameters as fine as 1/16th of an inch made of rushes chewed on one end to separate the fibers into usable points were used to paint details. Small brushes have been found that have been chewed so often that only three or four inches remain of what began as a foot-long tool. Paints were stored in individual three- to four-inch pottery cups, suggesting that each painter used only one color at a time.

As with every society, fashions—even artistic fashions—changed. Early in the Eighteenth Dynasty, for example, light gray backgrounds were generally chosen to set off painted subjects; later a bright white background gained favor, with yellow as an infrequent alternative. Yellow had become the primary background choice by the Nineteenth Dynasty. As time passed, the time-consuming carving necessary to produce bas reliefs became less common, and it was replaced, as in the tomb of Tutankhamen, by paint alone.

ARCHITECTURE

In addition to erecting the most massive stone building in the world (the Great Pyramid) and the largest place of worship (Karnak Temple), Egypt contributed several new forms to architecture: columns, pylons and at least three kinds of decoration. These innovations are discussed here; for the development of architecture, see Chapter 7.

Egyptians were the first people to erect stone columns—a fact of no great surprise since they were the first to build with durable materials. The first stone building, the pharaoh Zoser's Step Pyramid, included an entrance court lined on each side with two rows of near-columns. These columns were ribbed and formed of stone drums stacked one on top of the other—the harbingers of the great Greek fluted columns—although these served no architectural purpose, only an aesthetic one. Nor were they true columns because horizontal supports anchored them to the wall. The same architect carved other near-columns; these were only half-round, forming part of a wall in the face of a temple inside the enclosure, but faceted—the models for the freestanding, true fluted columns that had arrived in Egypt by the Middle Kingdom. That this was no accident or mistake is proven by their repetition in three other locations in Zoser's complex. Why the architect faceted his near-columns is not known.

Earlier wood examples certainly provided inspiration as demonstrated by the drooping, ribbed leaves at the tops of these stone columns. One possibility is that he copied wood poles tied together in bundles that were used at the time in house construction. This probably explains the engaged columns in the entrance court, which are ribbed like a bundle of trunks; however, this theory does not account for the carved leaves at the top. Perhaps these facets represented the marks an adz would make as it sliced down a circular trunk. Neither theory is plausible enough for us to feel we understand why this architect—or the Greeks at a later time—decided to flute otherwise circular columns. That it adds interest to the architecture is certain, and, in the end, that may be the only explanation.

Whatever their origin, true, freestanding fluted columns—predating Greek versions by a millennium and a half—had appeared in Egypt by the Middle Kingdom, primarily in rock-cut tombs of the governors of a central Egyptian province known today as Beni Hassan. Interestingly, the Egyptians did not greatly favor this form of column; they chose other types for more important buildings. Generally they erected perfectly round columns, composed either of stone drums or a solid block of stone, each of which tapered up to one of five different capitals. One characteristic capital depicted upswept palm fronds; another represented papyrus flowers opened as a tumbrel; two others showed lotus—one in closed buds and one in open flowers. Each of these four representations generally incorporated carved rope ties just below the capital. A fifth capital depicted the head of the cow goddess Hathor on each of four flat sides. Egyptians loved their columns and put them to use in both houses and temples. The imposing Hypostyle Hall of Karnak's Amun temple, for example, has twelve seventy-foot-high columns that form a central aisle, bordered by a forest of 80 slightly shorter columns.

Karnak Temple also illustrates another Egyptian innovation—pylons. Pylons, after first appearing in the New Kingdom, became standard features of temple entrances thereafter. At the end of the Eighteenth Dynasty, Akhenaten used their drama to provide a grand entrance to his palace, but this is the only known private use of pylons. Many Egyptologists think a door placed between a pair of pylons symbolized the sun rising between two mountains.[8] Perhaps this demonstrates something about the imagination of Egyptologists; there is no good reason to believe ancient Egyptians viewed their pylons in this way. A simpler

explanation would be that pylons gave an appearance of greater size with less work than other sorts of entrances, while providing a large area for carved scenes.

A sixty-foot-high wall of bricks, especially without mortar, is at constant risk of collapse unless the base is wider than the top and the walls tapered. Taking such architectural precautions would automatically produce a pylon. With such structures fronting a temple, the whole building would appear to be equally tall, permitting lower side and back walls without losing the impression of size. Pylons were used solely to support flag poles at the front of the temple and to anchor the entrance doors set between each pair, a result which could certainly have been accomplished by different means.

Egypt made three contributions to decorative architecture: the cavetto cornice, torus molding and the kheker frieze. Cavetto cornices add interest to the tops of walls by gently curving outward. Even as early as Zoser's Third Dynasty Step Pyramid complex, wall tops often project, but without any curve. By the Fifth Dynasty, the curve actually appears and, from that point on, a row of horizontal ribs is etched into it at intervals, with the cornice at times painted yellow. Prehistoric illustrations of reed shrines suggest similar curved tops leading to the theory that this cornice replicates in stone either the tops of reeds or palm fronds.[9] At several inches apart, the etched ribbing seems wider than that of a reed, although yellow is typically used to indicate reeds in Egyptian painting. But, while the ribbing of palm fronds is the correct width, it would be unlikely that they would naturally all bend in the same outward direction, and they would be painted green, not yellow. Cavetto cornices, whatever their original model, served as signature decorative elements on pylons and kiosks throughout most of Egyptian history and thereafter in the architecture of other cultures.

Almost always cavetto cornices stand just above a torus molding. This simple molding consists of a rib with etched indications of wrapping, strongly suggesting that some sort of rope material served as the model.

OPEN PAPYRUS BLOSSOM CAPITALS *sit atop the gigantic columns supporting Karnak's Great Hypostyle Hall.*

Unlike cavetto cornices and torus molding, kheker friezes, although common in Egyptian architecture, seldom appeared in other cultures. Kheker friezes comprised rows of horizontal elements, shaped something like a flame above a round base. In this case, the model seems clear. Papyrus plants send out a fan "flower," like a giant dandelion thistle. In prehistoric times, shrines were constructed of standing papyrus reeds whose tops protruded above the roof. The "flower" was gathered together for neatness by tying the petals near their tops and again, separated by a bit of space, twice more near the bottom. The bottom two ties formed a rough circle; the top tie elongated the petals into a dart. This unusual decorative motif appeared at the top of so many walls that a picture of a single kheker became the hieroglyph for decoration in general.

Ceramics and Glass

Egyptian pottery adequately served its purpose, but it never achieved the quality of Egyptian sculpture, painting and architecture. Bowls could convey charm, however, as in the case of small predynastic "footed" ones which rested on two tiny human feet. The most interesting pottery also dates back to such early times. Two-color pots were produced by oxidizing iron impurities in the clay which fired it to a red color, while the top of the pot lay buried under the fire's ashes to carbonize black. The finished product, which could be as thin as an eighth of an inch for a pot over a foot tall, exhibits a distinct shine that came not from a glaze but from being burnished with a smooth stone before firing.

Something like a potter's wheel was invented during the Old Kingdom, if not before. A heavy circular stone rested on a pivot for turning by hand or foot, at a level lower than our modern version. It spun more slowly, but produced round vessels of consistent thickness. The kiln was also an early invention. In the Egyptian version, a tall, conical brick structure held a fire at the bottom while a shelf supported the unfired clay above the ashes. In this simple way pots were produced—for cooking, storing and carrying—during all ancient Egypt's history. Because they were utilitarian objects, their makers seldom paid much attention to their beauty.

When artisans turned their attention to ceramic amulets, however, they invested more imagination and care and produced thousands of images—from the tiny to a foot in height—depicting gods, the magical eye of Horus (for health), the *djed* pillar (of stability), the sacred scarab beetle (for long life) and even images of servants, called *ushabtis*, which each person took to his tomb to magically work for him during his afterlife. These figures, generally colored a rich sky blue, aqua or green, were not molded from clay, but from a material of Egyptian invention. Called Egyptian faience, it consisted of a core produced from finely ground quartz coated with a glass-like glaze. Composed of a solution of natron and quartz dust, it could be shaped by hand or pressed into a clay mold. When fired, it solidified into a solid mass harder than soft stone.

The glaze consisted of natron again, mixed in solution with malachite or another oxide of copper. The solution, which was washed over the object to be glazed then heated to fuse with the silicon of the quartz, produced a blue or green glass that was literally bound to the object. Instead of washing the coloring agent over the object, it could instead be mixed in with the quartz powder before firing. When heated, it would rise to the surface as a self-glaze.

In addition to making delicate figures by the thousands, Egyptians used their faience to manufacture small bowls and dishes of rich blue. They even learned, by changing the oxide, to produce red and yellow versions and to create objects in two and three colors. One early experiment produced the first glazed tiles in history. A room in a second tomb of Zoser, called the Southern Burial, was found lined with rows of lovely green-blue tiles, about three inches long by an inch and a half wide. A method to fix them to a wall was lacking, however. The tiles were attached to the wall by a string through a hole in the back of each.

A SHALLOW FAIENCE BOWL *with blue glaze, c. 1425 B.C.E. The aquatic imagery—two fish carrying lotus stems with buds and opened blossoms in their mouths—suggests the powerful themes of rebirth and regeneration.*

Egyptian glaze not only shone like glass, it actually was glass, so Egyptians must be counted among the very first glass producers. Some pure glass may have been manufactured as early as predynastic times, but evidence that the process was understood and intentional remains unclear.[10] Glass results from fusing sand with an alkali and mixing in additives for color as desired. Sand existed in inexhaustible supply in Egypt and natron, an alkali, was available from a place where it covers the ground so extensively that the area is called the Wadi Natron. Egyptians were unable to produce temperatures high enough to make clear glass, hardly a matter of concern since all their glass was intentionally colored for use as ornaments. Since glass blowing originated in later Roman times, Egyptians produced glass objects either by pouring molten glass into molds or by dipping a sandy clay core into molten glass, then, in a process called marvering, rolling the glass-covered core over a stone to smooth its surface. After hardening, the core was scraped out. Alternatively, rods of glass, often of different colors,[11] could be wrapped around a core to form a vase or bowl. One special treatment was to drag a tool up and down the still viscous bands to produce attractive waves of color in the final product.

By the time of the New Kingdom, glass had become an industry which turned out thousands of excellent inlays, beads, vases, bowls and amulets. Strangely, production had declined by the Twentieth Dynasty, two dynasties later, and disappeared entirely during the Late Period, not to be resurrected until many centuries later by the Ptolemies.

CARPENTRY

Egyptian carpentry dates from predynastic times when coffins were constructed of lap-joined planks held together at the corners with lashing tied through holes. By the First Dynasty, construction had become more sophisticated, resulting in admirable work. One box, about ten inches by four inches, consists of one large compartment and another of the same size divided into four spaces.[12] The corners were lap-joined with the bottom rebated into the sides, and all was fastened with leather tied through angled holes. A sliding lid sealed the box. Even at this early time, carpenters had mastered the craft of producing flat pieces of wood, then cutting and joining them into a well-built box. Predynastic tombs contained boxes with inlayed panels and mortise and tenon joints for the rails and stiles, mitered corners and inlays of ivory strips or even faience plaques attached by tree resin to a gesso base. Splendidly carved bull's feet with sinews and fetlock accurately depicted in ivory for use as the feet of beds or chairs serve today as museum exhibits.

Carpenters had gotten off to a precocious start, barely hampered by the absence of glue and of nails. Glue, made from boiling down the bones and cartilage of animals, did not come into use as an adhesive until about the Fifth Dynasty. By the Fourth Dynasty, boxes with barrel or gabled lids, others with cavetto cornices and some with curved sides, show that shaping presented no problem. Sloping lids rising to a curved peak attained the height of complexity in the Sixth Dynasty. Rope handles tied through side holes aided carrying, or, in the case of larger boxes,

THIS 11.3 × 11.8 × 14–INCH WOODEN BOX *from the first century B.C.E. may have been used in temple rituals. Glue wasn't used as an adhesive until the Fifth Dynasty, but by the New Kingdom, dowel hinges and intricate openwork carvings were common.*

copper loops on the box bottom secured carrying poles that slid out when not needed. Lids were locked by a string tied to a knob on the front, the top, or both.

Plywood composed of six eighth-of-an-inch-thick pieces of imported Syrian cypress, pegged together with grains running in different directions for strength, were used in a coffin as early as the Third Dynasty. Later, even thinner veneer, as thin as one-thirty-second of an inch, was used to cover cheaper material, sometimes pieced together, to masquerade as more costly woods. One funerary box from the Eighteenth Dynasty contained such a clever locking mechanism that its excavator had to break it open. Afterward he discovered that when the lid was pushed closed a tongue swung down into a tenon, locking the box. No means for unlocking it had been provided.[13] Dowel hinges also existed by the New Kingdom, along with such intricate design techniques as openwork carving; inlaying with contrasting woods, ivory, faience, stone and glass; and gilding using tissue-thin sheets of gold.

In addition to boxes in many styles and designs, carpenters produced wooden beds and small tables that stood on three or four legs. Chairs tended to have low seats, less than ten inches above the ground, and almost straight backs, often intricately cut out. Some examples of folding stools have been found with leather seats that could collapse for transport to the battlefield or the hunt.

All these objects were produced with simple woodworking tools. Saws with two-foot-long blades attached to a wood handle were pulled, not pushed as ours are today, which meant the far end aimed high and was drawn down with two hands toward the user. Pictures show upright logs lashed between poles with a sawyer working his way down to shape a plank. Several kinds of drills existed. One type, more of an awl, was twisted by hand; another was a drill driven by a bow that moved back and forth. After sawing wood to its approximate measurements, an adz could be used to achieve an exact size quickly. A chisel, driven by a round wood mallet, worked the area even more finely before its final sanding with blocks of sandstone the ancient equivalent of sandpaper. Neither wood planes nor lathes existed in these times; the Egyptian carpenter compensated for the absence of these tools with his infinite patience.

Although ancient Egypt did not grow the best woods, available material proved adequate for carpenters when supplemented by imports.[14] Egypt grew no tall trees for tall ship masts, large coffins and towering temple doors. For these uses, tall cedar from Lebanon or cypress trees were imported. Tough, elastic ash was imported from Syria for use in bows and chariots. Beautiful, hard dark ebony, whose name derives from the ancient Egyptian word *hbny*, was imported from tropical Africa and Punt (Somalia) for the solid furniture of the rich and for inlays and veneers for those on a budget. From Palestine (Israel) came elm for strong chariot axles and supports; yew from Persia was imported for coffins. Egypt was not, however, without its own lumber. Acacia grew tall enough for shorter ship masts and boat planking. Date palm trunks provided roof beams, though its fibrous wood made it inappropriate for furniture. Sycamore, which served many uses, from boxes to coffins, proved to be one of the most useful native woods. The shorter tamarisk tree provided wood for boxes and some coffins, though much pieced together. Wood from willow trees became knife handles and parts of some boxes.

LITERATURE

Although probably less than 5 percent of Egypt's population was literate, Egypt, like any other great civilization, employed a large bureaucracy to collect taxes, record business transactions and preserve the country's history—all tasks that required writing. Besides being crucial for the business of the country, written work provided the literate minority with both instruction and pleasure.

A common misconception about Egyptian writing is that hieroglyphs picture the subjects written about; that the appearance of a bird or a rabbit in a text, for example, indicates a discussion of those animals. Hieroglyphs are actually phonetic, like our own letters, in which signs represent word sounds. When an ancient Egyptian sculptor carved a hand followed by a rectangular reed mat and a loaf of bread on a temple wall he was indicating the sound *d*, *p* and *t*, spelling the word *dpt*, ancient Egyptian for "boat." If he wanted to make the meaning doubly clear, he could add the boat hieroglyph at the end of the word. Hieroglyphs used in such a manner are called determinatives because they help the reader determine the meaning.

The classical Egyptian alphabet served its people for 3,000 years. Egyptians did not generally symbolize their vowels because a reader familiar with the language would know which vowels were meant without being told. The ancient Hebrew alphabet followed the same design. Still, some of their signs could be used, if someone wished, when writing a modern name. Thus the Egyptian vulture sign is not an exact equivalent of our letter "a" but may be used in its place. The arm hieroglyph may be used in place of our "e," and so on.

In addition to an alphabet of single sounds, other hieroglyphs, called biliterals, represented two consecutive sounds. The hieroglyph of a house plan ⊏⊐ represented the combined *p* and *r* sounds, pronounced something like *per*. Our word "pharaoh" comes from an Egyptian word made up of two biliterals: ⊏⊐ (the bottom bilateral was pronounced "aha" and meant "great"). Thus the *per-aha* was the one who lived in the great house. Another group of hieroglyphs represented three sounds—triliterals, such as the hieroglyph ☥, pronounced *ah-n-kh*, the ancient Egyptian word for life. A scribe used about five hundred common hieroglyphs in all, but several thousand others were written occasionally or rarely.

In addition to record keeping and religious writing, literature, where the craft was as important as the content, existed as well. Wisdom literature, simply called "Instructions" by their authors, were texts that first appeared during the Old Kingdom to guide younger generations. Their aristocratic authors, princes and viziers, thus instructed their sons how to attain and prosper in high offices. The "Instructions to Kagemni" advise modesty.

> The respectful man prospers.
> Praised is the modest one.
> The tent is open to the silent.[15]

This theme is repeated throughout wisdom literature; modesty, calmness and restraint are all virtues to be cultivated and will lead to advancement. Kagemni is advised further,

> Gluttony is base and is reproved.
> A cup of water quenches thirst,
> A mouthful of herbs strengthens the heart.[16]

In a set of thirty-seven maxims, the vizier Ptahotep gives his son, and us, a view of the moral system of the ancient Egyptians: one should know one's place.

If you are among guests
at the table of one greater than you,
Take what he gives as it is set before you.[17]

And reason, rather than emotion, should be followed.

The trusted man does not vent his belly's speech,
He will himself become a leader...
The great hearted is god-given,
He who obeys his belly belongs to the enemy.[18]

Ptahotep also counsels against woman and greed. "In whatever place you enter, beware of approaching the women!" "Guard against the vice of greed . . . The greedy has no tomb." Mixed with the advice of restraint—in lovers, eating and speech—runs the belief that justice will prevail. In an equivalent of our "Crime does not pay," Ptahotep proclaims, "[c]rime never lands its wares, In the end it is justice that lasts."

The Egyptian sense of order, with everything and everyone in its proper place led to the highly structured society reflected in wisdom literature. Know your place and be restrained; the rich are supposed to be rich, so do not rock the boat. The pharaoh Khety counseled,

Don't reduce the nobles in their possessions.
Beware of punishing wrongfully,
Do not kill, it does not serve you.
Punish with beatings and detentions,
Thus will the land be well ordered.[19]

In spite of the aristocratic tone, justice is always paramount.

Make firm your station in the graveyard,
By being upright, by doing justice,
Upon which men's hearts rely.
The loaf of the upright is preferred
To the ox of the evildoer.[20]

By the time of the New Kingdom, a growing class of well-to-do non-aristocrats required their own wisdom literature which encouraged the same virtues as in the Old Kingdom texts, but preached those values from the mouths of scribes, rather than kings and princes. Any, a scribe of Queen Ahmose-Nefertari, instructs his son,

Don't indulge in drinking beer, lest you utter evil speech,
and don't know what you are saying.
If you fall and hurt your body,
none holds out a hand to you;
Your companions in drinking
Stand up saying: "Out with the drunk!"[21]

This is the way a working class man tells his son to stay out of bars.

Although wisdom literature had the practical purpose of instruction, a large body of fiction literature was written for pure entertainment. Since most Egyptians were unable to read and those who could, in most cases, were unable to afford a papyrus for mere entertainment, these short stories were probably read at gatherings, much as Middle Eastern storytellers entertained the illiterate until modern times. Egyptian short stories deal with magic and mystery, heroes and bravery, and almost always have happy endings. Probably the most famous is the "Tale of Sinhue."[22]

Sinhue, an aristocrat and a loyal courtier of the Middle Kingdom pharaoh Senusert I, flees Egypt for the northern lands of Syria-Palestine when his pharaoh dies. He endures hardships, almost dying of thirst and hunger, but is finally rescued by a Syrian prince who recognizes Sinhue, having met him on an earlier trip to Egypt. Sinhue's skills and virtues enable him to prosper in his new land, and the tale chronicles his rise to respectability. He marries a princess and becomes an owner of cattle and large tracts of land but, as in any good tale, there is a villain. A local warrior, jealous of Sinhue's wealth and status, challenges him to mortal combat—the equivalent of two gunfighters shooting it out. After preparing his bow, arrows, shield and dagger, Sinhue marches toward his enemy while a crowd cheers him on. The villain fires first from a distance that allows Sinhue to sidestep the arrow and continue forward until he draws close enough to fire back. Sinhue pierces his enemy's neck. Moving in for the kill, Sinhue dispatches him with his battle ax. As is traditional, Sinhue appropriates his rival's cattle and goods to become even more wealthy. He fathers numerous children and enters his twilight years as one of the most respected men of his adopted tribe.

In spite of Sinhue's successes, however, he remains an Egyptian at heart, realizing that, if he dies abroad and is not mummified, he will lose his chance for immortality. When the son of the pharaoh Sinhue originally served hears of Sinhue's desire to return to Egypt he sends an entourage to escort him home. The story proclaims Sinhue's joyful and triumphant return, as he is welcomed by the new pharaoh and his children and is given land and a grand house so he can spend his final days in comfort. Although the "Tale of Sinhue" is intended as entertainment, it contains the clear message that there is no place like home, especially if home is Egypt.

Because magic was such an integral part of their daily life, Egyptians loved tales of wonder and mysterious beings. "The Shipwrecked Sailor" is a fantasy similar to those in *The Arabian Nights*.[23]

As a high official sails home to Egypt, despondent because of an unsuccessful royal mission, one of his shipmates attempts to cheer him by telling of a time when he too thought all was lost before his fortunes changed. The sailor had been a crewmate of 120 others, all skilled and brave, but a terrible storm sank their ship, killing everyone but the sailor telling the story. A great wave washed him onto the shore of an island. After recovering from his initial fright of the unknown island, he explored it and discovered a tropical paradise filled with figs, incense, vegetables, grapes, fish and fowl. In the midst of his wonder at all this bounty, he hears a noise like the roar of the sea that emanates from the mouth of a gigantic, forty-five-foot-long cobra, wearing a pharaoh's false beard made of lapis lazuli.

Petrified, the sailor throws himself on his belly before the cobra. The cobra bellows angrily, "Who brought you to my island?" When the sailor is unable to reply, the cobra threatens to reduce him to ashes. Finally the sailor stammers out the story of the shipwreck and the loss of his comrades. Moved by the tale, the cobra assures the man he has nothing to fear, even predicting that in four months a great ship from Egypt will rescue him from the island. Then the cobra gently carries the man in his mouth to his den where he tells the shipwrecked sailor of his own woes—a tale of woe within a tale of woe within another tale of woe. When the cobra was young, he lived with his family, seventy-five in all. One day, when he was away from his house, a meteor fell from the sky, setting his house on fire and killing all his family. Like the shipwrecked sailor, he alone was spared.

Four months later, as the cobra had foretold, a boat arrived to rescue the shipwrecked sailor. At his departure, the cobra gives him gifts of incense, perfume, elephant tusks, ivory, monkeys and baboons. The man promises to repay these many kindnesses but the cobra tells him they will never meet again, that the enchanted island will return to beneath the sea.

Love poetry also existed in Egypt, becoming particularly popular during the New Kingdom. As in all love poems, separated lovers pine for their loved ones, extolling the pleasures of ecstasy (sometimes in graphic detail). Women are compared to the beauties of nature, and couples scheme how to meet.

> I will lie down in my house
> and pretend to be dying.
> When the neighbors come to see me,
> perhaps my love will come with them.
> She will make doctors unnecessary.
> She knows what's wrong with me![24]

Egyptian poetry often refers to the Nile as the transport for a lover to his adored. At other times it is a barrier, but even a raging river and crocodiles do not deter a true lover.

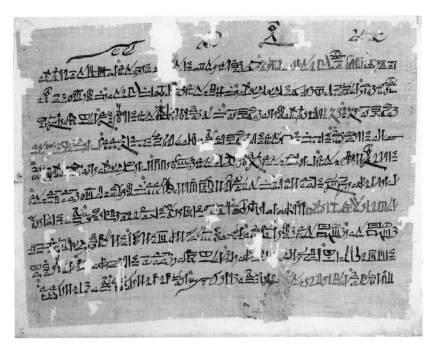

"THE TEACHING OF KING AMENEMHAT I," *a poem written by royal scribe Inena in 1204 B.C.E. Red dots mark the ends of verses.*

My love is over on one side,

the river between us.

The river is high now,

and there's a crocodile on the sandbank.

I dive into the river and brave the current.

My heart is strong.

The crocodile seems small to me,

the torrents are like ground under my feet.

Her love makes me strong;

It makes a water spell for me.[25]

AN EXACT MAP
of the River
NILE done
by Mr. Lucas.

The Cataracts of ye Nile p.38

French Leagues

Fortress of ye

Pyramids

p.138. Asuana in ruins

p.137. Tombs of ye Arabian Cheeks

Maafallu where there is a Custom House p.132. p.137. Maffa Fort where is a garison of Janizarys

Sicut
Ruetia
Velolie

Benesalem

Lojojoue

Beuechigare

Benut

Abouliosous

Beniay

p.137. Huts of ye Arabians

Fuisare

Mesare

Ceoterangoa ruin'd place

Boniamera

Masera

p.137. Ruinous Temples

Huts

Column like ye of Pompey

Sola once a great Town

Neloae a fine Town

Reromont

B. Ulade Mouse so call'd because ye Inhabitants say twas ye Country of Moses. p.136.

mummys ye th
g within
a Com
vade

Beedi a place where ye Turks cannot live p.132.

Roda

Seguiet moava

Cude

Minio

Tougar

Lanalut

Colesene

Benjemot

Abougirge

Chex Zeiade

Care

Nazou

Negalo p.136.

Tombs of Arabian Cheek

Barbambou C.

Cheronne

Clouque

Yagaadit

Fesene

Tougaie

Bibe

Amanurar

Tlebbe

Benesules p.131.

Mangors

Bouche

Lellan

Demene

Menon

Benedeore

Commadire

p.135. Caa a City from whence they transport corn & Pulse to Mecca

Habou Jhoua Tomb of a Cheek

Hus a ruin'd Town

Bagioura

Egeronne

Joule

uife

id

Yoabe

Gourturu

Zauxic

Rione

Arislaux

p.133. Aquemin where are fine ruins

Suaiffe

Boubas

Latfit

Dabay

Davou

Manegonne

Chaubat

Loen

Acharfas

9

TECHNOLOGY AND CONSTRUCTION

E VEN WITH ALL OUR MODERN ADVANCES IN ENGINEERING, ancient buildings like Rome's Colosseum, the Inca's Machu Picchu and Egypt's pyramids still have the power to awe. How could ancient people accomplish these feats without modern machines or the engineering we take for granted today? In ancient times builders not only erected grand monuments but also invented the means, the engineering, by which they could be built, in the process creating their marvels. By understanding the challenges confronting ancient builders and their solutions, we gain appreciation for and insight into the thinking and ingenuity of these people from long ago.

In particular, construction in ancient Egypt was complicated by the composition of its land—much of it either soggy, marsh soil or shifting sand. For this reason, Egyptians never developed the grand system of roads that civilizations like the Romans did, although this is not to say there were no roads in Egypt. Where solid ground existed, Egyptians laid gravel, when available, or smoothed and tamped the soil to create a surface suited to rapid chariot movement for its army, foreign diplomats and merchants.

Still, the main highway of Egypt was a wide natural thoroughfare called the Nile River. The river served as the most efficient means of moving heavy objects over long distances, shifting the burden from humans to the divine river. Still, transporting loads from the Nile to a building site was a problem. Since wheels proved of little use in transporting heavy objects across a marsh or sand, the Egyptians invented sleds, which could glide over wet or soft soil. Egyptian sleds

A C. 1716 MAP OF THE NILE RIVER, *the main highway of ancient Egypt.*

had two joined wooden runners that curved up at the front, and normally served their purpose well, even when, in shifting sand, they required someone riding on the front of the sled pouring water to help the runners glide. Nonetheless, transporting objects that weighed many tons proved difficult. Rather than a constant steady pulling motion, what was needed were spurts of pulling power that could jerk the sled with force when it stalled.

Egyptians found that nothing was better than man-power for such tasks; indeed, one surviving picture shows 172 men pulling on four separate ropes to drag a stone statue that must have weighed sixty tons or more. Although oxen sometimes hauled heavy sleds, when the load was truly great, nothing proved better than a team of men all pulling together. Incidentally, although Egyptians bred tens of thousands of horses, they used them only for transporting people.

Just as geography significantly affected construction techniques in ancient Egypt, so too did the availability of a huge workforce. Throughout history nations have sought to increase the efficiency of individual workers so that fewer people would be required for given projects, freeing up others for assignment elsewhere. Ancient Egypt was an exception. Thanks to the "miracle" of Nile floods that replenished their farm soil every year, abundant crops were reaped regularly by the Egyptians, ensuring that food, the dominant concern of most civilizations, was relatively easy for them to produce. With fewer citizens required to feed the population, more were available for other tasks, such as construction and manufacturing. If someone took a month to carve a stone jar, there were still plenty of people available for other projects while that craftsman was occupied.

A third important factor affecting construction techniques in ancient Egypt was the fact that, since this civilization flourished before humans learned to work iron, it had to make do without iron or steel tools during most of its history. Throughout the five hundred years of the Old Kingdom, the strongest metal Egyptians knew for tools was copper. Later, bronze was discovered; but it took another five hundred years before iron became commonplace. Copper's virtue, its relatively low melting temperature, permitted it to be poured into molds of any shape. But its less beneficial characteristic, extreme softness, meant that, when forged into a tool with a sharp edge, it blunted with the first blow to a hard object. Because bronze is much harder than copper—similar to wrought iron but much easier to melt and mold into various shapes—its discovery and increasingly common use during Egypt's Middle Kingdom made carving stone significantly easier in that period.

Yet, as early as the Old Kingdom, Egyptians, equipped only with copper tools, managed to construct the massive stone structures of both the Great Pyramid and the Sphinx. During this early time, they quarried and carved huge blocks of granite, a substance harder than steel; they raised blocks weighing as much as sixty tons up a pyramid 480 feet tall; they constructed 200-feet-long ships without nails; and they leveled their pyramids to a precision that cannot be bettered today. They accomplished all this with only the most primitive tools. How did they manage such feats? In some cases the answer remains unknown, but in other cases detective work reveals the solutions to these ancient mysteries.

Building a Pyramid

Because of their immense size, building pyramids posed special problems of both organization and engineering. Constructing the Great Pyramid of the pharaoh Khufu, for example, required that more than two million blocks weighing from two to more than sixty tons be formed into a structure covering two football fields and rising in a perfect pyramidal shape 480 feet into the sky. Its construction involved vast numbers of workers which, in turn, presented complex logistical problems concerning food, shelter and organization. Millions of heavy stone blocks needed not only to be quarried and raised to great heights but also set together with precision in order to create the desired shape. These problems became even more complicated because of time constraints: since it was a tomb, the pyramid had to be completed before the pharaoh, Khufu, died. How did the ancient Egyptians overcome such obstacles?

In the case of Khufu's Great Pyramid, they first selected a site, a plateau of about fifty acres in the desert, then assembled more than 25,000 workers and set them to transforming the desolate, uninhabited terrain into a kind of boom town. The workers were free citizens, signed up by recruiters who had roamed the country seeking healthy, patriotic men willing to work for a national cause. They were certainly not the slaves that Hollywood so often portrays. They labored for the gratitude of their pharaoh, a person whom they believed would resurrect as a god, so a promise of free food and shelter was merely a bonus. Most were farmers who were accustomed to hard labor but had never traveled far from their villages. They came for a great adventure.

Before construction could begin on the pyramid, a sufficient number of houses, bakeries and breweries to sustain a workforce of tens of thousands through decades of labor had to be built. That is, an entire city had to be created. Workers had to excavate a four-mile canal to the Nile so supplies could be floated from all over Egypt directly to the work site, and they had to dig a harbor and construct docks to receive the tons of supplies necessary for this workmen's city.

There then remained a pyramid to be built. The first problem of construction was aligning the future building precisely with the four points of the compass, for when the dead pharaoh was resurrected, as the religion of the ancient Egyptians foretold, his new self would travel to the Polar Star, situated directly north. To orient the building so the pharaoh would not miss his way, engineers relied on their observation that the stars rotate around a fixed point in the sky. That point is true north and the Egyptians determined its exact orientation by one of two fairly simple methods.

Engineers could plant a stick so that it cast no shadow at noon. If the stick's shadow was then marked sometime before noon and marked again the same amount of time after noon, true north would lie exactly half way along a line connecting the two shadow marks. If precision was important, as it probably was, the process could be repeated for several days and the results averaged.

A second method entailed constructing a temporary wall, with as level a top as possible, that faced approximately northward. If a mark were made where any given star was first sighted rising in the night, and if a second mark were made where the same star disappeared later, a mark exactly half way between these two would point directly north.

With true north determined, the land had to be readied for the immense structure it would support. Since the pyramid would be constructed of stone blocks merely resting atop other blocks, its base had to be almost perfectly level; an even slightly tilted structure would tumble with the first earthquake. Pyramid engineers superbly accomplished their assignments: the difference in elevation from one corner of the Great Pyramid to the next, a distance of 756 feet, is less than an inch; because of this stable foundation, the structure has managed to survive the tremors of four millennia. We would be hard pressed with all our complex modern instruments to do much better. While no record describes how Egyptians accomplished such precision, the feat was most likely achieved by simple means, probably by digging a shallow trench around the perimeter of the future pyramid and filling it with water. The water's surface would have functioned as a gigantic carpenter's level, with gravity ensuring that the water evened to exactly the same elevation along the entire trench. The surrounding land could then simply be dug down to match the level of the water.

Clever Egyptian engineers even found a way to save the work and time of installing several thousand blocks at the center of the Great Pyramid by only excavating the stone at the perimeter of the building site. They saw no reason to level the natural mound only to have to build it back up later. So the first few courses of the Great Pyramid simply consist of a natural hill covered with an outer casing of cut stones.

When it was finally time to begin serious building, the first row of blocks was moved into position. But a problem had to be addressed before a second row could be added: at what angle should the sides of the pyramid incline as they rose to meet at the top? The angle was not ordained by any religious dictate: various pyramids across Egypt rise at different angles. Nonetheless, there were considerations. If the angle was too steep, the building might collapse; too gradual and the sides would meet too quickly, making it impossible to form a pyramid of impressive height. Engineers for Khufu's pyramid set the angle at a middle ground of 51.84 degrees. Once decided, the angle had to be maintained on each of the pyramid's four rising sides, or they would not meet together in a point at the top. To ensure consistency, engineers most likely constructed a wooden template in the form of a right triangle whose hypotenuse inclined at the proper angle and placed it on top of each completed row to determine the proper indentation for the next.

The engineers had to build quickly if the Great Pyramid were to be ready by the time their Pharaoh died. We know that Khufu reigned for about twenty years so the pyramid had to be completed in less time than that. The math indicates that, with about 2 million stones to place and at most twenty years to position them, given a work-year of 350 days and a work-day of ten hours, approximately thirty blocks were placed per hour. That is, one block was delivered to its position in the pyramid every two minutes. That is a very tight schedule.

How could thousands of two-ton blocks be raised hundreds of feet in the air in a manner that allowed such rapid delivery, given that Egyptians used people, not animals, to haul heavy loads?

Some theorists believe Egyptians used a kind of hoist. But, since the sides of a pyramid slanted inward, a straight pull to the top—necessary for a hoist—was impossible. Separate hoists on every completed row would involve untying a stone from its hoist when it was raised up one level and retying it to the hoist on the next level up. The tying and retying would take time, making it impossible to lift a block up ten or twenty levels within a two-minute-per-block schedule. Multiple hoists on each level could allow multiple blocks to be lifted at the same time, of course, but this would necessitate hundreds of hoists and thousands of people hoisting. While this might work at the pyramid's lower levels, as the building narrows to a point near the top, there would be less and less space available for hoists.

Another theory proposes that a ramp was used to haul blocks up pyramids. Such ramps certainly were employed by the Egyptians since ramp remains still survive near some ancient construction sites. It is unlikely that a ramp was used for Khufu's pyramid, however. As with hoists, a ramp might work for the lower part of a pyramid, but would cause difficulties for the higher levels. The problem is one of physics. The steeper the angle of an incline, the more effort necessary

THE METHOD OF CONSTRUCTION FOR KHUFU'S 480-FOOT PYRAMID *is a mystery. Over a twenty-year period, 25,000 workers arranged two million blocks—some weighing more than sixty tons—into a perfect pyramidal shape.*

to move an object up that incline. So, in order for a relatively small number of men, say ten or so, to drag a two-ton load up a ramp, its angle could not be more than about eight percent. Geometry tells us that to reach a height of 480 feet, an inclined plane rising at eight percent would have to start almost one mile from its finish. It has been calculated that building a mile-long ramp that rose as high as the Great Pyramid would require as much material as that needed for the pyramid itself—workers would have had to build the equivalent of two pyramids in the twenty-year time frame.

A modification of the ramp theory has also been proposed. It conjectures that a ramp was attached to the pyramid and followed its sides, as a road might circle up a mountain. Resting against the pyramid, such a ramp would not need to be self-supporting and could therefore be less massive and require less material than a straight ramp. But this idea is also problematic. While the mass of an Egyptian pyramid consisted of piled rectangular blocks, an outermost coating of finer limestone blocks with angled outer faces filled in the steps to create a true, smooth pyramid. Such a coating remains visible today at the top of the pyramid next to Khufu's on the Giza plateau. According to the modified ramp theory, the ramp covered the outside of the pyramid, so the blocks that form its smooth sides could only have been put in place after the ramp was removed. That is, workmen would have to begin at the top and work down as the ramp was disassembled because, once the ramp was removed, there would be no way to transport blocks to the top. But a top-down sequence is impossible because each casing block rests on the one below it, not the one above. Additionally, at the time the first casing blocks were placed at the top, the ramp would still encircle the pyramid, hiding its lower sides from view, a serious problem given that the only way to ensure the pyramid's 51.84 degree angle of incline is by sighting along its corners, an impossibility if the circling ramp was hiding the pyramid's corners.

A radical new theory about how the Great Pyramid's blocks were raised has recently been proposed by Jean-Pierre Houdin, a French architect.[1] His idea also involves a ramp, but one on the interior, not the exterior, of the pyramid. He believes that during the early stages of construction a straight, external ramp was used to haul stones up to about the first third of the pyramid's eventual height. Since this ramp would only rise a hundred feet or so, it would not need to be very long or involve vast amounts of material. As the first part of the pyramid was being built using this ramp, engineers created a corridor inside, which followed the outer walls and rose at about the eight-percent slope that would allow a small team of men to advance a two-ton stone. Each new level would include an addition to the corridor so it would ascend along with the building itself. Then the remaining two-thirds of the structure could be built with blocks hauled up this inner corridor. As an added advantage, the interior corridor-ramp was hollow which would mean that fewer blocks were needed to create the pyramid. Mr. Houdin even speculates that the blocks to finish the pyramid could have been those recovered from the first, external ramp when it was dismantled. The corridor could not be much wider than the blocks hauled through it, however, or this spiraling hole in the pyramid might cause structural problems.

Nonetheless, rooms do exist in the pyramid. Intended as a tomb, space had to be left inside for the burial of the pharaoh and the treasures he intended to take with him to the next world. Corridors were necessary, as well, to lead from the pyramid entrance to the burial room so that the body could be transported there after death. Three rooms are known to exist inside Khufu's pyramid, along with a network of corridors leading to them.

The reason that two extra chambers were built, in addition to the one needed for the pharaoh's tomb, was because no one knew when the pharaoh might die. The first burial chamber was built as soon as the plateau was leveled so that, even if the pharaoh died as soon as work began on his pyramid, he would still have a place ready for his eternal rest. This chamber is a rectangular room carved into the bedrock at the center of the pyramid below the lowest level of blocks. The pharaoh did not die early, however, so this chamber was never completed. After about six more years, with the pharaoh still living, work began on a second burial chamber. It too is in the center, directly above the first chamber, but this time it is constructed inside the pyramid proper. Today it is referred to as the "Queen's Chamber" since the earliest Egyptologists thought that multiple rooms must indicate that more than one person had been buried in the building. Today, however, we know that each of Khufu's queens had her own small pyramid near her husband's massive one. Finally, as the building neared completion, a third chamber was constructed about three-quarters of the way up the pyramid. Again, it is located in the center, directly above the other two and would count as a large living room by modern standards at thirty-by-fifteen-feet. This room was completed with perfectly smoothed walls. A granite coffin still remains inside. Unfortunately, nothing else, and certainly no body, was found inside when the first modern explorers entered.

Children building with blocks know that special treatment is necessary if they leave open spaces inside their creations, otherwise the construction collapses. Egyptian engineers faced exactly this problem when they built rooms inside their massive block structures. The limestone blocks they used were easier to mine than harder stone but so weak that a long block, say fifteen feet in length, would crack and break under its own weight. Even harder granite which could easily span fifteen feet without breaking would nonetheless fracture from the weight of the massive stone pyramid pressing down above it. Egyptian engineers found two different solutions to the problem of spanning a distance with stone inside a pyramid.

Their first solution was to invent what today we call a corbelled arch. Instead of stones piled to form vertical walls, engineers overlapped each course of stones a little further into the room, but not by much, merely a few inches. As the wall rose, the room became narrower as course upon course lapped further into the room. The walls ascended until they had grown close enough together that only a narrow ceiling needed to be spanned. Even soft limestone could cover such short distances. Of course this device created rooms that, if they were appreciably wide, had extremely high ceilings. We see such a dramatic effect in the Grand Gallery of Khufu's pyramid.

Engineers did not apply this solution to the pyramid's final burial chamber, the one where Khufu presumably was buried, however. It has vertical walls even though its ceiling is fifteen feet wide. How was this managed? In the first place, the fifteen-feet-long blocks that span the ceiling are hard granite, not the softer limestone that would

THE CORBELLED ARCH *was one solution for creating open spaces within pyramids. This arch is found within Sneferu's Red Pyramid in Dahshur.*

crack due to its own weight. Still, thousands of tons of pyramid rise above this ceiling, altogether a weight that would fracture even granite. What the Egyptians did was to divert the weight above the room away from the room's ceiling to rest it on the solid surrounding portion of the pyramid. They accomplished this with a set of massive granite blocks forming a gigantic inverted "v." A row of these v-forms above this chamber follows the long walls of the room, so the weight from the pyramid above rests on these massive supports. The ceiling of the chamber bears no weight at all.

Year after year stones were quarried by gangs of men, carved into oblong blocks by other gangs, then hauled up ramps (presumably inside the building) to be set in place by still other gangs. One block arrived every other minute for sixteen years or more. An outer coating of the finest limestone, polished gleaming white, completed an extraordinary, gigantic pyramid that reflected the sun and moon as a beacon for all to see and wonder at.

STONEWORK

How were the ancient Egyptians able to quarry the millions of tons of stone and shape it into the millions of blocks used to build the most massive stone building in the history of the world? The answer has to do with their love for the material. They adored stone, working it into beautiful, finely polished shapes that lovingly revealed whatever natural colors and veining lay inside the rock. The attraction began before 4000 B.C.E. and continued throughout the long history of their civilization. Egyptian stoneworkers even had a kind of patron saint, the god Ptah, the god of creation. Whether creating tiny vessels less than half an inch high or soaring obelisks 100-feet tall, Egyptians attained complete mastery over the art of working with stone, from soft limestone to hard-as-steel granite. Lacking hardened steel tools and diamond-hard abrasives, their stonework depended more on infinite patience than efficient machines. Their approach was to labor over a stone for days, weeks or years, getting to know it intimately.

Even if Egyptians had the time, stone cannot be carved without tools of a substance hard enough to cut stone. Stone comes in many varieties of hardness, from limestone to granite, so a tool that cut soft stones might be inadequate for the harder ones. Special tools were required to quarry a stone from its bed, while other tools shaped the freed stone into a finished product, and still others produced a fine finish. Before bronze was available, Egyptians found ways to quarry and shape limestone—used to construct the original pyramids—and even granite, used at places in the pyramids and for the coffin of the Great Pyramid's owner, the pharaoh Khufu.

The reason the pyramids were built on the Giza Plateau was because the site itself provided their material—it was a pure limestone hill. What tools cut the limestone blocks from the bedrock? Ordinarily, copper chisels would lose their cutting edge after one strike, but recent analyses of ancient Egyptian tools have revealed how the Egyptians overcame copper's natural softness. In the first place, Egyptians were fortunate in that their copper ore was not pure—it contained percentages of tin mixed in. Since bronze is simply copper with tin added, Egyptian "copper" was partial bronze; that is, it was harder than copper alone would have been. Analysis shows that it was, in fact, within 15 percent of the hardness of bronze.[2] Second, Egyptians had discovered that if the edge of a copper tool is hammered after it cools, a more durable edge is produced. Even so, limestone can be hard enough to blunt such chisels after a few blows, requiring continual sharpening. But just as freshly cut wood is softer than after it dries, limestone freshly cut from under the earth, before it dries in the open air, is exceedingly soft. It is soft enough for Egyptian copper chisels to do their job. We know that copper chisels were employed in quarrying stones for the pyramids, but they probably were not the only tools.

When Egyptologists examined an ancient waste site near the Pyramids' limestone quarries, they found tons of limestone chips and powder, as expected, but also thousands of pieces of flint.[3] It appears that Egyptians also quarried limestone with flint chisels. Flint is an unusual material, extremely hard, even slightly harder than granite, yet easily flaked to create a knife-sharp edge. If flint were chipped into the form of a chisel and hit against a hard object with a stone hammer, however, it would likely shatter. But, if struck instead with a softer wooden mallet, the wood would absorb some of the blow yet still transfer sufficient force to the flint to drive it into limestone without shattering. Since flint is harder than copper, it holds a sharp edge longer, and, if a bit of its edge should chip off, it would leave another sharp edge behind. Flint chisels appear to be the primary tool used to quarry Egyptian limestone.

Flint (or copper) chisels could also have shaped the freed limestone into the block shapes composing the pyramids, but there was a better tool to speed the rough shaping process. Examples of copper Egyptian saws have survived, although in ancient pictures they are usually shown cutting wood. A different version of a saw, however, one without teeth, could be employed to cut a limestone slab into a block of desired dimensions. After sand was placed in a groove in the stone, the toothless copper saw, moving back and forth over the sand, would abrade a quick cut through the stone because sand is composed primarily of tiny, sharp pieces of quartz, an extremely hard stone. In fact, such quartz pieces are the coating for most ordinary sandpaper today. The same process could even saw through hard granite, although much more slowly, given its hardness.

Sawing would take too long to free a block of dense granite from its granite bed, however, and flint chisels would take years to painstakingly chip a large piece free. A different means had to be found to quarry this stone. Fortunately, a partially quarried slab of granite, an obelisk that fractured before it was finished, still remains in an ancient quarry near Aswan. It seems that a line of workmen stood along the piece to be quarried, each holding a ten-pound ball of hard dolerite rock. Each man would simply bend and drop his rock over and over, letting the weight of the rock do the work of fracturing the granite into powder. Eventually a trench would form. The men knelt in this trench, continuing their pounding until they reached the desired depth. A second trench to the same depth would be pounded on the opposite side, probably by a second team. Then, either smaller dolerite balls pounded holes into the underside of the stone or flint chisels picked similar holes. When these holes reached far enough under the block, strong wooden levers could crack it free. Of course, this process would take weeks or months, so granite was a prized stone primarily used for religious or royal purposes.

So much for securing a suitable chunk of granite, but how would the piece be carved into a desired shape? The saw-grinding-sand method could be used to remove whatever big chunks were unwanted, but other processes were necessary for finer carving. Flint picks, or copper or bronze picks, shaped the piece much as a modern sculptor does with his chisel. Then the object would be painstakingly sanded smooth, erasing the marks of the picks, either by rubbing with sand or by rubbing with a piece of sandstone, which is essentially sand in a compact form. These methods, although tedious, can shape the hardest stone into any shape desired. It only takes time.

Jars of various shapes were the most common stone objects in ancient Egypt. To create the shape of a jar out of stone, however, the stone must be hollowed out. Ancient Egyptians ingeniously adapted the bow—the first human machine—to this task. First the bowstring was wrapped around a stick. Then, the lower end of the stick was fitted into a metal sleeve; the upper end was fit into a depression carved into a palm-sized stone. The depression was lubricated, making it easy for the stick to spin. A craftsman held the stone in place and moved the bow back and forth, making the stick spin, while the weight of the "capstone" applied force to the metal sleeve at the bottom end. When sand was placed on the object to be hollowed, the motion of the bow spun the sleeve in the sand, abrading the stone to be drilled out.

Such bow drills, without the metal sleeve or sand, became fire makers when rapidly spun in a depression in a piece of wood. The friction of the wood tip against the piece of wood created enough heat to ignite dried grasses placed alongside. Another variation for such drills was to carve a y-shaped fork in the end of the stick in which a crescent-shaped piece of flint was lashed. As the drill spun, the flint would grind out a larger hole in the stone vessel than the narrower metal sleeve. Egyptians even learned to tie a pair of stones to the top of these drills to save effort. As the drill spun, the stones would fly around the drill both stabilizing it and exerting pressure on the bit through their weight.

METALLURGY

Metal is a hard material, difficult to melt and not easy to find, all of which caused problems prior to the invention of modern excavating machines and furnaces. Egyptians naturally worked metals in the easiest ways at first but learned how to perform more sophisticated operations through cleverness and trial and error.

Producing a metal object involves, first, melting metallic ore, second, transferring the still molten metal from the fire and, third, pouring it into a prepared mold to give the metal its desired shape.

Even soft copper does not turn from raw ore into a liquid until heated to at least 1,000 degrees.[4] This is several times the temperature produced by a normal fire, so Egyptians had to invent furnaces capable of producing such temperatures. They dug a pit in the ground and lined it with stones so the heat would be concentrated and reflected back to the center. Favorite sites for these kilns were areas where continual wind naturally fanned the fire. For fuel they used charcoal, which burns at much higher temperatures than wood does. Still, the charcoal fire of a backyard barbeque does not attain temperatures sufficient to melt metal. Something had to heat the charcoal to an even higher temperature. Since oxygen is the necessary catalyst for any fire, the more oxygen, the hotter the fire, so Egyptians used blowpipes to force oxygen into the burning charcoal to raise its temperature above the necessary 1,000 degrees. These "pipes" were simply hollow reeds with clay fixed to the end in the fire so that the tip of the reed would not burn. Instead, the heat turned the clay to pottery allowing the blower's breath to raise the fire's temperature as it passed into the burning charcoal.

At least two people would need to blow continually to produce sufficiently high temperatures, but Egyptians later invented a machine that allowed one man to generate the necessary oxygen. Leather covers were securely attached to each of two large, flat bowls with a hole in their sides from which a hollow reed ran into the charcoal. The worker stood on both of these contraptions holding a string tied to the leather top. As he raised one foot he uncovered a hole in the leather and, by pulling the leather up by its string, drew in air to fill the container. At the same time, his other foot came down on the membrane of the second container, forcing its air out into the furnace. With this bellows device one man could work the smelter just by marching in place, first one leg and then the other continuously forcing oxygen into the fire.[5]

The steps for producing a metal object began with mining ore. After the raw ore had been mined, it was crushed into powder. The powder was poured into a pottery container and placed in the sort of furnace described. Several hours of heating liquefied the ore. Now—assuming it began with copper ore—the container held pure copper at its bottom with lighter impurities, called slag, floating on top. The container could be transferred from the heat using a pair of wooden sticks, freshly cut so their moisture would prevent them from burning from proximity to the boiling metal. The container could then be carefully tipped to pour the molten copper into any desired mold, leaving the lighter slag behind.

Egyptians used two kinds of molds. Sometimes they simply pressed a shape in wet sand. When molten copper was poured into this depression, it flowed to take the depression's shape. Other times they made a mold of clay and heated it to turn it into pottery which has a much higher breaking temperature than even molten metal. Liquid metal poured into the pottery mold would flow into its shape, and, if the mold had separate halves, the mold could be removed from the cooled metal and reused.

This technology is sophisticated and the art of making a mold that would produce an intricate statue or utensil is complex, so Egyptians used metal in a different way at first. They poured molten copper into a slight, flat depression in sand to form a copper sheet. The sheet was then beaten with hammers to make it thinner and larger. Such sheets could be bent by hand or hammered to form a pot or other utensil, held together, if desired, with a metal pin. Using this technology, a metal statue was produced near the end of the Old Kingdom that stands almost six feet tall. It consists merely of copper sheets pressed and nailed onto a wood core. Yet, by the end of the Old Kingdom, molds were being used to produce fine metal statuary, which became more sophisticated in the Middle Kingdom and common by the New Kingdom.

The first molds produced statues with solid cores. A wax model of the desired statue was carved then coated with clay. Since plenty of beehives existed in Egypt to satisfy Egyptians' sweet urges, wax was abundant. When the clay was heated in a fire, the wax melted and ran out while the outer clay turned into hard pottery, preserving the features of the wax model. This is known as the *lost wax method*. Molten copper, bronze, silver or gold could be poured into the pottery form. When the metal cooled, the pottery shell was broken and the metal statue freed. Later, craftsmen realized that a pottery mold with back and front halves did not need to be broken to free the metal inside, so this mold could be reused to produce many identical statues. Early statues required a lot of metal, however, since they were metal throughout. Since metal was hard to mine and difficult to melt, molded objects were expensive. By the Middle Kingdom, craftsmen learned how to produce hollow objects, thus saving precious material. All that was required was to form the rough shape of a statue in very sandy clay before covering the clay with wax that could be easily and finely carved. The whole was then covered with another layer of regular clay with a hole somewhere, usually at the bottom. When this assemblage was fired, the outer coat of clay hardened, the sandy clay dried and the wax ran out through the hole. Molten metal was poured into this same hole to create a metal statue inside of which was clay that would crumble and fall out, if chipped at with a stick.

Masterpieces of sculpture were produced in this manner, from delicate miniatures to others over three feet tall, proudly displayed in museums today. Indeed fragments of statues have been found whose complete originals would have towered above a man. To allow for more complex designs, parts sometimes were cast separately and later attached to the body. Thin ribbons of gold were pressed into indentations scratched in the metal to introduce glowing designs or hieroglyphs. One special statue of the god Amun, in pure gold and displayed at New York's Metropolitan Museum, is as lovely as anything humans have ever produced in metal.

AN INTRICATE GOLDEN COLLAR *topped with the head of the feline goddess, Sekhmet. Metal workers probably casted the broad collar (wesekh), counterpoise (mankhet), and divine head separately in order to create its complex design.*

Ship Building

Ancient Egyptian life centered on the mighty Nile River, which provided precious water for irrigation while serving as the most convenient highway for travel. Prevailing winds on the Nile blow in the direction opposite to the current's flow which means a boat can sail upstream and float downstream. Oars and man-power only sped the process. In addition, the upper quarter of Egypt, the delta area, was a maze of rivers, streams and marshland that made boats more practical for travel than walking. It is no surprise that boats are pictured in the oldest images ever found in Egypt, perhaps from as long as six thousand years ago, but what is surprising is that, although sharing a long border with the Mediterranean Sea, Egyptians came very late to sea travel.

The first Egyptian boats were constructed of reeds, especially papyrus, a free material, abundant throughout the country. Since reeds are hollow, they float, which meant constructing a boat involved merely tying a bundle of cut papyrus together. A man with a pole could stand on such a skiff and propel himself. Such vessels were used by citizens throughout the long history of Egypt, since, with material available for the taking, they cost only a little time and effort. Every family living in the delta region probably had its own boat.

This sort of craft tipped too easily for sailing on a large river, such as the Nile, but with a little more work, reeds could be laid and tied to produce a vessel with sides. A seated sailor would provide sufficient stability to prevent capsizing in normal river use. Crafts made from nothing but fragile reeds, however, posed problems for attaching a mast, since the weight and pressure of a vertical mast-pole would push through a fragile reed hull. To counter this problem, Egyptians joined two smaller poles at their tops and lashed their bottoms to opposite sides of the boat, forming an inverted "v." Not only was the weight less than that of a single, more substantial pole, but the weight was distributed so that no part of the boat had to support as much. An added bonus was that this mast, held to the boat in two places, stood more securely than a single pole could. Attach a rectangular sail of linen or one woven from flattened papyrus and a pleasant sail along the river would result. The popular archaeologist, Thor Heyerdahl, even constructed a large vessel of papyrus in just this way and sailed it with a crew for more than three thousand miles across the Atlantic Ocean.[6] Nonetheless, there are no indications that Egyptian reed boats ever attained such great size as Heyerdahl's, or were ever used to transport heavy objects or sail the open ocean. The construction of the original small, fragile vessels did, however, teach shipwrights valuable lessons they employed on larger craft.

Egyptians constructed their larger boats out of wood. But, using the principles learned from their reed vessels, the resulting ships presented an appearance quite unlike modern versions. For hundreds of years we have constructed ships on the model of an animal's body; that is, their structure

MODEL OF AN EGYPTIAN RIVER BOAT, *c. 2050 B.C.E. Small vessels were made of reeds, while larger "sewn" ships were constructed of wood planks tied together with rope.*

consists of an internal assemblage of "bones" to which a less substantial "skin" is affixed. Thus, modern ships start with a keel at the bottom, like our spine, to which substantial ribs are attached, like, well . . . like our ribs. This skeletal structure forms the ship's shape so that its hull can simply be joined to the "skeleton" creating its external appearance. This keel-plus-ribs assemblage provides the solidity a ship needs, so the "skin," hull, of a modern ship could not support itself without its internal structure.

Egyptian ships were different—they consisted of nothing but the outer shell. This meant that, rather than bending the hull material to the shape of internal ribs, Egyptian hull planks were carved into an appropriate inward-arc and affixed to nothing but each other. How were these planks joined together? Using the knowledge gained from their reed boats, Egyptian shipwrights tied their planks together, producing what is appropriately termed a "sewn" ship. Holes were bored into adjacent planks, and then ropes were thread through the holes to tie the planks together. This is not as foolhardy as it may seem. Nails would have caused a problem since wood swells and shrinks as it gets wet then dries, enlarging the area surrounding any nail and loosening it over time. This, in turn, loosens the planks, creating space that lets water into the vessel. The ropes used by Egyptians shrank when wet and drew the planks more tightly together.

An Egyptian ship constructed in this manner would appear reasonably familiar to us from the outside with sides curving up to a pointed bow. The stern would look a bit different, however, because it, too, generally rose and was pointed, giving the whole vessel a giant canoe-shape. Inside, however, crosswise struts instead of modern ribs lent some support to the hull. The mast might not be the single upright we are used to but instead an inverted "v," consisting of two poles attached at their tops and then to opposite sides of the hull. Of course, with a pointed stern there is no place to attach a rudder, so huge oars were fixed to opposite sides of the stern. Used in tandem, they turned the ship as a canoer at the rear of his craft does by angling the blade of his oar. There might be a cabin on the deck, but there was no living space below. Altogether, this ancient Egyptian craft would look like a proper ship but with a few elegant differences.

How do we know so much about ancient Egyptian ships? True, there are numerous pictures of vessels on temple walls and in tombs, even a few illustrations of ships being built, but these pictures do not record small details such as how the wood was held together. The reason that ancient Egyptian ships are so thoroughly understood is because good fortune presented a complete vessel to Egyptologists fifty years ago.

While a young archaeologist, Kamal el-Mallakh, was helping clear sand from around the Great Pyramid, he noticed that part of an ancient wall enclosing the pyramid was fifteen feet closer to the pyramid on its south side than on the other sides. Curiosity aroused, he speculated that the reason must be to hide something under that portion of wall. He convinced the authorities to clear away part of the wall which revealed forty-one limestone slabs, covering a large pit cut into the natural rock. The limestone blocks had been sealed with plaster, creating an air-tight environment that preserved a ship in the pit for more than four thousand years.

It had been completely disassembled into carefully stacked pieces, more a boat-kit than a vessel. In all it consisted of 1,224 parts: Experts toiled for years to put it together, thereby discovering how ancient Egyptians constructed at least this one vessel. The hull consisted of cedar planks almost six inches thick, with some as long as seventy feet. Both the stem and bow ends rose high in the air, ending in a knob of planks which spread out like a fan—similar to the ends of a reed boat, where the reeds spread apart after the last compressing lashing. Sometimes Egyptians even carved a replica of this lashing on a wooden ship's stern. The planks were joined together with thick ropes, complimented by wooden pegs. The boat had no keel or ribs, although crosswise struts provided some stability. Wood pieces and poles formed a cabin on the deck toward the rear. Reconstructed, the boat was 144-feet long, slim and elegant of line. But there was no mast and only six pairs of oars, which were certainly too few to propel such a large craft. In all likelihood, the oars were used only for steering, so the ship would need to be towed to its destination. This indicated that it was a ceremonial vessel intended for some religious purpose such as magically carrying the pharaoh through the sky to the North Star.[7]

Although much was learned about Egyptian ships from Khufu's buried example, clearly, this was not a normal, working ship. Text and drawings from various temples and tombs, however, provide details about functioning vessels.

A working ship might have a single mast, rather than the inverted "v" composite type, since, not being made of reeds, it could support it. Sails were generally rectangular, to catch as much breeze as possible, and they were attached rather high on the mast so their bottom ends would not sit in the water when the ship heeled. These masts could be tilted back and laid horizontally, and the sail could be lowered for travel against the wind when oars replaced sail power. Most working ships lacked the irrelevant soaring ends fore and aft that terminate in knobs of the ceremonial boat of Khufu. Large vessels generally incorporated one additional, unusual feature, however, to keep them rigid from stem to stern since they lacked the keel that performs this function in a modern vessel. Huge ropes, often several, ran from the bow of the boat to the stern on elevated struts above the deck, tying the front of the ship to the back. Called "hogging trusses" today, these devices included a pole stuck crosswise between the twisted ropes that could be turned to tighten or loosen the pressure.

Egyptian ships carried both commodities and people through the length of the country. Unlike a modern ship, however, cargo was not stored in holds under the deck since the hull was not strong enough to support its extra weight; instead, the load was carried on the deck, which necessitated buttressing the deck with numerous struts to the hull to distribute the weight as widely as possible. Since truly enormous granite statues and obelisks dot the land of Egypt, and granite was only quarried at modern Aswan in the extreme south, some gigantic transports must have ferried these megaliths to their eventual sites in the north.

One such scene, pictured at the Dier el Bahari Temple of Queen Hatshepsut, shows two obelisks, end to end, carried on a single ship towed by thirty smaller vessels that are being propelled by oarsmen. This massive craft, properly called a barge, was a huge ship. Hatshepsut's known obelisks range from 60-foot— normal sized—to 100-foot megaliths. Most likely, the obelisks she was proudest of, which certainly would be the 100-footers, would be the ones chosen for this depiction on her temple walls.

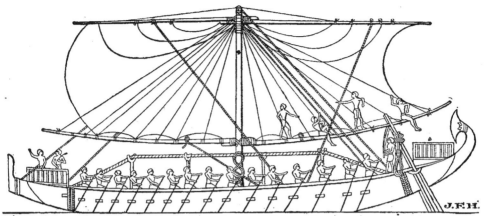

Egyptian ship on the Red Sea, about 1250 B.C. [From Torr's "Ancient Ships."]
Mr. Langton Cole calls attention to the rope *truss* in this illustration, stiffening the beam of the ship. No other such use of the truss is known until the days of Modern engineering.

THIS ILLUSTRATION OF AN EGYPTIAN NEW KINGDOM SHIP *highlights the huge ropes— commonly known as "hogging trusses"—that extended from the front to the back of the boat, keeping it rigid.*

How large would a barge need to be in order to transport two 100-foot-long solid stones? The vessel might have been over two-hundred-feet long to fit cargo of that length on its deck. The ship would additionally need to support a weight of almost 500 tons, the estimated poundage of two slabs of granite almost 100 feet long. No wonder thirty towing vessels are pictured dragging this behemoth, powered by as many as sixteen pairs of oarsmen each. Almost a thousand sets of arm muscles must have strained at the load, for this would be a ship that would turn the eyes of modern people accustomed to mammoth tankers and cruise ships.[8]

It is surprising that, despite their undeniable ability to construct large ships, ancient Egyptians were not great seafarers. They preferred sailing on their river, generally relying on foreign nations to ferry trade goods to them. Indeed, they never developed the navigational skills to sail across open sea. The major foreign import carried on Egyptian vessels was a commodity needed in abundance for their own ships. As mentioned earlier, the land of Egypt was poor in native wood, lacking tall trees, and large ships need long planks and tall masts that can only be hewn from tall trees. Fortunately, a hundred miles or so from Egypt, along the coast of the Mediterranean Sea, lies modern Lebanon, famed in ancient times for its abundant tall cedar forests. Egyptians regularly sailed transport ships to Lebanon and returned with loads of lumber for their shipwrights. This would not have been a difficult voyage, since the ships could hug the coast all the way with no great navigational skill required. Ocean-going ships would need to be stronger than those intended for travel along a placid river, however. A scene on Hatshepsut's Temple walls depicts five vessels built for a trip to Somalia, the fabled ancient Land of Punt, which lay south of Egypt, down the Red Sea. That this particular sea voyage was a rare event, in contrast to the more regular trips to Lebanon, is proven by the fact that Hatshepsut chose to memorialize it on the walls of her temple, while Lebanon trips are rarely pictured anywhere. But her pictures do show one accommodation that ocean voyages demanded: The hogging trusses, mentioned previously, are depicted in these ocean scenes as even more substantial than those shown on river transports, a necessity to make the hull strong enough to withstand the battering of ocean waves.

ERECTING AN OBELISK

Even after solving the myriad problems of quarrying, carving, and transporting a solid slab of granite obelisk up to one hundred feet in length to its site, one final difficulty remained. Transported in a horizontal position, the stone needed to be raised vertically when it reached its intended position. It might weigh as much as 250 tons. Since ancient Egyptians had no cranes or hydraulic jacks, how did they manage this feat?

While no certain answer to this question has been found by Egyptologists, they believe that the combination of a ramp, strong ropes, and abundant manpower could accomplish the feat. A long ramp that ended abruptly at the place intended for the erect obelisk could be constructed. It would have to be long so that its incline would be gentle enough to allow the massive weight of the stone on several sleds to be dragged by manpower along it. The obelisk would be hauled on this ramp until almost half of its weight teetered over the ramp end. As everyone knows, once more than half of the weight hung over the edge, the object would begin to fall. What the Egyptians needed was a very controlled fall. Strong ropes held by scores of men would gradually pull more and more of the obelisk over the edge. Meanwhile, still more scores of men would pull on more strong ropes that had been looped over the top of wood towers to exert an upward force on the stone and slow down. If the fall were gradual enough, even more ropes and men could guide the end of the stone to the desired position on a previously prepared base. This would have been a most anxious time. If the stone fell too quickly, it might break, wasting months and months of hard labor spent freeing it from its quarry, carving it beautifully and ferrying it to the site. Even if it settled intact but missed the exact spot on its base, the whole erection process would have to be laboriously repeated until it sat where it was intended.

Thus, an alternative theory has some supporters. It includes the same ramp and the same principle of tipping the stone over the edge, but instead of the obelisk falling through the air, this theory proposes that the bottom of the tipped obelisk would rest on sand inside a large brick container built for a special purpose. This container would have been constructed around the intended obelisk base and then filled with local sand. When the obelisk rested on the top sand, some bricks could be removed from the bottom of the container to let sand out. As sand streamed from the bottom of the container, the level of sand at its top would gradually lower and the obelisk would descend along with it. In this scenario the rate of descent could be controlled simply by the adjusting the rate of removal of sand from the bottom hole. Perhaps ropes and men hauling on them could be used at the end of the process when the obelisk was just a few inches from its destination to make final, precise adjustments.

Whichever method was actually used, it was certainly successful since scores of obelisks have been found standing tall all around Egypt, serving as visible proof of the industry and intelligence of the ancient Egyptians.

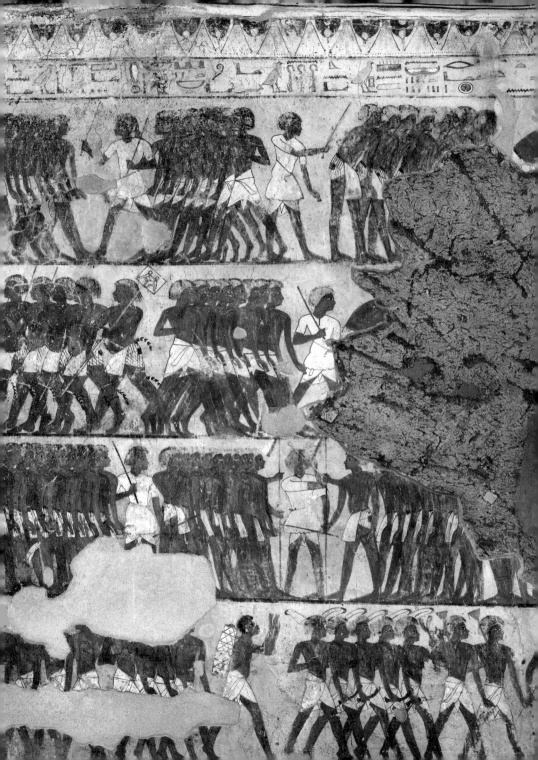

10

WARFARE

PHARAOHS DEMONSTRATED THEIR GREATNESS BY RAISING IMPOSING buildings or by waging successful wars—then boasting over and over again about their accomplishments. None ever bragged that his reign was peaceful. Successful military campaigns increased a pharaoh's prestige because they reinforced every Egyptian's view of his country as superior to others, and they served the economy by ensuring a flow of foreign goods to Egypt. Today we only view war as justified when it corrects great wrongs and we consider hostilities that begin without formal declarations to be "sneak" attacks. In ancient times, aggression was acceptable, even expected; undeclared wars were a way of life.

Wars recurred in ancient times because of the nature of military operations. The Egyptian army invaded to seize whatever booty was available, not to annex land. The army thus marched south into Nubia for gold or north to Syria for cattle and slaves, but, as soon as victory was achieved and the booty collected, everyone returned home to Egypt. Seldom were garrisons of troops stationed in conquered territories, and the government usually remained, as before, in local hands. Before leaving, Egyptian leaders exacted a promise from the invaded country to send an annual tribute, but without a continued army presence there was little incentive to comply. So each year the troops sallied out again to force payments. This system of raid and retreat meant that Egypt never built a true empire—it dominated its neighbors but did not expand its territory.

Amazingly detailed accounts of battles—with numbers of casualties, enemy killed, prisoners taken, even the names of the king's war horses—have come down to us, thanks to the pharaohs' custom of carving boasts on temple walls to tell their people how brave and mighty they had been. As a result, battles

A PAINTED RELIEF OF WARRIORS *in the tomb of Tjenuny, an army general under pharaoh Tuthmosis IV (1419–1386 B.C.E.).*

are better recorded than any other Egyptian events. Today we might think it inappropriate to paint scenes of slaughter and pillage on a church wall, but the ancient Egyptian saw no conflict: war was condoned by their gods as part of the divine order. There was even a god of war, Montu, whose name some pharaohs adopted, becoming Montuhotep, or "Montu is pleased."

This warrior tradition went back as far as Egypt's origin as a nation. The oldest Egyptian historical record, the Narmer Palette, shows the first pharaoh menacingly wielding a mace at a captive. Egypt took its first steps toward becoming an international power soon after Narmer unified the country; centralized government controlled by a single king inevitably led to an army. In fact, it may have been Narmer himself who first led troops beyond the borders of Egypt, since a pottery fragment inscribed with his name has been found in southern Israel.[1] At first, Egypt's army ventured cautiously beyond Egypt's borders. Not until seven centuries after Narmer could the pharaoh Sneferu boast that he had subdued the Bedouin tribes on the adjoining Sinai Peninsula, pacifying it to exploit its turquoise mines.

No records from this early period describe the original armies, but undoubtedly they were composed of conscripted or volunteer farmers who went to war when the Nile's inundation made farming impossible, although Egypt's ability to grow surplus food did eventually support a standing army. While not a profession of great status because of the long marches, difficult conditions and dangers, soldiering attracted men for the captured booty which, after the pharaoh's share had been subtracted, was disbursed among the troops. Before modern times, war was fought hand to hand; a soldier looked directly into his enemy's eyes before killing him. In this kind of battle, the king was expected to lead his troops in person, unlike the president of the United States, who, as commander in chief of the armed forces, makes his decisions at a safe distance from the battle.

ARMS

By the time of the Middle Kingdom, Egypt's army was professional, disciplined and divided into units. Tomb models display corps marching in orderly columns of ten. Archery divisions were considered elite troops, and entire units of these were composed of Nubians who were famed for their skill with the bow.

(Egyptians even referred to Nubia as the "Land of the Bows.") Most archers were right-handed so they held their bow with the left—the arm generally protected from the snap of the string by a leather arm guard—and drew the string with the right hand. The bow, consisting of two basic parts, the body and the string, is the first tool in history designed to concentrate energy. When an arrow is notched on the string and drawn toward the archer, the bow's body stores the tension that will propel the arrow forward upon release. The bow's advantage over a mace or sword was its ability to kill at a considerable distance—how far depended on the amount of tension. If your bow had greater range than your opponent's, you could injure him while standing safely out of his range, an advantage that led to the world's first arms' race.[2]

The earliest Egyptian bows were made from the acacia tree, one of the few native sources of wood available, and were simply convex in shape. By putting a reverse curve at both ends of the bow—shaping it like an upper lip—the string lay closer to the body of the bow, increasing the distance it traveled when drawn back and hence the amount of tension. This invention armed Egypt's oldest troops. But an ideal bow would combine strength with flexibility, which no single wood can do. Woods that bend easily store little energy; those that store more energy break rather than bend. The solution was to combine different materials in one bow, thus extending its range. These "composite bows," made of animal horn, animal tendons, wood and glue, were constructed by first gluing together woods from several types of trees to produce a core. The part facing the string (called the belly) was strengthened with two sections of strong animal horn, one on either side of the hand grip. The back of the bow (the part away from the string) was covered with animal sinews for flexibility and to prevent the wood from splitting. After shaping the composite bow into a double convex form ⌐⌐) to add power, its effective range became nearly a quarter of a mile.[3]

Of course, a bow is useless without well-made arrows. Because the shaft had to be straight, light and strong, it was generally made of wood, occasionally of reed. The arrowhead, which needed to be hard, was made of flint or metal and was either leaf-shaped or triangular. The arrow shaft fit into a socket in the head, or else an extension of the head (tang). To ensure that the arrow flew straight, feathers of various birds—eagle, vulture or kite—fletched the end. Because the archer fired many arrows during a single battle, Egyptian leather quivers, holding from twenty to thirty arrows, were worn over the shoulder to free both hands to load and shoot what the Persians called "messengers of death."

Slings were similar to bows in purpose. Originally designed by shepherds to keep foxes from their herds, these simple weapons, composed of a rectangular piece of leather with two strings attached, could inflict damage at a distance. A stone was placed on the leather, which became a pouch when the ends of the strings were held together in one hand. The sling was swung round and round to build momentum, then one of the strings was released, which opened the pouch and sent the missile on its way. David from the Bible aside, the problem with this weapon was accuracy, but corps of slingmen served in conjunction with archers to rain missiles on massed enemies.

For closer combat, the arsenal expanded. Javelins were medium-range weapons, similar in principle to an arrow but propelled by hand. They consisted of a wooden shaft (approximately five feet long) with a metal tip fixed to it with either a socket or a tang. When hurled by a skilled thrower, javelins could be lethal at more than one hundred feet. Spears, larger and heavier than javelins, were intended for thrusting, rather than throwing.

The oldest hand-to-hand weapon was the mace featured on Narmer's Palette. This simple but lethal weapon consisted of a stone fixed to the end of a stick whose short handle, about eighteen inches long, allowed quick swings. The lethal end consisted of a carved pear-, disc- or apple-shaped rock about the size of a fist with a hole in one end for the handle, replacing a modern ax head. Unlike an ax, however, the mace was designed to smash rather than cut. Although it was an impressive weapon, it was replaced by the battle ax when enemies began to protect their heads with metal helmets. The close combat arsenal also featured lethal-looking but overrated swords. Two basic kinds were employed. A straight version was intended for stabbing, so its metal blade was pointed at the tip and honed sharp along both edges. A striking sword, on the other hand, was sharpened only along one edge and curved, like a sickle, to slice as it was pulled back. The problem with both versions was that they consisted of long pieces

THIS RELIEF SHOWS MEMBERS OF HATSHEPSUT'S TRADING EXPEDITION *to the "Land of Punt" bearing shields, spears, and battle axes, the preferred weapon for hand-to-hand combat.*

of bronze which ancient metalsmiths could not forge strongly enough to do damage without bending, chipping or breaking. Battle axes, which evolved over the centuries in response to changes in warfare, were preferred for hand-to-hand combat because they carried a smaller, thicker, more durable metal blade. The first axes were cutting weapons, so their blades were broad, and often curved for a larger cutting surface. The blade was attached to a short wooden handle either by the tang or the socket method and reinforced with cord so it would not fly off during battle. Armor caused the axe's undoing: cutting blades made no dent in chests of mail or metal helmets. A more pointed blade, better suited for piercing, was developed later.[4]

To counteract all these weapons, soldiers carried shields as barriers between themselves and the enemy's weapon. Always something of a compromise, they were either large and heavy, providing excellent protection but slowing the soldier's attack, or small and light, affording little protection. A shield light enough to carry in one hand but strong enough to ward off an enemy's blows was eventually developed by combining materials. Egyptian shields were round-topped rectangles that extended from the chin to the knee. Wood formed their core, hardened by a tough animal-hide cover, a combination that made the shield difficult to penetrate while keeping it light and maneuverable. Soldiers held shields in their left hands to ward off arrows, axes and swords, while attacking with a weapon in their right. Since each country's shield shape was distinctive, ancient representations of battles distinguish the good guys from the bad not by the color of their hats but by the style of their shields.

For over 700 years, the Egyptian arsenal hardly changed until the unthinkable happened: a foreign army invaded Egypt and won. There are no records of the invasion—the Egyptians never recorded defeats—so Egyptologists have reconstructed a probable scenario. The invaders, called Hyksos by the Egyptians, or "foreign rulers," arrived from the north and ruled Egypt for more than a century (1663–1555 B.C.E.). Although Egypt was a more advanced civilization—the Hyksos were illiterate—with a population that vastly outnumbered the invaders, defeat was inevitable because this enemy brought a new superweapon with them: the chariot. Until the Hyksos, the Egyptians had never seen a horse; no word for this animal existed at the time in their language.

Three factors determined the outcome of any battle: firepower (arrows, axes, spears and so on), defense (shields and armor) and mobility. The chariot was never intended as a troop transport since an army's rate of march is constrained by its slow infantry. Rather, the chariot was a mobile platform from which javelins could be hurled and arrows shot. Pulled by two horses, these light, two-wheeled vehicles provided a tremendous advantage against foot soldiers. A weakness in the infantry lines could be reinforced by chariot troops before the enemy could take advantage; a weakness in the enemy lines could be overcome by horse-driven reinforcements before reinforcing foes arrived. Even if endangered, a chariot could quickly retreat to safety and fire from a distance. Chariots held a pair of soldiers—a driver and an archer, or sometimes a javelin thrower. A skilled driver controlled his horses with one hand while his other held a shield to fend off enemy arrows, allowing his partner to fire away in safety. In addition to the chariot, the Hyksos may have introduced the composite bow into Egypt. Such a twofold advantage—in firepower and mobility—would give them an unbeatable edge. After their victory, the Hyksos ruled Egypt from the north, allowing Thebes and southern Egypt to manage itself, but hostile parts of Egypt could not coexist forever. Two artifacts tell the story of the eventual expulsion of the Hyksos: a papyrus and a mummy.

Papyrus Sallier describes the end of the Hyksos domination when the Hyksos ruler, Apophis, governed from his capital at Avaris in the Delta and Seqenenre Tao II ruled in the south from Thebes. According to the papyrus, Apophis sent Seqenenre an inflammatory letter stating that the hippopotami in Thebes (500 miles away) were keeping him awake and had to be silenced. The papyrus breaks off before relating the result, but Seqenenre's mummy with five serious head wounds leaves little doubt about his violent end. (In the photograph, two upper left arrows and the one on the lower right point to probable ax wounds, with the arrow furthest right showing where a blunt instrument, perhaps a mace, delivered a blow that broke nasal and facial bones, causing a break in the skin, as indicated by the arrow on the bottom left. In addition to these four injuries, a sharp weapon, perhaps a spear, was thrust into the skull below the left ear. With the exception of the blow to the nose, any of the four other injuries could have killed Seqenenre.)

The probable outcome of the Hyksos challenge to Seqenenre is that he marched north to fight Apophis and died in battle, most likely far from professional embalmers' workshops. (Although his viscera were removed through the traditional incision on the left side, little else was done to preserve his body.) The wounds suggest a probable scenario for Seqenenre's last moments. First he was stabbed by a spear beneath his left ear that either killed or knocked him unconscious, then four blows to the head were delivered while he lay on the ground. Given the fact that three different weapons were used to hasten his demise, it appears that two or three separate enemies cooperated in dispatching him to the netherworld. Writing boards found by Howard Carter in 1908, in the vicinity of a Seventeenth-Dynasty tomb, tell us that Seqenenre's son (or, perhaps, brother) and successor, Kamose, continued the struggle against the

Hyksos with a second military campaign against Apophis at Avaris. It provides a clear end to the story:

> When the sun shone forth on the land I was upon him like a falcon. When the time for perfuming the mouth [lunch] came, I defeated him, I destroyed his wall, I killed his people. I caused that his wife go down to the river bank. My soldiers were like lions upon their prey, carrying off slaves, cattle, fat and honey, and dividing their possessions.[5]

Initially, the text was believed to be a literary boast rather than a historical document, but when a large stele uncovered at Karnak repeated the tale of Kamose's victory over Apophis, it counted as some confirmation. The stele includes the detail that when Apophis was surrounded in his walled city, he sent a messenger south with a letter to the Kushite king, asking him to come with reinforcements so that they could defeat Kamose together and divide Egypt between them. Kamose gleefully relates how he intercepted the messenger and fought against "the horses of the Hyksos."

The experience of the Hyksos wars so clearly proved the power of the chariot that, ever after, chariot divisions formed the heart of Egypt's army. These forerunners of light tanks required skilled woodworkers for their manufacture, a craft to which Egyptians brought centuries of experience in working with imported woods. Their skill at wood bending enabled them to make a spoked rather than solid wheel, reducing the weight of the chariot to aid its maneuverability. While elm, which bent easily, was used for the wheels, ash formed the carriage because of its strength. The floor on which the archer and his driver stood was woven from leather that acted as a shock absorber in stabilizing the platform. Chariots involved considerable investment. In addition to the expense of imported woods and skilled craftsmen, stables of horses and horse trainers had to be maintained. Egyptians bred their horses only for war, so all the raising, feeding and training expenses counted as military expenses. Because chariots also required continual maintenance—they broke easily despite the care that went into their production—military campaigns included hundreds of wheelwrights, chariot builders, spare horses and trainers. When an army marched out with its chariot corps, it displayed the kind of significant military investment only a superpower of the time could afford.[6]

Whereas Narmer, the first king of Egypt, portrayed himself smiting enemies with his mace, kings of the Eighteenth Dynasty are shown terrorizing their foes in chariots. As evidence of their prowess, they are often depicted controlling the chariot alone, without a driver, and pharaohs are even shown managing their horses with the reins tied around their waists so they could use both hands to shoot arrows. Chariots had become a status symbol, the jet fighters of the ancient world.

Fortifications

Storming Avaris was a substantial feat because ancient cities, fortified by massive walls, typically could withstand sustained attacks for years. Kamose's brother Ahmose, for example, spent three years laying siege to a fortified city in Palestine before it fell. Since cities generally crowned hills and water supplies lay in valleys outside the walls, a city's greatest survival problem during a siege was the need for water. One solution was to dig a deep pit inside the city leading to a tunnel running uphill to a well so the water could flow to the pit by gravity. Food could be gotten from animals stabled within the walls and some crops could be grown inside as well, so the addition of a secure water supply meant a long wait for a besieging army. Since Apophis felt he had the time to send a messenger all the way to Nubia for reinforcements, Avaris must have been such a well-fortified, well-provisioned walled city.

To allow defenders to rain missiles safely on besiegers from the tops of walls— arrows, stones, boiling oil—battlements were designed with what looked like rows of giant teeth, whose gaps, called "embrasures," provided spots where archers could fire at the enemy, then quickly retreat behind the "teeth," called "caps" or "merlons." Egyptian armies employed two strategies for attacking a foreign city: penetration and siege. Penetration could be achieved from above, from below, or through the wall, but none of these methods was easy. To penetrate from above, ladders were brought so the walls could be scaled. Naturally, the defenders attempted to throw down the ladders and hurled stones on the men as they climbed; at the same time, the attacker's archers tried to maintain a steady volley of arrows to chase the defenders from the parapet. Tunneling through a massive wall, on the other hand, was time consuming and inevitably led to a considerable loss of men. All manner of tools were used—axes, picks, spears—but battering rams were the primary weapon. A metal tip at the end of a long wooden beam was shoved into the wall and maneuvered up and down, left and right, to dislodge stones and bricks, thereby creating a breach through which the army could charge. The major problem with the battering ram was that it exposed the men who worked it to attacks from the wall. Before long a portable shelter was devised under which the men could work, protected from the rocks and arrows hurled from above. Some of these shelters fixed the battering ram to ropes hanging from their ceilings so it could be swung into the wall repeatedly with minimum effort. Because penetration could also be attempted through the gates to the city, the doors were usually covered with metal so they could not be set on fire; however, troops could attack the hinges in an effort to remove the doors completely. Penetration from beneath the wall was probably the least dangerous of the three possible routes, but it could prove disastrous. Miners would tunnel underground, often at night, to surprise the enemy within their walls. Of course, if the defenders discovered the tunnel, they organized an appropriate reception committee.

The alternative to taking a fortified city by penetration was to besiege it: surround the city and starve the defenders into submission. Although it was time consuming, it was generally the least dangerous method. Sieges became such standard tactics that they are described in detail in the Bible.

> When thou shalt besiege a city a long time, in making war against it to take
> it, thou shalt not destroy the trees thereof by forcing an axe against them:
> for thou mayest eat of them, and thou shalt not cut them down (for the tree
> of the field is man's life) to employ them in a siege. Only the trees which
> thou knowest that they benot trees for meat, thou shalt destroy and cut
> them down; and thou shalt build bulwarks against the city that maketh war
> with thee, until it be subdued. (Deuteronomy 20:19–20)

CAMPAIGNS

After expelling the Hyksos, the Egyptian army grew large and hierarchical, with commanders, generals, divisions, corps and so on beneath its commander in chief, the pharaoh. The Eighteenth Dynasty managed an unprecedented period of military successes as its second pharaoh, Amenhotep I, began his reign with a military expedition as far south as any expedition had ever gone—to the third cataract of the Nile.

Navigating the Nile south of Aswan, Egypt's southern border, was dangerous because collections of huge boulders formed cataracts hazardous to ships. Passage could be made only during April, May or June when the water was low and the boulders were revealed, allowing the boats to be controlled from the riverbanks and guided around the rocks with ropes. The second cataract, the "Belly of Rocks," was the most dangerous at this time, with temperatures often reaching 120°F by the time an expedition reached it. To avoid the blistering sun, boats were towed by moonlight, or in the early morning. In fact, the methods used by Amenhotep I's army to negotiate these cataracts were marveled at by British troops when they used the same plan 3,000 years later on their way to Khartoum in the nineteenth century.

The long, difficult trip to Nubia was an adventure expedition members remembered for the rest of their lives. Fortunately, military

BUHEN FORTRESS, BUILT C. 1860 B.C.E. *on the West bank of the Nile, is now covered by Lake Nasser. Battlements along the tops of walls allowed archers to fire at the enemy and then quickly retreat behind the teeth-like merlons.*

men often inscribed autobiographies on their tomb walls so the gods and posterity could appreciate their accomplishments. One of these was Ahmose-son-of-Ibana, a member of Amenhotep's expedition, whose account provides many colorful details of the 350-mile journey.[7] After navigating the cataracts and defeating some local tribes along the way, the expedition reached Gebel Barkal, a sacred mountain that resembles a cobra, where the final battle was fought. Ahmose describes his bravery: "Meanwhile I was at the head of our army; I fought incredibly; his majesty saw my bravery. I took two hands and brought them to his majesty." Ahmose referred to the Egyptian military practice of cutting off the right hands of dead enemies, after which, in a great ceremony, the hands were piled high for military scribes to count formally the number of enemy dead. Ahmose was rewarded for his bravery. "His majesty presented me with gold. Then I brought away two female slaves in addition to those that I had taken to his majesty, who appointed me, 'Warrior of the King.'"

The outpost Amenhotep established at Gebel Barkal would later become a great Egyptian stronghold, used by his successor Tuthmosis I, an even more accomplished military leader than Amenhotep I, who became the model of the pharaoh-as-warrior emulated by subsequent kings. In the first year of his reign, when news arrived that the Nubians were raising an army and had sent raiding parties to the Egyptian border, Tuthmosis led his army, including, for the second time, Ahmose-son-of-Ibana, south into Nubia. The expedition pushed deep into foreign territory, this time to the fourth cataract, reaching a part of the Nile that amazed them: suddenly the Nile flowed the "wrong" way—from north to south—all caused by a sharp S-turn in the course of the river before it curved back to resume its natural northern journey. Tuthmosis described it as "water that turned one who wanted to go north into one who rather went south."[8] If the army had used the river's flow as an indicator of direction, they would have found the sun rising in the west! To complicate matters, this thirty-mile stretch of river contained the roughest water on the Nile. Despite the heat and the raging waters, Tuthmosis pressed on. As a reward for successfully maneuvering the fleet through the cataract, he promoted Ahmose-son-of-Ibana to admiral. "I showed bravery in the King's presence, in the bad water, in the towing of the fleet in the reverse river. His majesty appointed me overseer of the sailors."

Once past this obstacle, the army camped on Mongrat Island, one of the largest in the Nile (about the size of Manhattan) and where the Nile calmed, allowing easy transit by night from their wooded stronghold to the east bank in preparation for the attack on neighboring villages. They fought a confederation of three tribes: the Iwntyu Seti, the Nehsi and the "sand dwellers," who were probably Bedouins living near desert wells. All the accounts of Tuthmosis' performance in battle agree he was ferocious: "Like a panther, his majesty threw his first lance which remained in the body of the fallen one . . . their people were brought off as living prisoners."[9] The chief of the Iwntyu Seti was captured by Tuthmosis for transport back to Egypt. Since by now it was July and the Nile was beginning to flood, making passage impossible, the army probably used the time to pillage the land, taking grain, cattle and anything else of value as they proceeded south. At Kurgus, where a large boulder, known as Hagar el Merwa, presents a natural landmark visible for miles, Tuthmosis built a fortress of mud brick with walls eighteen feet thick which would facilitate Egypt's access to central Africa and control the Nubians' route to Egypt. He also erected a stele proclaiming Egypt's control of the land which said that anyone who opposed him would have his head cut off, his family murdered, and "he would have no successor."[10] Egypt's southern frontier had been established.

When the floodwaters receded, the expedition, led by Tuthmosis' "Hawkship," returned to Karnak, where a crowd gathered to greet the pharaoh and view the captured leader of the Iwntyu Seti, who was hanging upside down from the prow of the flagship.

A later pharaoh, Tuthmosis III, deserved his reputation as Egypt's greatest military leader. Within a period of sixteen years he led fourteen separate campaigns into Syria-Palestine, crossed the Euphrates River and conquered the land of the powerful Mitanni. But the battle of Megiddo, one of Tuthmosis' early campaigns, demonstrates that he had to learn his craft. It also illustrates that although Egypt's army had become increasingly professional, military strategy was practically nonexistent: firepower and a commander's character were the primary determinants of success in the field. If a leader suffered a character flaw, as Tuthmosis did at the beginning of his career, the results could be disastrous.

In the spring of 1468 B.C.E., as Tuthmosis marched north to do battle with the nations of Syria and Canaan (who had grown independent of Egypt), the ruler of Qadesh marched his army south from the Orontes River to join forces against the advancing Egyptians. Near Megiddo (called Armageddon in the Bible), a strategic location because it controlled access to the north, Tuthmosis convened a council of his commanders to hear spies report on enemy strength and intent. Three separate approaches led to the city, one of which his officers rejected because troops would have to proceed through a narrow valley single file ("horse behind horse"). Despite their objection that a smaller force could easily ambush the Egyptians with drastic effect, Tuthmosis chose this route so the enemy could not say, "His Majesty set out on another road because he has become afraid of us."[11] Tuthmosis was lucky; because the enemy expected the Egyptians to travel by either of the other two roads, it had stationed its forces elsewhere. The Egyptians emerged safely from the valley and gathered forces for a dawn attack which routed the enemy encampment in front of the city, forcing them to retreat inside their walled city. Instead of destroying the disorganized troops, the Egyptian army stopped to loot the camp, allowing the king of Qadesh and his troops to escape north. As a military scribe put it: "[N]ow if His Majesty's troops had not set their hearts to plundering the possessions of the enemies, they would have [captured] Megiddo at this moment."[12] By failing to seize the moment, seven months of siege were required before the city finally fell: Megiddo was admirably provisioned and its engineers had dug through 65 feet of solid rock to excavate a horizontal tunnel 10 feet high and 200 feet long to a well that supplied the city with fresh water.

Two hundred years later, another young pharaoh named Rameses II displayed similar carelessness and risked an even more fatal outcome. He led one of the largest professional armies the world had ever seen, with infantry numbering more than 20,000 men wielding battle axes, spears and swords, along with a substantial chariot corps. The Hittites, successors to the earlier Mitanni, at this time controlled the city of Qadesh. Their main weapon was a heavy, three-man chariot that carried a driver, a shield bearer and a javelin thrower; in effect, an infantry on wheels, well suited for close fighting after a charge. The

TUTHMOSIS III, CONSIDERED EGYPT'S GREATEST MILITARY LEADER, *smites Canaanite enemies during the Battle of Megiddo (c. 1468 B.C.E.) in this scene from the seventh pylon at Karnak.*

Egyptian army was more diversified with chariot-riding archers who could do damage at a distance and infantry who handled hand-to-hand combat. Both armies supplemented their troops with foreign mercenaries when they could, but coordinating these diverse troops required great administrative skills.

On the ninth day of the second month of summer in the fifth year of his reign, Rameses led 20,000 foot soldiers and his chariot corps north to Syria. The soldiers, who were divided into four divisions of 5,000, each named after a god of Egypt—Amun, Ra, Ptah, and Seth—averaged 15 miles a day, covering the 450 miles through Palestine to Qadesh in Syria in about a month. Like other pharaohs of the period, Rameses had accompanied his father on campaigns while still a youth and was experienced in the conduct of campaigns. Already convinced that Qadesh could not stand against him, he was fortified by the fact that the journey north met no resistance: "All the foreign lands trembled before him up through Galilee."[13]

When the troops entered Syria they saw vast areas of green meadows, perfect for chariots, and wildflowers unknown in Egypt. In the distance stood the snow-capped mountains of Lebanon, probably the first time most of his troops had ever seen frozen water. Rameses camped within a day's march of Qadesh, but, eager to reach his goal, he rose early, donned his battle garments and led the division of Amun toward Qadesh, while his other three divisions stretched for miles behind him. As Rameses neared Qadesh, two local tribesmen met the entourage and told him that the Hittite king, Muwatallis, had learned of Rameses' approach and had fled north to Aleppo, 120 miles away. This seemed perfectly reasonable to Rameses, so he pressed on to Qadesh, leaving his other three divisions to catch up as they could. When the fortified city came into sight, Rameses' exhausted division pitched camp on top of a knoll. The next day Qadesh and all its treasures would be his.

In the meantime, sentries caught two Hittite soldiers and beat the truth out of them. The local tribesmen who reported that the Hittites had run away had been Hittite spies sent to lull Rameses into a false sense of security; in fact, Muwatallis was waiting with 40,000 soldiers on the far side of Qadesh. While the Egyptian troops were settling in, repairing chariots, tending to tired feet, distributing supplies and feeding Rameses' pet lion, and while Rameses met hurriedly with his officers to make emergency plans, Hittite charioteers charged the lagging Ra division, cut it in half and almost destroyed it. Other troops made straight for Rameses' camp and attacked the unprepared Egyptians. A barrier of shields enclosing the Egyptian camp stopped the Hittite chariots only momentarily, but then they burst through and sent the Egyptian troops in every direction. Rameses called out:

> Stand ye firm, steady your hearts, my army that you may behold my victory.
> I am alone, but Amun will be my protector, his hand is with me.[14]

RAMESES II, POISED ATOP A CHARIOT *with a bow and arrow during the Battle of Qadesh (1274 B.C.E.), attacks enemy Hittites in what may be the largest chariot battle ever fought.*

Rameses rallied those immediately around him, jumped into his chariot, said a prayer to Amun and charged. It never occurred to him that he could lose. The surprise of his bold attack provided just enough time for Egyptian reinforcements to arrive. After organizing the new arrivals and what was left of the Amun Division, Rameses charged the Hittites six times. Finally, the enemy chariots were forced to flee across the river back to their camp.

Muwatallis, waiting to move in for the kill with his horde of infantry, was shocked to see his crack chariot companies retreating, some fleeing into the fortified city, others retreating across the river. The Orontes River is narrow enough to throw a stone across, but deep enough that chariots had to cross at shallower fords. In their rush to safety, some headed directly across the river instead of locating a ford. Accounts of the battle carved on Egyptian temple walls showed one prince from Aleppo who swallowed so much water trying to escape that he had to be held upside down by his ankles to be emptied.

What was left of the division of Ra after their ambush by the Hittites arrived to finish off the enemy stragglers. A rout had been transformed into a victory. It was time to cut the right hands off the dead Hittites so scribes could count the enemy casualties. Rameses called his officers around him to chastise them for not being there when he needed them. From his throne of gold he said,

> What ails you, my high officers, my infantry, and my charioteers, who know not how to fight? . . . Did you not know in your hearts that I am your wall of iron? . . . I defeated millions of foreign counties being alone with my great horses, Victory-in-Thebes and Mut-is-Content.[15]

Both armies spent the night preparing for final battle the next day. The Hittites now outnumbered the Egyptians, but the Egyptian chariots were the superior fighting machines. Egyptian chariots carried bowmen which allowed them to strike at a distance; the Hittites' transported spear throwers who were good only for close combat. All told, the armies were about evenly matched. When the two forces faced each other, they hurled taunts and postured, but neither side initiated a fight—they had reached a standoff. The Hittite troops were too well trained and numerous to be defeated; Rameses had demonstrated his prowess. Muwatallis offered Rameses a peace treaty: both parties would accept the status quo and agree never again to attack each other. Rameses agreed and never returned to Qadesh.

Not surprisingly, with one notable exception, Egyptian battle records all describe land engagements since Egypt had no navy. Hemmed in by deserts on the east and west and the Sudan in the south, Egypt's only water border was the Mediterranean to the north. The Egyptians, skilled in plying the placid Nile, never developed open-water navigational or sailing skills and seldom sailed the Mediterranean; their ideal river conditions had spoiled them. In fact, their extensive trade with both Greece and Cyprus depended on sailors from those seafaring lands.

The only Egyptian record that describes a real naval battle was fought by Rameses III against a mysterious group called the Sea Peoples. This enemy was comprised of populations of different nationalities who came from Asia Minor and later occupied various territory around of the Mediterranean.[16] One segment of the Sea Peoples were called the Peleset, who gave their name to Palestine. They wore distinctive feather-topped helmets; their primary weapon was the long, straight sword; and they carried round shields. A smaller, but important group of the Sea Peoples, called the Sherdens, gave their name to Sardinia. They too carried round shields, but wore horn-topped helmets.

Rameses depicted two battles with the Sea Peoples on the walls of his temple at Medinet Habu: one on land, another on water. According to the text accompanying the battle scenes, "[T]he foreign countries made a conspiracy in their islands . . . they were coming forward toward Egypt." A powerful confederation had set their sights on Egypt which would have to fight for its existence.

The land battle, shown in traditional style, was a complete victory for the Egyptians and a total defeat for the enemy. Two details are of interest, however. Behind the enemy infantry and chariots, carts are pictured carrying noncombatants—women and children. This suggests that the Sea Peoples intended to settle in Egypt if they won. That they were migrating is the reason different groups of Sea Peoples settled in different Mediterranean countries after their defeat. The other interesting detail is that the Sea Peoples are depicted without an archery corps; they could engage in nothing but close combat.

Although Rameses boasts that he destroyed the Sea Peoples on land, the records show that a sea battle was also necessary, even if it was not the sort of naval encounter we normally think of because there was no maneuvering on open water. The conflict probably took place in the Delta where the Nile branches out into the Mediterranean. Since narrow streams provided no space to sail, ships on both sides served merely as platforms for infantry. The temple wall account of the battle shows several important differences between the Egyptians and the opposing troops, any one of which could explain Rameses' victory. First, the Egyptian ships were fitted with both sails and oars; those of the Sea Peoples had only sails, giving the Egyptians the advantage of greater control and maneuverability in close river-fighting. Also, Egyptian archers were able to inflict damage at a distance, but the Sea Peoples, lacking archers, could only try

RAMESES III DOMINATES THE SEA PEOPLES *in this relief from Medinet Habu. The temple walls also depict Egypt's only recorded naval battle, which occurred against these seafaring raiders around 1175 B.C.E.*

to board Egyptian ships which maneuvered out of their way while raining arrows on them. Finally, while more Egyptian archers shot arrows from the shore, men with slings hurled stones at the Sea People from the crow's nests of their ships. The temple walls show the outcome in graphic detail: no hand-to-hand combat, only enemies pierced by arrows falling into the Nile.

CONCLUSION

The Egyptian armament and style of campaign served the country well for a thousand years, allowing Egypt to dominate surrounding countries during that time with superior manpower. Egypt's control was finally reduced by new superpowers who raised warfare to a science with more modern methods.

Assyria created the idea of an empire. Unlike the Egyptians and their earlier contemporaries, who simply raided and returned home with their booty until it was time to raid again, the Assyrians subdued territory, cowed the population with harsh measures and installed governors to rule the conquered people. In this manner they added troops to their army with every conquest. Where a large Egyptian army might comprise from 20,000 to 30,000 troops, Assyrian armies reached 100,000 men. Not surprisingly, Assyria conquered Egypt in the seventh century B.C.E. Assyria was overcome by Persia, a warrior society that conscripted every able-bodied man to fight for his country rather than hoping for enlistments to create an army larger than comparable populations could field against them. After borrowing the idea of empire from Assyria, their superior army added territory after territory, creating a hegemony that stretched from Egypt through modern Turkey. Drawing on this huge conquered population, Persia could field an army half a million strong.

Persia remained invincible until militant Greeks, under Alexander the Great, used superior tactics to turn the numerical superiority of the Persian army against it. No one had fought more often than the Greeks, even if generally against other Greeks, which had permitted them to develop advanced strategy. The Greeks concentrated their inferior numbers on one part of a larger Persian force to rout it, panicking the remaining Persian troops.

Egypt endured through the rise and fall of one militant superpower after another, rebelling when it could, joining forces with other countries in opposition, or simply biding time. It could not, however, endure the invincible Romans who created an empire never equaled before or since. They made Egypt their province and bled it dry.

11

MEDICINE AND MATHEMATICS

PHYSICS, CHEMISTRY AND BIOLOGY WERE NEVER STUDIED BY ancient Egyptians; true science with its controlled experiments, careful observations and testable results did not exist until long after their early, superstitious times. Still, Egyptians approached injuries and diseases more objectively than their contemporaries, and mathematics, essential for the complex and precise buildings that Egyptians erected, was taught in every school.

MEDICINE

Diseases

Although ancient Egyptians were shorter than we are today—the average male stood five feet six inches tall, as opposed to almost five feet ten inches in the United States—in every other way, they resembled modern people and, consequently, were subject to most of the same diseases. One scourge of countries with damp, hot climates, schistosomiasis, which still afflicts 10 percent of Egypt's population today, seems to have been rampant in ancient times. One study found remains of the eggs that cause this disease[1] in fifteen of twenty-three examined mummies.[2] The cause is a parasite, carried by snails living in the still waters of canals and in the Nile's riverbanks, that burrows through the feet of waders, enters their veins, and then swims to the body's bladder and rectum to deposit eggs. The worms finally migrate to the urinary tract, causing blood in the urine (hematuria), and after the eggs hatch, they cause severe anemia, urinary infection and liver ailments.

A BEAUTIFULLY PAINTED RELIEF *of the "eye of Horus," often worn as an amulet to ensure good health.*

Since the ancient Egyptians never suspected that a virtually invisible worm caused these problems, all they could do was try to relieve the discomfort. Medical papyri specified a potion consisting of the tail of a mouse mixed with onion, meal, honey and water, all strained before using, then drunk for four days.

Egyptians also suffered from a high incidence of lung disorders. Tuberculosis, in particular, was more common then than in modern times. This disease, which affects the lungs, sometimes destroys bone as well and shows up in mummies as osteomyelitis of the spine (Pott's disease) because tuberculosis affects the disks between vertebrae. Even more common was sand in the lungs which hindered breathing (sand pneumoconiosis), to be expected in a desert country where every breeze carried sand into the respiratory system. As a result, persistent coughs plagued the Egyptians—their version of the modern black lung disease of coal miners.

Dental problems were a major concern. Tooth decay was prevalent, not because of a diet rich in sugars—Egyptians had no pure sugar nor could the average person afford honey—but because teeth were worn away until their pulp was exposed, making them vulnerable to infection. A double dose of sand plus grit in the ancient diet, which came from bread that was made by grinding a stone against another stone to produce flour, caused the wear. Examinations of mummies, both young and old, found severely worn teeth, even abscesses that can prove fatal. Although Egyptians had specialists for many medical problems, dentistry was not one of these; Egyptians with these problems simply suffered. With dental infection so common, foul breath was a major social problem, and Egyptians invented the first breath mints: a combination of frankincense, myrrh and cinnamon boiled with honey and shaped into pellets.

Surprisingly, arteriosclerosis, or the hardening of the arteries, affected ancient Egyptians just as it does modern people, leading to a restricted flow of blood both to the brain, which can cause senility, and to the heart, which can cause heart attacks. Since the primary cause of this disease is a buildup of fatty deposits on the interior walls of the arteries, and since the ancient Egyptian ate far less fat than found in modern diets, it had been assumed that arteriosclerosis was a purely modern disease until examination of the arteries of mummies revealed numerous cases.[3] Because the ancient Egyptian diet included little meat or other sources of fat, this affliction remains a puzzle.

Infections of various kinds were incurable before the discovery of the penicillin family of medicines during our century. Malaria plagued ancient Egyptians who lived near marshes and lakes—a large percentage of the population—and neither its cause nor any effective treatment was known before modern times. Cancer of soft tissues is one disease that plagues modern people much more than it afflicted ancient; less than a handful of documented cases have ever been found in mummies. Without tobacco or artificial additives for food and with fewer pollutants in the air, ancient people had little to fear from this dreaded modern disease.

Medical Treatment

Egyptians took two approaches to their medical problems—clinical and magical—with the type of illness determining which was used. As long as the cause of a medical problem was known to Egyptians, as in the case of broken bones and crocodile bites, they treated it in a clinical manner. For example, the prescription for a crocodile bite was to sew the wound closed before placing raw meat over it. If, however, the affliction was something like a fever whose cause was unknown, it was attributed to demons or malicious magic and treated with magical cures. Some afflictions, to be sure, fell entirely outside the understanding of the Egyptians and were left to a specialist in what they termed "unknown diseases."

Whether clinician or magician, most physicians came from the ranks of priests. Because Sekhmet, the lioness-headed goddess, was associated with medical arts, her priests were considered superior doctors, although some were skilled in clinical, others in magical, medicine. A man named Nedjemou was chief of the priests of Sekhmet as well as chief of the physicians; while another, named Heryshefnakht, was chief of magicians, high priest of Sekhmet, and royal physician. It is ironic that Sekhmet became the patron deity of medicine since, in mythology, she had been feared for her temper that almost destroyed mankind. The gods Isis, Horus and Toth were also associated with healing.

Isis was claimed as the patron both of clinical and magical specialists because she had reassembled her deceased husband, Osiris, after he had been hacked to pieces by his evil brother Seth—rather fancy surgery—and, as the goddess of magic, her supernatural powers were eagerly sought. Because an important myth told how Horus' eye was magically restored to health after it was almost destroyed in battle, he, in turn, became the patron of eye doctors. Toth, the god of wisdom, usually depicted as an ibis-headed god (but sometimes as a baboon), was the fabled inventor of writing and so was also called upon for clinical matters. Ancient Greek authors tell us that Toth inspired a series of forty-two encyclopedic books, of which thirty-six, according to Clement of Alexandria, dealt with philosophy and general knowledge; the remaining six concerned medicine. One volume covered anatomy, another diseases, others surgery, remedies, diseases of the eye and diseases of women. Because the Greeks identified Toth with their own god Hermes, these works became known as the Hermetic books.

These famous books have disappeared, but quite a few ancient Egyptian medical works survive. These works fell into the same two categories—clinical and magical—as did the medical practitioners. The most famous clinical writings, *The Edwin Smith Surgical Papyrus*, which dates from approximately 1700 B.C.E., was a copy of a much older papyrus from the Old Kingdom. The papyrus, which deals intelligently with physical injuries, such as fractures and broken bones, indicates that whoever wrote it possessed extensive, direct knowledge of these problems. Some Egyptologists speculate that the original author was the revered Imhotep, architect of the Step Pyramid at Saqqara, who, along with his duties as royal architect, served as royal physician. This position could have provided him with firsthand knowledge of the breaks and fractures that must have occurred to workmen during the construction of the world's first large stone building.

Forty-eight specific injuries are discussed in the papyrus, each preceded by a title such as, "Instructions Concerning a Wound on the Top of His Eyebrow." This is followed by "The Examination," where the surgeon is told how to probe the wound and what to look for. Each case ends with a "Diagnosis." The physician is told to state what the injury is, then whether he can treat it by saying

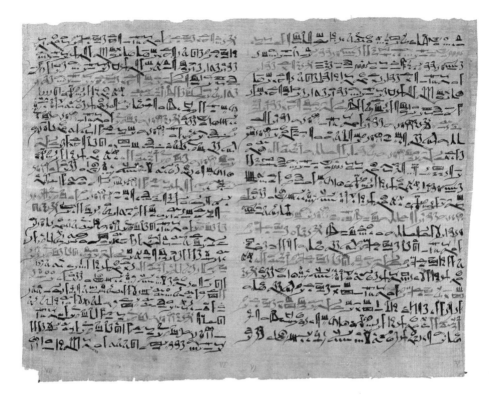

THE EDWIN SMITH SURGICAL PAPYRUS *(c. 1700 B.C.E.) includes treatments for ailments ranging from physical injuries to infections. The plates featured here discuss facial trauma.*

one of three things: "an ailment which I will treat," "an ailment with which I will contend," or "an ailment not to be treated." These diagnoses divided his cases into those he could cure, those he hoped to cure and those he could not. Fourteen cases described in the papyrus were so severe the physician was instructed to say they could not to be treated, including bulging tumors in the breast and fractures of the temple so severe that blood flowed from the nose and ears of a patient unable to speak. The intention of such a hopeless diagnosis was not for the patient's good, but to protect the reputation of the doctor—business would suffer if he treated too many patients who died.

The papyrus covers ailments from the top of the head to the spinal column, although blank space at the end of the papyrus suggests that, if the scribe had completed his copy, he would have included injuries to the legs and feet. Three examples involving exposed brains present enough detail to show the author had carefully observed this crucial organ. He calls the material surrounding the brain (the meninges) *netnet*, in hieroglyphs ⌒⌒⌒ . The first four symbols show how the word was pronounced (*nt-nt*), and the final sign, called a determinative, indicates to what kind of thing the word applied. In this case, the determinative is an animal skin, which makes sense because the meninges is a kind of skin. Equally accurate is the author's description of the brain's convolutions, which he likens to "ripples which form on molten copper."[4] He also made a start in understanding the functions of the brain, for he mentions the possibility that a severe head injury might affect the limbs, one symptom of which could be a limp. While this does not prove the writer understood how the brain controlled the limbs, at least he had observed that one problem occurred with the other. (Actually, the papyrus states that the affected limb will be on the same side of the body as the brain injury, which is incorrect because the left side of the brain controls the right side of the body.) Despite this good beginning, Egyptians developed specialists in eye ailments, gynecological ailments and a few other medical problems, but not those of the brain.

For the "cases to be treated," recommended remedies are surprisingly similar to modern treatments: bandages, splints, plaster, tape and sutures to help the patient mend. Still, one curious discussion deviates from the clinical approach. In a case concerning a crushed forehead, magic is advised. A poultice of grease and ostrich egg was to be applied to the wound, probably because the shell of the ostrich egg resembled the frontal bone and the hope was that the bone would knit to form a solid sphere like the eggshell. Before applying the poultice a spell was to be recited:

Repelled is the enemy that is in the wound!
Cast out the [evil] that is in the blood,
The adversary of Horus [on every] side of the mouth of Isis.

This temple does not fall down;

There is no enemy of the vessel therein.

I am under the protection of Isis;

My rescue is the son of Osiris.[5]

Why would an author describe forty-seven cases so clinically and then include one purely magic cure? Perhaps the scribe who copied the original work inserted one example from a different book. In any case, the spell provides an interesting literary first. In the process of his copying, the scribe omitted a word. Where the missing word belonged, he inserted a small red "x," then wrote the word above the line—the first, but far from the last, caret in history.

Although called *The Edwin Smith Surgical Papyrus*, the work contains no discussion of surgery. The practitioner is told only how to remove bone fragments, dress the wound and so on, not what to cut or saw. Examinations of hundreds of mummies indicate that Egyptian physicians seldom practiced surgery, which would have been a difficult undertaking using only bronze knives and lacking anesthesia. Yet Egyptians did perform circumcisions. Such a scene is shown on the walls of the tomb of Ankh-ma-Hor, overseer of the works of King Teti from the Sixth Dynasty. Two adult men stand as they undergo circumcision by two others. One of the patients is held by a fifth man to whom the circumciser says, "Hold him fast, don't let him fall." The only other evidence for surgery is what appear to be surgical instruments carved on the back wall of Kom Ombo Temple in Upper Egypt, although some doubt exists about their purpose since the hieroglyphs around the scene make no mention of surgery or refer to the tools in any way.

Papyrus was expensive enough that both sides were typically used. The reverse side of the *Edwin Smith Papyrus* consists of a second medical work based on principles of magic, consisting of a hodgepodge of spells on such diverse topics as what to do for a woman whose menstrual flow has stopped and treatments for hemorrhoids. The most intriguing is titled "How to Transform an Old Man into a Youth," the forerunner of medieval alchemists' elixirs of life. The Egyptian version consists of a wrinkle cream for smoothing the skin made from a fruit called *hemayet* (a word still untranslated). Whatever the fruit was, it was crushed, husked and winnowed like grain, then placed with water in a new container to boil. When the mixture reached the consistency of clay, it was removed from the fire and spooned into a jar until it cooled, then placed on linen to strain over a jar opening, after which it was stored in a vase of costly stone. The spell promises that, if the cream is spread on the face, it will remove wrinkles, blemishes, in fact every sign of age, and ends with the assurance that "it has been shown to be effective millions of times."

While this side of this papyrus contains exorcisms of demons and incantations to gods, it also hints at something very much like modern germ theory. The first eight spells concern "The Pest of the Year," an epidemic that afflicted the Egyptians annually. Spells say the disease came on "the plague-bearing wind," could be carried by flies, was lodged in food and beds or bed linens and entered the body through the mouth and throat. Of course, the text does not mention germs—malicious gods and demons, even Sekhmet, are cited as causes of the plague—still, Egyptian doctors had made an interesting observation about how diseases spread. For example, while the title of one spell calls the cause of the disease "the demons of disease, the malignant spirits, messengers of Sekhmet," it suggests that they come on the wind:

> Withdraw, ye disease demons. The wind shall not reach me, that those who pass by to work disaster against me. I am Horus, who passes by the diseased ones of Sekhmet, [even] Horus, Horus, healthy despite Sekhmet. I am the unique one, son of Bastet. I die not through thee.[6]

This spell had to be spoken by a man who carried a stick of deswood in his hand as he circled his house, thus drawing a circle of protection around his abode; the stick, of course, was a magic wand, a common tool of Egyptian magicians. These same words could also be uttered while drawing a circle around a bed to protect a sleeper from scorpion bites.

Another spell for a man who has swallowed a fly asserts that his mouth will become as clean as a newborn calf who has never eaten, and that the fly will pass out of him in his excrement without injuring his stomach. The use of a special spell to rid the body of a fly suggests that Egyptians realized flies carry disease. There was also a general spell for cleaning everything, including beds. Altogether this collection of spells against "The Pest of the Year" makes "disease demons" resemble modern bacteria.

Physicians of ancient Egypt grappled to understand the cause of disease as well as they could. Although they never quite grasped the ideas of bacteria or germs, they created a theory centering around a noxious substance they called *wechdu*, which resided in the lower intestine. They believed *wechdu* caused most diseases. This substance could travel from the bowel through the vascular system, they thought, coagulating the blood and changing it to pus. Such "rising" of *wechdu* produced heat (fever) that could affect the pulse rate.[7] *Wechdu* also caused aging because its slow absorption led to body decay. Since this foul substance caused disease, the Egyptian cure was to get rid of it. When a fever or infection grew serious, doctors prescribed an enema, or, simply as a preventative, purges were recommended to rid the body of *wechdu*. The Greek historian Herodotus noted during his visit to Egypt that these people purged themselves as a health measure for three days of each month. Today, we can see the errors in this view of disease, but the theory shows a rational, clinical approach to trying to understand and treat ailments.

Egyptian physicians had some knowledge of anatomy as well. The *Edwin Smith Papyrus* illustrates that some of their knowledge came from treating accident injuries: when a skull was severely fractured in a construction mishap, the attending physician could sometimes view the living brain. Additional opportunities for study were provided by war and mummification. Since physicians traveled with the troops, they could inspect internal organs and bones while they repaired battle wounds. Constrained by the need to move quickly from one battle victim to the next, however, they were unable to perform the careful examination that could lead to a precise anatomical description. Anatomy lessons learned during mummification had even greater limitations. Since the brain, for example, was intentionally pulverized inside the cranium before extraction, any possibility of discovering its structure was eliminated. On the other hand, although various internal organs were removed whole from the body and could be thoroughly inspected, embalmers, who occupied the lower end of the social scale, were not physicians and lacked both the interest and training to contribute to medical knowledge.

TEMPLE OF HATHOR AT THE DENDERA COMPLEX, *which specialized in miracle treatments. At the nearby sanatorium, visitors bathed in sacred waters and consulted gods in dreams for an appropriate cure.*

Since Egyptians did not perform human autopsies because of their religious belief in resurrection, much of their anatomical knowledge came from animals. Most Egyptians would have witnessed animal slaughter and had ready access to the local butcher shop. Hieroglyphs for various internal parts of the human body clearly show that animal anatomy was the source for information about human anatomy. The word for womb, *idt*, depicts the bicornuate (two-horned) uterus of a cow (the next to the last symbol from the right) rather than the unicornuate human uterus, a misunderstanding that persisted up to the seventeenth century when dissection of human cadavers became standard practice in medical schools.[8] Even the hieroglyph for heart, is a bovine, not a human, heart. Since mummification left the heart inside the body, a cow's heart was more familiar than a human one. The hieroglyphs for many other human bodily parts—backbone, ribs, intestines—depicted animal anatomy as well. While the physicians of ancient Egypt were recognized as the most skilled of their time in the world, their knowledge of human anatomy fell far short of modern standards. They did not even have a word for the human pancreas.[9]

The Egyptians had no hospitals, only home care, but, since most of their physicians were priests, people often sought healing at temples where they were treated with a combination of medicine, theology and magic, then sent home to recover. In addition, several temples with reputations for effecting miraculous cures became pilgrimages for the ill. Dendera in southern Egypt specialized in several types of miracle treatments. Water that dripped from statues inscribed with healing spells was channeled to basins so the diseased could bathe in holy water or drink it. Alternatively, patients could recline in small, dark crypts with special lamps, hoping to converse with appropriate gods in a dream to learn their cure. A Greek who visited an Egyptian temple for this kind of cure recorded his dream.

> It was night, when every living creature except those in pain slept, but divinity showed itself more effectively; a violent fever burned me, and I was convulsed with loss of breath and coughing, owing to the pain proceeding from my side. Heavy in the head with my troubles, I was lapsing half conscious into sleep and my mother, as a mother would for her child . . . was sitting without enjoying even a short period of slumber, when suddenly she perceived—it was no dream or sleep, for her eyes were open immovably, though not seeing clearly, for a divine and terrifying vision came to her from observing the god himself or his servants, whichever it was. In any case there was some one whose height was more than human, clothed in shining raiment and carrying in his left hand a book, who after merely regarding me two or three times from head to foot disappeared. When she had recovered herself, she tried, still trembling, to wake me, and finding that the fever had left me and that much sweat was pouring off me, did reverence to the manifestation of the god, and then wiped me and made me more collected . . . everything that she saw in the vision appeared to me in dreams. After these pains in my side had ceased and the god had given me yet another assuaging cure, I proclaimed his benefits.[10]

The temple at Deir el Bahri, also in southern Egypt, was another famous pilgrimage site. Long after Queen Hatshepsut, its New Kingdom builder, had been forgotten, medical miracles were reputed to take place on the upper terrace of her temple. On the terrace, dedicated to two famous Egyptian physicians, Imhotep and Amenhotep, son of Hapu, the walls of a small "healing" room still retain the graffiti written by those whose prayers were answered. One reads, "Andromachos, a Macedonian, a worker for hire, came to the good god Amenathen: he was sick and the god succored him on that very day. Farewell."[11]

Priest physicians who healed were called *wabu*: lay physicians were called *sunu*. Careful regulation of the medical profession by the government with stiff penalties for improper practice ensured that, whether associated with a temple or not, all doctors were thoroughly trained. The difference between priest and lay doctors was that the lay doctors could draw from all available sources for his cures, not just those connected with a single god.

While both priest and lay physicians used a combination of clinical medicine and magic, a third kind of healer, magicians, employed only incantations, amulets and other magical cures. Unfortunately, most surviving "medical" papyri come from this third class of medical men, for magicians required the exact words to be recited whereas the average doctor does not need his textbook at hand to treat most ailments. As a result, our information about the Egyptian medical profession is skewed toward its least scientific practices. The most extensive magical work is the sixty-eight-foot-long *Papyrus Ebers*, a disorganized collection of more than eight hundred magical concoctions and spells to alleviate suffering—from how to stop a baby from crying (make a potion with opium as an ingredient) to how to speed up a woman's labor (apply peppermint to her bare posterior).

All these remedies are based on a belief in the magical principle of similars, a kind of ancient homeopathy. In place of something essential to health (like blood) a substance similar in color, texture or function could be substituted (a potion of red plant dye, for example). G. Elliot Smith, a physician interested in ancient Egyptian medicine, who examined a grave of several small children who had died more than 5,000 years ago, discovered that they had eaten skinned mice just prior to their death. Egyptians believed the life-giving Nile created mice because these animals mysteriously emerged from cracks in the mud after the Nile receded each year. Since life substitutes for life, according to the principle of similars, mice were administered to these critically ill children in a desperate effort to sustain their lives.

Following the principle of similars meant Egyptian remedies used some unusual ingredients, such as the testicles of a black ass, milk of a woman who has borne a son and cat's dung, and listed specific spells to enhance the potency of these ingredients.

Blindness, for example, called for two dehydrated pig's eyes, without indicating how they were reduced to that state (perhaps with natron, as in mummification). Mixing the dried eyes with collyrium (red lead) and wild honey produced a paste that was injected into the ear of the patient while the physician said, "I have brought this thing and put it in its place. The crocodile is weak and powerless." Repeating this seemingly inappropriate spell twice was supposed to cure the patient of his blindness instantly. Numerous prayers to gods who made people "see darkness during the day" suggest that blindness was far from rare. If a patient had cataracts, a spell could be recited over the brain of a tortoise mixed with honey which was then applied to the eyes, unless the eyes were discharging matter, in which case a ground-up statue would be mixed with the honey along with leaves from the castor tree. The principle of similars dictated that the solidity of the statue was exactly what was needed to stop the running eyes. For coryza, a disease of the nose, a plug made from fragrant bread and the milk of a woman who bore a son was inserted in the nostrils. While the plug was prepared, the magician had to repeat four times that foulness was rising from the earth. Just as the spell would cause the foulness to come out of the ground, so it would pull the foulness from the nose.

Egyptians never explained what gave potency to various ingredients, so it is not clear what was special about the milk of a woman who had bred a son. It may be that Egyptians believed that this milk was actually different from the milk of a woman who had had a daughter, since even the Greek philosopher Aristotle, in his *Healing of Animals*, Book VII, Chapter 4, says that mothers of sons are stronger than mothers of daughters. More likely, however, the magic of similars again was at work. This milk was similar to that of the goddess Isis, who was

A HORUS-STELE FEATURES HORUS THE YOUNGER, *son of Isis, with the head of the child-protector god, Bes, above him. Water poured over this stone slab was believed to absorb magical spells that protected those who drank it from harm.*

the mother of a son, Horus. Since she was also the goddess of magic, such milk was perhaps believed to include her magical potency. In any case, this special milk was first stored in a vessel shaped like a woman holding a fragile child in her lap. After incantations, the milk was transferred to a similar vessel with a robust child figure, then the milk was ready to heal.

Magical treatments continued into the latest periods of Egyptian history, although during the Greek occupation of Egypt (332–30 B.C.E.), papyri included Greek ideas and words such as those in the *London-Leiden Papyrus*. Written in demotic, a late form of the Egyptian language, the main subject of the papyrus is magic and medicine. One spell for curing a man with gout in his foot calls for magical words written on tin or silver which is bound by a deerskin to the foot of the man, who is then called "fleet skin" because the skin of the nimble deer will render the lame foot well. The Greek addition is a stipulation that this procedure should be done when the moon is in the constellation of Leo, an astrological constellation unknown to ancient Egyptians.

The principle of similars applied not only to functions but to appearances as well: plants that resembled afflicted body parts were often prescribed. Mandrake was considered both an aphrodisiac and fertility drug because it takes the shape of male genitals; indeed, one Arabic name for the plant is "devil's testicles." Paul Ghalioungui, one of the great authorities on ancient Egyptian medicine, gives an account of how the mandrake was picked in antiquity.

Mandrakes could be picked only on certain nights, by moonlight, or with the morning dew. The picker stopped his ears with wax, tied the plant to a dog, and ran away; the dog running after its master uprooted it and then dropped dead, for the mandrake was said to utter out when torn away such a horrible cry that anyone who heard it or touched it ran mad or died on the spot.[12]

Egyptian magic was not pure mumbo-jumbo—several ingredients used by the ancient doctors have been proven effective today. Ground malachite, for example, was recommended for open wounds, and when mixed with animal fat it created a green eye makeup. In fact, this mineral contains cupric carbonate, shown in recent laboratory tests to kill infectious bacteria such as staphylococcus/anseus.[13] The *Kahun Gynecological Papyrus* recommendation that a pubic area infection be painted with green eye cosmetic would actually reduce inflammation and permit the healing process to progress naturally. Honey, one of the most common ingredients used by ancient physicians, especially on wounds, has been shown to have significant antibacterial properties because it is hyper-tonic, killing microorganisms by drawing the water from them. Propolis, collected from bees, was used as an antiseptic until the beginning of our century.[14]

Those skilled at gathering the plants physicians needed were the ancient equivalent of our pharmacists. When the Greek traveler Herodotus visited Egypt around 450 B.C.E. he was struck by the degree of specialization.

The practice of medicine they split up into separate parts, each doctor being responsible for the treatment of only one disease. There are, in consequence, innumerable doctors, some specializing in diseases of the eyes, others of the head, and others of the teeth, others of the stomach and so on.[15]

The surprise in this list is the mention of teeth specialists. Since no evidence exists of dental surgery—no filled teeth, no dental bridges—Herodotus' reference was most likely to dispensers of potions to relieve tooth pain.

He was certainly right about the degree of specialization: one entire medical papyrus was devoted to snake bites. Lethal cobras and vipers were plentiful in Egypt; the serpent was such a common danger in the ancient Middle East that the Bible makes it the archetype of evil. Ancient Egyptians believed that when they traveled across the sky to the netherworld, snakes would try to stop them, and magical spells would be needed to counter their venom. So it is not surprising that magical papyri are full of spells to protect the living from snake bites, and one is devoted to their treatment. The Brooklyn Museum's *Snake Bite Papyrus*[16] is similar to *The Edwin Smith Surgical Papyrus* in that it takes a nonmagical approach. Its first section lists types of snakes, their distinctive features, the seriousness of each bite, and the god associated with that snake.

Snake	Characteristics	Prognosis	God
Viper	Quail-colored, no horns	Can be saved	Horus
White *henep*	White, four teeth	May die	Selket
Apep (cobra?)	Red with white belly, four teeth	Die quickly	Was itself a god

Today we know the action to take after a poisonous bite is to stop absorption of the venom either by applying a tourniquet or by cutting open the bite and withdrawing the poison, but neither of these treatments appears in the snake bite papyrus. "Treatment with the knife" is occasionally indicated, but merely to reduce swelling and release fluids. Sometimes the physician is instructed to bandage the wound with a poultice of salt or natron, which would indeed reduce the swelling by osmosis just like the Glauber's salts (magnesium sulfate) used today, but it would not remove the poison. Instead, the main treatment, listed twenty-seven times in the papyrus, suggests giving the victim an emetic concoction of onions, salt, *sam*-plant and beer which would induce vomiting but not affect the venom circulating in the bloodstream. While physicians did not understand the mechanisms by which venom killed, they were certainly familiar with its effects. Several treatments were designed to "cause the throat to breathe" or "open the throat," which was a priority since cobra venom blocks impulses from the nerves to muscles, paralyzing the muscles involved in respiration.

We do not know whether obstetrics was a medical specialty, although a pregnancy test crops up in several papyri, usually under the heading, "Another test to see if a woman will bear a child or if she will not bear a child." The woman urinated on two test patches of emmer and barley seeds for several days. If either grew, she was pregnant; if only the barley sprouted, she would have a boy; if only the emmer, it would be a girl. This method was recently tested and found to be partly effective.[17] When emmer and barley seeds were watered with the urine of forty pregnant women, one or both sprouted in twenty-eight cases while grain watered with nonpregnant urine sprouted in only 30 percent of the cases—a 70 percent accuracy rate. It was not useful, however, in predicting a child's sex.

Egyptian women gave birth sitting down so gravity assisted the baby's exit, permitting less forceful contractions. Doctors probably did not assist at childbirth. The woman sat on a special birthing stool, generally made of bricks (giving rise to the Egyptian slang phrase "sitting on the bricks" for giving birth), and the hieroglyphs for birthing 𓄿𓃀𓏏, pronounced *meswet*, show a woman sitting in such a birthing position, as the head and arms of the baby emerge. A few carvings of births exist on temple walls, usually to establish the divine birth of kings and queens, but a physician is never shown. The mother is attended by females, either because of her modesty or because the process was considered so natural that it required no physician.

MATHEMATICS AND MEASUREMENT

Egyptians built massive temples, palaces and pyramids without the sophisticated mathematics engineers would use today, since simple arithmetic was all the Egyptians knew. Their expertise extended only to addition and subtraction, not even multiplication or division. Lacking a theoretical understanding of numbers, they substituted clever tricks and found practical ways to arrive at the solutions they needed.

Multiplication was achieved by clever addition, called the Method of Doubling. If a scribe wanted to multiply 18 by 7, he started by writing 18 once, then below it doubled the number and continued doing so, while to the left of each doubling he wrote the number of times it had occurred (see Figure 1). When the numbers in the left column added up to 7, he knew the total of the right column would be the correct answer, 126.

Division was accomplished by a similar procedure, just a bit more complicated. If a scribe had to divide 184 bronze chisels among 8 workers, he treated the problem as a doubling (multiplication) problem (see Figure 2). After asking himself what he had to multiply 8 by to get 184, he began his doubling. He stopped at 128 because he knew the next doubling (256) would be larger than the 184 he had to work with. He next asked, what in the right-hand column adds up to 184 without going over it? The answer is 128+32+16+8. He then put a slash mark next to those numbers and added the left column entries beside them; that is, he added 16+4+2+1 to get 23. Thus, 8 goes into 184 23 times: each worker gets 23 chisels.

The Egyptians worked with a base of 10, using hieroglyphs only for the number one and for numbers that are powers of ten (see Figure 3).

Symbols were repeated to indicate multiples of their values, thus the number 21,654 would be written: ⅢⅠ𓆼𓆼𓎆𓎆𓎆𓎟𓎟𓏤𓏤.

As to fractions, the Egyptians worked only with numerators of 1. They had no 3/4 or 6/7. Rather, 3/4 was written as 1/2+1/4, and 6/7 was 1/2+1/4+1/14+1/28.

Doublings	Sum
1	18
2	36
4	72
7	126 = answer

FIGURE 1

Doublings	Sum
1	8/
2	16/
4	32/
8	64
16	128/

FIGURE 2

Here too the scribe resorted to his doubling techniques to draw up long tables he could consult rather than redoing the tabulation each time.

Fractions were written by placing the hieroglyph that meant "part," represented by a mouth (⟨⟩), above the denominator so that 1/7 was (seven parts) and 1/10 was (ten parts). The only hieroglyph with a numerator other than 1 was 2/3, written. The fractions 1/2, 1/4, 1/8, 1/16, 1/32, and 1/64 used special hieroglyphs based on the myth of Osiris. After Osiris was killed by Seth, Osiris' son Horus (the falcon) avenged his father's death but lost his eye in the battle. Fortunately, the fragments were collected and restored by the god of magic, Toth. The distinctive markings of the feathers around Horus' falcon eye became the hieroglyphs for well-being, and, when broken into components, represented special fractions (see Figure 4):

Number	Hieroglyph
1	
10	
100	
1,000	
10,000	
100,000	
1,000,000	

FIGURE 3

Fraction	Hieroglyph
1/2	
1/4	
1/8	
1/16	
1/32	
1/64	

FIGURE 4

Of course, the Egyptians realized that these fractions added up to only 63/64, instead of 64/64 or unity, so they claimed the missing 1/64 was supplied by Toth's magic.

Egyptians used mathematics not for abstract intellectual exercises, but only for practical problems: fields had to be measured, quantities of grain recorded and supplies divided among workers. Such problems required standards for size, weight and volume that could be used with their arithmetic.

Since construction workers constantly had to measure, cut and mark off distances, they used parts of their bodies—hands, palms, fingers—for measurement. We call their basic unit the cubit: the distance between the elbow and the tip of the middle finger (cubitum is Latin for elbow). Although the length of a cubit or width of a palm varied from worker to worker, such standards proved adequate for many small projects. Major projects, such as temples or pyramids whose thousands of blocks had to be uniform in size, required greater precision. The royal cubit was set for this purpose at 52.3 centimeters (20 5/8 inches), slightly longer than the average Egyptian's elbow to middle fingertip. This royal cubit was divided into seven palms, approximately the width of four fingers without the thumb. Palms were further divided into fourths, called "fingers," making twenty-eight fingers to the cubit. The smallest unit Egyptian craftsmen used was 1/16 finger. Architects for major construction projects supplied cubit rulers for their overseers to maintain uniformity.

Land was measured by ropes cut in 100-cubit lengths, called a *khet*. An area one *khet* (100 cubits) on all four sides was a *setat*, the basic unit of surface area, about 2/3 of a modern acre. Volume was measured in *hekats*, which contained slightly less than a modern liter. The standard unit for liquids was the *hin*, a small jar about one-tenth of a *hekat*.

In a society that had no coin or paper money, commodities were the means of exchange and were measured for each transaction. For bread and beer, the staples of the Egyptian diet and of exchanges, there was even a measure of quality, the *pesu*. A *hin* of diluted beer was not worth as much as one that was full strength, nor was a heavily aerated loaf of bread equal to a dense loaf. The *pesu* indicated the number of jars of beer or loaves of bread obtained from 1 *hekat* of grain.

One equivalent of a mathematics textbook survives, *The Rhind Mathematical Papyrus*, a fifteen-foot-long scroll. Copied in the thirty-third year of the Pharaoh Apophis by a scribe named Ahmose, it presents dozens of math questions and their answers, which lend some insight into the kinds of problems Egyptians could solve. Included were such simple matters as dividing 6 loaves of bread among 10 men. Because the Egyptians did not use fractions with numerators other than 1, they could not give the easy answer of 6/10 of a loaf. Each man got 1/2 of a loaf plus 1/10 of a loaf. If there were 7 men for the 10 loaves, then the scribe got to use his one fraction with a numerator other than 1 (2/3) so each man got 2/3 + 1/30 of a loaf.

In other problems the student was asked to calculate the relative values of gold, silver and lead, or how much bread was needed to force-feed a certain number of geese for a certain period. There are even problems about the volume of a truncated pyramid. Overall, the impression conveyed by the *Rhind Papyrus* is of the utter practicality of Egyptian mathematics. It served the purpose well, even though, lacking a foundation in number theory, it contributed little to modern mathematics.

A SURVEYOR USES ROPE TO MEASURE *the height of crops before the harvest, from the tomb of Menna, c. 1400 B.C.E.*

The Egyptian Calendar

The Egyptian calendar differed slightly from ours. There were only three seasons: inundation (⟨glyph⟩, *akhet*), the period when the Nile overflowed its banks and covered the farms with water, lasting approximately from June 21 to October 21; emergence (⟨glyph⟩, *peret*), the time when the water receded, from October 21 to February 21; and summer (⟨glyph⟩, *shemu*), which lasted from February 21 to June 21. Each of these seasons consisted of four months of thirty days each, so there were 360 days in the standard year. With a 360-day calendar, however, periodic natural phenomena would have occurred five days earlier each year until the season called inundation would arrive when the land was dry. To correct the discrepancy, Egyptians added five days at the beginning of every year, and, in effect, devised the modern 365-day calendar.

New Year's day, which was called "the opening of the year," began not with an arbitrary date like our January 1, but with an event—the annual rise of the Nile—which occurred in roughly 365-day intervals. This took place around our June 20, and coincided with the first time the bright star Sirius appeared on the horizon at just before sunrise. These two natural events marked the beginning of the Egyptian year.

Living under a sky unobscured with industrial smoke or bright city lights, ancient Egyptians became keen stargazers, using the movements of the stars for their nighttime clock. They learned that the hour of the night could be determined by observing where each of their thirty-six major constellations appeared in the sky at that time. If an ancient Egyptian priest wanted to determine the end of the last hour of the night and a particular star appeared on the horizon just before dawn, he might try to use this star to fix the end of the twelfth hour of the night. But, because of the annual eastward motion of the sun, this star would rise earlier each day until it no longer served as a usable indicator of the end of night. Priests learned to select a larger object, the constellation next to this star instead and use that as the indicator of the end of the last hour of the night.

THIS CALENDAR AT THE TEMPLE OF KOM OMBO *shows days 26–30 of the second month of Akhet, the season of inundation. Egyptians divided the 365-day year into three seasons, each composed of four 30-day months. Five feast days followed.*

Despite Egyptians' keen observations of the night sky, their records contain no predictions of lunar or solar eclipses. They used their astronomy for practical purposes and saw no reason to involve themselves in abstract theories.

ACKNOWLEDGMENTS

Many people deserve thanks for their help with this book. David Moyer read the entire manuscript, found most of our errors, corrected our spelling and, in general, proved indispensable. Pat Remler worked hard and long securing illustrations and editing the text. Rivka Rago took valuable time from her own work as an archaeological artist to draw many of the illustrations. Our former editor at Greenwood Press, Emily Birch, deserves our humble thanks for her patience and astute suggestions. Last, but far from least, the Trustees of Long Island University graciously granted the authors sabbaticals from teaching to work on the first edition of this book.

NOTES

Chapter 1

1. Egypt vies with one other contender for the honor of being the first civilization: Sumer in southern Iraq holds equally strong credentials. Some archaeologists consider Egypt the first nation; others opt for Sumer.

2. For this and subsequent dates see Chronicle of the Pharaohs: The Reign-by-Reign *Record of the Rulers and Dynasties of Ancient Egypt*, by Peter A. Clayton (London: Thames and Hudson, 1994).

3. For a detailed description see *The Boat Beneath the Pyramid*, by Nancy Jenkins (New York: Holt, Rinehart & Winston, 1980).

4. Translated by Alan Gardiner, *Egypt of the Pharaohs* (New York: Oxford University Press, 1961), 109.

5. Ibid., 166.

6. Noted by Christiane Desroches-Noblecourt in *Tutankhamen: Life and Death of a Pharaoh* (New York: Penguin Books, 1984; a reissue of New York Graphic Society, 1963), 182. Desroches-Noblecourt claims that thirteen stretchers, not men, however, were required to transport the idol.

7. For the murder theory, see *The Murder of Tutankhamen*, by Bob Brier (New York: Putnam's Sons, 1998).

Chapter 2

1. Alan H. Gardiner, trans., *Hieratic Papyri in the British Museum*, Third series, vol. 1 (London: British Museum Press), 1935, 9–23.

2. Alexandre Piankoff, *The Pyramid of Unis* (Princeton, N.J.: Princeton University Press, 1968), 71.

3. E. A. Wallis Budge, *The Egyptian Book of the Dead* (New York: Dover Books, 1967), 198–202.

4. Ibid., 112–14.

5. E. A. Wallis Budge, *The Mummy* (New York: Causeway Books, 1974), 197–203.

6. E. A. Wallis Budge, *Egyptian Magic* (London: Routledge, Kegan, Paul, 1899), 185.

7. Ibid., 189.

8. Ibid., 195–96.

9. After the translation of Miriam Lichtheim, *Ancient Egyptian Literature*, vol. 2 (Berkeley: University of California Press, 1976), 91–92.

Chapter 3

1. This example from the First Intermediate Period was translated by Alan Gardiner, *Egypt of the Pharaohs* (New York: Oxford University Press, 1961), 109–110.
2. Modified from Gardiner, *Egypt of the Pharaohs*, 51.
3. See B. G. Trigger, B. J. Kemp, D. O'Connor, and A. B. Lloyd, *Ancient Egypt: A Social History* (New York: Cambridge University Press, 1983), 216.
4. Kemp's phrase, from Trigger, Kemp, O'Connor, and Lloyd, *Ancient Egypt*, 85ff.
5. See J. Cerny, "Consanguineous Marriages in Pharaonic Egypt," *Journal of Egyptian Archaeology* 40 (1954): 23–29. This situation changed, however, when the Greek Ptolemies took over during Egypt's final days. Cleopatra, for example, married her own full brother.
6. The guesstimate of Kemp, in Trigger, Kemp, O'Connor, and Lloyd, *Ancient Egypt*, 226.
7. Ibid., 214.
8. Ibid., 202.
9. Ibid., 301–309.
10. Very likely the Hebrews adopted this practice as a result of their stay in Egypt.
11. It seems the sandalbearer symbolized royal authority. The ancient Narmer Palette, which portrays the original conquest of the north, displays a prominent sandalbearer as part of every depiction of the pharaoh.
12. Gardiner, *Egypt of the Pharaohs*, 152.
13. For this and what follows, see Schafik Allam, *Some Pages from . . .Everyday Life in Ancient Egypt* (Cairo: Prism Books, 1985), 41ff.
14. Ibid., 30.
15. See Trigger, Kemp, O'Connor, and Lloyd, *Ancient Egypt*, 315.

Chapter 4

1. Cited by Pierre Montet, *Everyday Life in Egypt During the Days of Ramesses the Great* (Philadelphia: University of Pennsylvania Press, 1981), 168.
2. See B. G. Trigger, B. J. Kemp, D. O'Connor, and A. B. Lloyd, *Ancient Egypt: A Social History* (New York: Cambridge University Press, 1983), 328.
3. Quoted by Montet, *Everyday Life*, 256.
4. Quoted by Montet, ibid., 158.
5. Quoted by Montet, ibid., 159.
6. Shown in *The Theban Tomb Series*, edited by Norman DeGaris Davies and Alan H. Gardiner (London: Egypt Exploration Society, 1915) vol. 1, p. 8.

7. Bernd Scheel claims that no independent craftsmen existed with their own workshops. See his *Egyptian Metalworking and Tools* (Aylesbury, England: Shire Publications, 1989), 59.

8. See Montet, *Everyday Life*, 124.

9. Modified from Montet, Ibid., 96–97.

10. Ibid., 97–98.

11. See the description in William Hayes, *The Scepter of Egypt* (New York: Metropolitan Museum of Art, 1959), vol. 2, p. 26.

12. Currently in New York's Metropolitan Museum collection and described in Hayes, *The Scepter of Egypt*, 25–26.

Chapter 5

1. Kurt Baer, "The Low Price of Land in Ancient Egypt," *Journal of the American Research Center in Egypt* 1 (1962): 25–45.

2. Noted in William J. Darby, Paul Ghalioungui, and Louis Crevetti, *Food: The Gift of Osiris* (New York: Academic Press, 1977), vol. 2, p. 502.

3. Ibid., 503.

4. Only ancient Sumer offers a challenge to this claim. Whether beer was first brewed in Sumer or Egypt is still argued—the timing was close, whichever country won the race. One difference in beers of these two ancient countries is that Egyptians strained theirs as we do before drinking, Sumerians instead sipped theirs through a straw.

5. A. Lucas and J. R. Harris, *Ancient Egyptian Materials and Industries* (London: Histories and Mysteries of Man, 1989), 10–11.

6. Darby, Ghalioungui, and Crevetti, *Food*, vol. 2, p. 583.

7. Ibid., vol. 1, p. 337.

8. Cited in ibid., vol. 2, p. 399.

9. Ibid., vol. 1, p. 302.

10. Ibid., vol. 2, pp. 653 –95.

11. Ibid., vol. 2, pp. 697–99.

12. Ibid., vol. 2, pp. 791–807.

13. See Leonard H. Lesko, *King Tut's Wine Cellar* (Berkeley, Calif.: B.C.E. Scribe Publications, 1977), 23.

14. Cited in Alan Gardiner, *Egypt of the Pharaohs* (New York: Oxford University Press, 1961), 152.

15. One such model is reproduced in H. E. Winlock, *Models of Daily Life in Ancient Egypt: From the Tomb of Meket-Re at Thebes* (Cambridge: Harvard University Press, 1955), fig. 17.

16. Quoted in Darby, Ghalioungui, and Crevetti, *Food*, vol. 1, p. 139.

17. Quoted in ibid., vol. 1, p. 191.

18. Quoted in ibid., vol. 1, p. 221.

19. Claimed at least for early times in Ibid., vol. 2, p. 430.

20. Cited by Salima Ikram, "Food for Eternity: What the Ancient Egyptians Ate and Drank," part 2, "Greens, Bread, Beverages & Sweets," *KMT* 5, no. 2 (Summer 1994): 55.

21. Cited by Darby, Ghalioungui, and Crevetti, *Food*, vol. 1, p. 54.

Chapter 6

1. Cited in Philip J. Watson, *Costume of Ancient Egypt* (New York: Chelsea House, 1987), 20.

2. One requirement for priests was that all their hair had to be shaved. Perhaps wool was forbidden in temples because it was regarded as a kind of hair.

3. Pictured in William C. Hayes, *The Scepter of Egypt*, vol. 2, *The Hyksos Period and the New Kingdom* (New York: Metropolitan Museum of Art, 1959), 411.

4. For a discussion of dyes and mordant, see A. Lucas and J. R. Harris, *Ancient Egyptian Materials and Industries* (London: Histories and Mysteries of Man, 1989), 150–54.

5. Explained by Hero Granger-Taylor in *The British Museum Book of Ancient Egypt*, ed. Stephen Quirke and Jeffrey Spenser (London: Thames and Hudson, 1992), 188.

6. Noted by Flinders Petrie, *Arts and Crafts of Ancient Egypt* (London: T. N. Foulis, 1909), 147.

7. Pictured in Hayes, *The Scepter of Egypt*, 412.

8. Detailed by Mary G. Houston and Florence S. Hornblower in *Ancient Egyptian, Assyrian and Persian Costumes* (London: A. & C. Black, 1920).

9. See Cyril Aldred, *Jewels of the Pharaohs* (New York: Praeger, 1971), 144.

10. This is Lucas' argument in Lucas and Harris, *Ancient Egyptian Materials*, 83.

11. Ibid., 85–97.

12. Ibid., 92.

Chapter 7

1. See Alexander Badawy, *A History of Egyptian Architecture: The First Intermediate Period, the Middle Kingdom, and the Second Intermediate Period* (Berkeley: University of California Press, 1968), 25–27.

2. Somers Clarke and R. Englebach, *Ancient Egyptian Construction and Architecture* (Mineola, N.Y.: Dover Books, 1990; reprint of Oxford University Press, 1930), 209.

3. Badawy, *A History of Egyptian Architecture*, 46.

4. Ibid., 126.

5. The most recent survey is by Barry J. Kemp and Salvadore Garfi, *A Survey of the Ancient City of El-Amarna* (London: Egypt Exploration Society, 1993).

6. Considered harems by, for example, Badawy, *A History of Egyptian Architecture*, 82ff.

7. Ibid., 47–54.

8. Ibid., 224–25.

9. See Kemp and Garfi, *A Survey*, 50–57.

10. Technically, the prize for the oldest surviving true pyramid could be awarded to a subsidiary pyramid next to the Bent Pyramid at Dashur, although it is a relatively small affair.

11. Badawy, *A History of Egyptian Architecture*, 385.

12. Ibid., 407–22.

Chapter 8

1. A number of books on ancient Egypt beautifully illustrate the development of its art; see, for example, Kazimierz Michelowski, *Art of Ancient Egypt* (New York: Abrams, n.d.).

2. Occasional exceptions prove the rule, such as a fine, small, slate statue of the Second Dynasty pharaoh Khasekhem.

3. Noted, for example, by Waley-el-dine Sameh, *Daily Life in Ancient Egypt* (New York: McGraw-Hill, 1964), 55.

4. See Cyril Aldred, *Egyptian Art in the Days of the Pharaohs 3100–320 B.C.E.* (New York: Oxford University Press, 1980), 24.

5. Illustrated, for example, in W. Stevenson Smith, *Art and Architecture of Ancient Egypt* (New York: Penguin Books, 1958), 65.

6. See the discussion in A. Lucas and J. R. Harris, *Ancient Egyptian Materials and Industries* (London: Histories and Mysteries of Man, 1989), 1–6.

7. Ibid., 356–61.

8. For example, Aldred, *Egyptian Art*, 145– 46; and Jean-Louis de Cenival, *Living Architecture: Egyptian* (New York: Grosset and Dunlap, 1964), 89–90.

9. Alexander Badawy presents both views in *A History of Egyptian Architecture: The First Intermediate Period, the Middle Kingdom, and the Second Intermediate Period* (Berkeley: University of California Press, 1968), 79–81.

10. The evidence is critically assessed by Lucas in Lucas and Harris, *Ancient Egyptian Materials*, 179–84.

11. For a discussion of the different colors, see Lucas and Harris, *Ancient Egyptian Material*, 187–91.

12. Described by Geoffrey Killen, *Ancient Egyptian Furniture*, Vol. 2, *Boxes, Chests and Footstools* (Warminster, England: Aris and Phillips, 1994), 3–4.

13. Ibid., 38–39.

14. See the thorough discussion by Lucas in Lucas and Harris, *Ancient Egyptian Materials*, 429–48.

15. For a complete translation of "The Instruction Addressed to Kagemni," see Miriam Lichtheim, *Ancient Egyptian Literature* (Berkeley: University of California Press, 1972), vol. 1, pp. 59–61.

16. Ibid.

17. For a complete translation of "The Instruction of Ptahotep," see Lichtheim, *Ancient Egyptian Literature*, vol. 1, pp. 61–80.

18. Ibid.

19. For a complete translation of "The Instruction Addressed to King Merikare," see Lichtheim, *Ancient Egyptian Literature*, vol. 2, pp. 97–109.

20. Ibid.

21. For a complete translation of "The Instructions of Any," see Lichtheim, *Ancient Egyptian Literature*, vol. 2, pp. 135–46.

22. William Kelly Simpson, *The Literature of Ancient Egypt* (New Haven, Conn.: Yale University Press, 1972), 57–74.

23. Ibid., 50–56.

24. For a different version of this poem, see John L. Foster, *Love Songs of the New Kingdom* (Austin: University of Texas Press, 1992), 72.

25. Ibid., 193.

Chapter 9

1. See "How to Build a Pyramid" by Bob Brier (*Archaeology*, May/June 2007, Vol. 60, No. 3), pp. 25–27.

2. See *Experiments in Egyptian Archaeology: Stoneworking Technology in Ancient Egypt*, by Denys A. Stocks (London: Routledge, 2003), p. 61.

3. Reported by W.M.F. Petrie in *The Pyramids and Temples of Gizeh* (London: Field and Tuer, 1883), p. 213ff.

4. The following is based on the experiments of Denys A. Stocks in *Experiments in Egyptian Archaeology: Stoneworking Technology in Ancient Egypt* (London: Routledge, 2003). See pp. 34ff.

5. Ibid., pp. 37–40.

6. See Thor Heyerdal, *The Ra Expeditions* (New York: Doubleday, 1971). Heyerdahl was struck by the fact that pyramidal structures existed both in ancient Egypt and in Pre-Columbian America. He tried to show that ancient Egyptians could have sailed from Egypt to America to teach Pre-Columbian Indians how to build these uncommon shapes. On his second sail, Heyerdahl made it. There are great problems with his theory, however. First, there is no evidence that Egyptians built such large ships out of papyrus or sailed them on an ocean. Second, pyramids in America were built no earlier than the seventh or eighth centuries A.D.; by which time Egypt had not built such structures for almost three thousand years and was no longer the rich and powerful nation of previous times.

7. See Bjorn Landstrom, *Ships of the Pharaohs: 4000 Years of Egyptian Shipbuilding* (Garden City, NY: Doubleday & Company, 1970) for details about this and other ancient Egyptian boats and ships.

8. These calculations are based on Landstrom, *Ships of the Pharaohs*, p. 128ff. He believes that the obelisks are pictured end-to-end just to show there are two, whereas, they would have been transported side-by-side. He also wonders if the two obelisks shown on a single ship represent artistic license; in actuality, separate barges might have been used for each obelisk. However, he vastly overestimates the probable size of the load, since no completed obelisks as tall as 200 feet are known. Hence, our calculations are based on 100-feet-tall obelisks, the largest ever successfully erected in Egypt.

Chapter 10

1. Yigal Yadin, *The Art of Warfare in Biblical Lands* (New York: McGraw-Hill, 1963).

2. W. M. McLeod, *Self Bows and Other Archery Tackle from the Tomb of Tutankhamen* (Oxford, England: Griffith Institute, 1982).

3. For a discussion of the composite bow, see McLeod, *Self Bows.*

4. For descriptions of existing ancient weapons, see W. V. Davies, *Catalogue of Egyptian Antiquities in the British Museum: VII Tools and Weapons* (London: British Museum Press, 1987).

5. After the translation of Alan H. Gardiner, "The Defeat of the Hyksos by Kamose: The Carnarvon Tablet," *Journal of Egyptian Archaeology* 3 (1916): 95–110.

6. Because they were made of light wood, few chariots have survived from ancient Egypt. A rare exception are those found in Tutankhamen's tomb described by

M. A. Littauer and J. H. Crouwel, *Chariots and Related Equipment from the Tomb of Tutankhamen* (Oxford, England: Griffith Institute, 1985).

7. Miriam Lichtheim, *Ancient Egyptian Literature* (Berkeley: University of California Press, 1976), vol. 2, pp. 11–15.

8. A detailed account of Tuthmosis I's expedition is presented in "Following Thutmose I on his Campaign to Kush" by Louise Bradbury in *KMT* (Fall 1992): 51–77.

9. Ibid., 56.

10. Ibid., 57.

11. Lichtheim, op. cit., 35.

12. Ibid., 32.

13. A readable account of the battle of Qadesh is given by K. A. Kitchen in *Pharaoh Triumphant: The Life and Times of Rameses II* (Warminster, England: Aris and Phillips, 1982), 53–64.

14. Translated by Alan Gardiner, *The Kadesh Inscriptions of Ramses II* (Oxford, England: Griffith Institute, 1975), 11.

15. Ibid., 12.

16. See N. K. Sandars, *The Sea Peoples: Warriors of the Ancient Mediterranean* (London: Thames and Hudson, 1978).

Chapter 11

1. M. A. Ruffer, "Note on the Presence of 'Bilharzia haematobia' in Egyptian Mummies of the XXth Dynasty," *British Medical Journal* 1 (1910): 16.

2. R. C. Nutley et al. "Palaeoepidemiology of Schistosoma Infection in Mummies," *British Medical Journal* 304 (1992): 355–56.

3. Marc Armand Ruffer, "Arterial Lesions in Egyptian Mummies," in *Studies in the Paleopathology of Egypt*, Ray L. Moodie, ed. (Chicago: University of Chicago Press, 1921), 20–31.

4. James Henry Breasted, *The Edwin Smith Surgical Papyrus* (Chicago: University of Chicago Press, 1930), 165–66.

5. Ibid., 220.

6. Ibid., 447.

7. Robert O. Steuer and J. B. de C. M. Saunders, *Ancient Egyptian & Cnidian Medicine* (Berkeley: University of California Press, 1959), 4.

8. Andrew Gordon, "Origins of Ancient Egyptian Medicine," *KMT* (Summer 1990): 29.

9. Kent Weeks, *The Anatomical Knowledge of the Ancient Egyptians and the Representation of the Human Figure in Egyptian Art* (Ann Arbor, Mich.: University Microfilms International, 1970), 75; James H. Walker, *Studies in Ancient Egyptian Anatomical Terminology* (Warminster, England: Aris and Phillips, 1996).

10. Bernard P. Grenfell and Arthur S. Hunt, eds. *The Oxyrhynchus Papyri Part XI* (London: Egypt Exploration Society, 1915), 221.

11. J. Grafton Milne, "The Sanatorium of Dier-el-Bahri," *Journal of Egyptian Archaeology* 2, Part 1 (1914), 96–98.

12. Paul Ghalioungui, *Magic and Medical Science in Ancient Egypt* (Amsterdam: B. M. Israel, 1973), 143.

13. J. Worth Estes, *The Medical Skills of Ancient Egypt* (Canton, Mass.: Science History Publications, 1993), 66–68.

14. Ibid.; p. 69.

15. Herodotus, *Histories*, book II, A. de Selinecourt, trans. (New York: Penguin, 1954), 86.

16. Serge Sauneron, *Un Traité Égyptien d'Ophiologie* (Cairo: L'Institut Français d'Archéologie Orientale, 1989).

17. Paul Ghalioungui, et al. "On an Ancient Egyptian Method of Diagnosing Pregnancy and Detecting Foetal Sex," *Medical History* 7 (1963), 241–46.

GLOSSARY

ADOBE Mud, shaped into bricks and dried in the sun, used a material for buildings.

AMARNA PERIOD The reign of the pharaoh Akhenaten, called the Amarna Period after the modern name of the area where his capital was located—Tel el Amarna.

AMULET A small object worn or carried for magical protection, often in the form of a god.

ANTHROPOID Greek for "human shaped." Coffins in the shape of a person are called *anthropoid coffins*.

BA The personality or soul of an individual, usually represented as a human-headed bird.

BOOK OF THE DEAD A collection of magical spells written on papyrus intended to help the deceased resurrect in the next world.

CANOPIC JARS Four jars used to store the mummified internal organs of the deceased.

CAPITAL Architectural term for the carved top of a column.

CARTOUCHE An oval circling the name of a royal person.

CATARACT Boulders in a river that makes passage by boat difficult.

CENOTAPH A burial or tomb that never contained a body but was constructed for ritual or religious purposes.

DELTA The triangular fertile area of land north of Cairo where the Nile spreads wide before reaching the Mediterranean Sea.

DEMOTIC A cursive form of writing the ancient Egyptian language used towards the end of Egyptian civilization. From the Greek word demos meaning "people" because it was generally used for secular matters.

DYNASTY A method for categorizing a number of successive pharaohs together, supposedly by family descent, although not always accurately.

ENNEAD A group of nine gods central to Egyptian mythology: Atun, Geb (earth), Nut (sky), Shu (air), Tefnut (moisture), Isis, Osiris, Set and Nepthys.

FAIENCE A ceramic paste that when fired in a kiln hardens and glazes itself and resembles modern porcelain. It was often used to make small amulets, drinking vessels and ushabti figures. (See *ushabti*.)

GESSO A plastering material made from powdered limestone and water used to produce a smooth coating on a wall or other object.

HIERATIC An abbreviated form of hieroglyphic writing.

HITTITE A kingdom centered in northern Turkey which was the great rival of Rameses the Great.

HOLY OF HOLIES The most sacred part of an Egyptian temple, usually consisting of one or more small dark rooms where sacred material and the temple idol(s) resided.

HYPOSTYLE HALL A grand room in a temple with massive columns supporting a high ceiling.

INUNDATION The season when the Nile overflowed its banks and water covered the fields. In ancient times this took place in July–August.

KA The spiritual double of a person. One of several aspects that each individual was composed of (see *ba*).

MASTABA From the Arabic for "bench." These rectangular chapels, mainly for the nobility, were built over Old Kingdom burials.

MEMPHIS The capital of Egypt during the Old Kingdom, located near modern Cairo.

MIDDLE KINGDOM The period consisting of Dynasties 11 and 12 (2040–1782 B.C.E.).

MORTUARY TEMPLE A temple where daily offerings could be made to a deceased person.

MUMMY A dead body dried of its moisture to preserve it.

NATRON A naturally occurring compound of chemicals used to dehydrate the body during the mummification process. Composed primarily of sodium carbonate, sodium bicarbonate and sodium chloride—basically baking soda and table salt.

NEW KINGDOM The period consisting of Dynasties 18–20 (1570–1070 B.C.E.).

NILOMETER Device used to measure the height of the Nile when it rose. Usually carved on a boulder at the river bank, sometimes Nilometers were stone pillars inside a building on shore.

NOME Ancient Egypt's equivalent of the states of the United States of America. For administrative purposes, Egypt was divided into 22 nomes for Upper Egypt and 22 nomes for Lower Egypt.

NUBIA The foreign territory south of the city of Aswan from which Egypt got much of its gold. Today it is modern Sudan.

OBELISK A tall pillar with squared sides, usually of granite, with a small pyramid (pyramidion) on top. Almost always, obelisks were erected in pairs at the entrances of temples.

OLD KINGDOM The period consisting of Dynasties 3–6 (2686–2181 B.C.E.).

OSTRACON A broken piece of pottery, often used in ancient Egypt in place of scrap paper to write notes, drawings or lists on.

PAPYRUS A tall species of reed. Also the name given to writing material made by pounding papyrus flat and gluing it together to form pages.

PECTORAL A necklace in the form of a broad collar that covered the upper chest.

POLYTHEISM Any religion that worships more than one god.

PREDYNASTIC The earliest period of Egyptian history.

PYLON Two large towers forming a gateway in front of a temple, usually carved with scenes of the pharaoh in battle.

SARCOPHAGUS A stone rectangular box that held the wood coffin containing the mummy.

SCARAB A beetle that the Egyptians believed gave birth to its young without mating and thus was associated with creation. Small stone scarabs were often carved and worn as amulets.

SISTRUM A rattle-like musical instrument used primarily in religious rituals by priestesses of the goddess Hathor.

SPHINX A mythical creature composed of a human head on a lion's body.

STELLA A round-topped stone carved with an inscription to commemorate an event.

THEBES The name the Greeks gave to the ancient Egyptian city of Waset, the religious capital of ancient Egypt during the Middle and New Kingdoms. It is called Luxor today.

USHABTI Small statues placed in the tomb that were intended to answer for the deceased if he were called upon to do any work in the next word. From the ancient Egyptian word *usheb*, which means "answer."

WADI A dried river bed.

SELECTED BIBLIOGRAPHY

Aldred, Cyril. *Egyptian Art in the Days of the Pharaohs 3100–320 B.C.* (New York: Oxford University Press, 1980). A broad, accurate and intelligent survey of all forms of Egyptian art.

———. *Jewels of the Pharaohs.* (New York: Praeger, 1971). The standard work on royal jewelry, including Tutankhamen's.

Allam, Schafik. *Some Pages from . . . Everyday Life in Ancient Egypt.* (Cairo: Prism Books, 1985). A quirky book that nevertheless contains specific information on marriage contracts.

Archaeology Magazine. (36 – 36 33rd St., Long Island City, NY 11106). This magazine covers the whole ancient world but almost every issue includes at least one article on ancient Egypt.

Arnold, Dieter. *Building in Egypt: Pharaonic Stone Masonry.* (New York: Oxford University Press, 1991). The definitive book on how Egyptians quarried and worked with stone.

Badawy, Alexander. *A History of Egyptian Architecture.* Vols. 1–3. (Berkeley: University of California Press, 1966–1968). The most detailed account of Egyptian architecture with many examples.

Baer, Kurt. "The Low Price of Land in Ancient Egypt." *Journal of the American Research Center in Egypt* 1 (1912): 25– 45. Explains the technical aspects of ownership in ancient Egypt.

Benson, D. S. *Ancient Egypt's Warfare.* (Ashland, Ohio: Bookmasters, 1995). Contains accounts of major Egyptian battles along with descriptions from the Egyptian records.

Betro, Maria Carmela. *Hieroglyphics: The Writings of Ancient Egypt.* (New York: Abbeville Press, 1995). Descriptions of all the hieroglyphs with good illustrations.

Bradbury, Louise. "Following Thutmose I on his Campaign to Kush." *KMT* (Fall 1992): 55–77. A detailed presentation of one ancient military campaign.

Breasted, James Henry. *The Edwin Smith Surgical Papyrus.* (Chicago: University of Chicago Press, 1930). Provides good information about clinical medicine.

Brier, Bob. *Ancient Egyptian Magic.* (New York: William Morrow, 1982). How the Egyptians practiced magic, including many spells.

————. *Egyptian Mummies*. (New York: William Morrow, 1994). The details of Egyptian mummification.

————. *The Murder of Tutankhamen*. (New York: G. P. Putnam's Sons, 1998). Presents the life and possibly violent death of the famous young king.

Budge, E. A. Wallis. *The Egyptian Book of the Dead*. (New York: Dover, 1967). A translation of a complete Book of the Dead along with the actual hieroglyphs.

————. *Egyptian Magic*. (London: Routledge, Kegan, Paul, 1899). An older book containing examples of magic spells seldom presented elsewhere.

————. *The Gods of the Egyptians*. 2 vols. (New York: Dover, 1904). This reprint of an old book is dated but encyclopedic.

————. *The Mummy*. (New York: Causeway Books, 1974). A reprint of an old book that remains useful for its details of the funerary customs of ancient Egypt.

Cerny, J. "Consanguineous Marriages in Pharaonic Egypt." *Journal of Egyptian Archaeology* 40 (1954): 23–29. Discusses all known cases of nonroyal brother-sister marriages.

Clarke, Somers, and R. Englebach. *Ancient Egyptian Construction and Architecture*. (Mineola, N.Y.: Dover Books, 1990). (Reprint of Oxford University Press, 1930). Some good information about building in Egypt, though superseded in some cases by more recent books.

Clayton, Peter A. *Chronicle of the Pharaohs: The Reign-by-Reign Record of the Rulers and Dynasties of Ancient Egypt*. (London: Thames and Hudson, 1994). A superior reference for all the kings and queens and their dates.

Darby, William J., Paul Ghalioungui, and Louis Crevetti. *Food: The Gift of Osiris*. 2 vols. (New York: Academic Press, 1977). Encyclopedic treatment of food in ancient Egypt.

Davies, Norman DeGaris, and Alan H. Gardiner, eds. *The Theban Tomb Series*. Vol. 1. (London: Egypt Exploration Society, 1915). Abundant pictures of tomb scenes.

Davies, W. V. *Catalogue of Egyptian Antiquities in the British Museum: VII Tools and Weapons*. (London: British Museum Press, 1987). Presents clear examples of ancient Egyptian weapons.

De Cenival, Jean-Louis. *Living Architecture: Egyptian*. (New York: Grosset and Dunlap, 1964). A general discussion of Egyptian temples and houses.

Desroches-Noblecourt, Christiane. *Tutankhamen: Life and Death of a Pharaoh*. (New York: Penguin Books, 1984). Fine pictures of the life and times of Tutankhamen.

Erman, Adolf. *Life in Ancient Egypt*. (New York: Dover, 1971). This reprint of a century-old book still provides useful information and contains abundant illustrations.

Estes, J. Worth. *The Medical Skills of Ancient Egypt*. (Canton, Mass.: Science History Publications, 1993). A solid survey of Egyptian medical skills.

Faulkner, Raymond. *The Egyptian Book of the Dead*. (San Francisco: Chronicle Books, 1994). An excellent recent translation of *The Book of the Dead*, with lovely color illustrations.

Fletcher, Joann. *Chronicle of a Pharaoh: The Intimate Life of Amenhotep III*. (Oxford: Oxford University Press, 2000). A well illustrated, readable biography.

Foster, John L. *Love Songs of the New Kingdom*. (Austin: University of Texas Press, 1992). Beautiful translations of love poems including the hieroglyphs in some cases.

Gardiner, Alan H. *Egypt of the Pharaohs*. (New York: Oxford University Press, 1961). Provides much material about the history of ancient Egypt, with some idiosyncratic comments.

———, trans. *Hieratic Papyri in the British Museum*. Third series, vol. 1. (London: British Museum Press, 1935). Presents the actual words of ancient Egyptians.

———, trans. *The Kadesh Inscriptions of Ramses II*. (Oxford, England: Oxford University Press, 1960). A complete presentation of how Rameses wished the public to view his largest military campaign.

Ghalioungui, Paul. *Magic and Medical Science in Ancient Egypt*. (Amsterdam: B. M. Israel, 1973). A solid book on the connections between magic and medicine in Egypt.

Ghalioungui, Paul, et al. "On an Ancient Egyptian Method of Diagnosing Pregnancy and Detecting Foetal Sex." *Medical History 7* (1963): 241–46. A modern experiment to assess the reliability of an ancient Egyptian pregnancy test.

Gillings, Richard J. *Mathematics in the Time of the Pharaohs*. (Cambridge: MIT Press, 1972). The best survey of mathematics in ancient Egypt.

Gordon, Andrew. "Origins of Ancient Egyptian Medicine," *KMT* (Summer 1990): 26–29. Presents the view that Egyptians studied animals to learn about human anatomy.

Grenfell, Bernard P., and Arthur S. Hunt, eds. *The Oxyrhynchus Papyri Part XI*. (London: Egypt Exploration Society, 1915). Presents a variety of magical spells.

Hackett, John. *Warfare in the Ancient World*. (New York: Facts on File, 1989). Stirring accounts of ancient battles and the techniques used by both sides.

Hayes, William C. *The Scepter of Egypt*. 2 vols. (New York: Metropolitan Museum of Art, 1959). Covers the extensive Egyptian collection of New York's Metropolitan Museum with abundant details of objects of daily life.

Herodotus. *Histories*. A. de Selinecourt, trans. (New York: Penguin Books, 1954). Still interesting for tidbits and an ancient Greek view of the ancient Egyptians.

Houston, Mary G., and Florence S. Hornblower. *Ancient Egyptian, Assyrian and Persian Costumes*. (London: A. & C. Black, 1920). Although dated, this work shows how clothing was made and worn in ancient Egypt.

Ikram, Salima. *Death and Burial in Ancient Egypt*. (London: Longmans, 2003). An excellent survey of the ancient Egyptian view of resurrection and mummification.

————. "Food for Eternity: What the Ancient Egyptians Ate and Drank." *KMT* 5 (Summer 1994). A good summary of the Egyptian diet.

Jenkins, Nancy. *The Boat Beneath the Pyramid*. (New York: Holt, Rinehart & Winston, 1980). A readable account of the only complete pharaonic boat ever found.

Kemp, Barry J., and Salvadore Garfi. *A Survey of the Ancient City of El-Amarna*. (London: Egypt Exploration Society, 1993). The detailed and up-to-date presentation of what Akhenaten's city must have looked like.

Killen, Geoffrey. *Ancient Egyptian Furniture*. Vol. 2 *Boxes, Chests and Footstools*. (Warminster, England: Aris and Phillips, 1994). A scholarly study on furniture with clear drawings that show the construction.

Kitchen, K. A. *Pharaoh Triumphant: The Life and Times of Rameses II*. (Warminster, England: Aris and Phillips, 1982). An authoritative account of the life of Rameses the Great.

KMT: A Modern Journal of Ancient Egypt. P.O. box 1475, Sevastapol, CA 95473. Devoted entirely to ancient Egypt with readable articles in every issue. Illustrated in full color.

Landstrom, Bjorn. *Ships of the Pharaohs: 4000 years of Egyptian Shipbuilding*. (Garden City, N.Y.: Doubleday & Company, 1970). Through exceptional illustrations and drawings, ancient Egyptian ships are analyzed and explained.

Lehner, Mark. *The Complete Pyramids*. (London: Thames and Hudson, 1997). A comprehensive survey of all the pyramids with fine photographs and computer-generated diagrams.

Lesko, Leonard H. *King Tut's Wine Cellar.* (Berkeley, Calif.: B. C. Scribe Publications, 1977). A comprehensive discussion of the largest ancient wine cellar ever found.

Lichtheim, Miriam. *Ancient Egyptian Literature.* 3 vols. (Berkeley: University of California Press, 1972–1980). The best collection of ancient Egyptian stories, prayers and records.

Littauer, M. A., and J. H. Crouwel. *Chariots and Related Equipment from the Tomb of Tutankhamen.* (Oxford, England: Griffith Institute, 1985). A thorough description of the most complete chariot ever found.

Lucas, A., and J. R. Harris. *Ancient Egyptian Materials and Industries.* (London: Histories and Mysteries of Man, 1989). Detailed and technical discussions of how Egyptians made things.

McLeod, W. M. *Self Bows and Other Archery Tackle from the Tomb of Tutankhamen.* (Oxford, England: Griffith Institute, 1982). Descriptions of Tutankhamen's bows and arrows.

Michelowski, Kazimierz. *Art of Ancient Egypt.* (New York: Abrams, n.d.) A survey of the best in Egyptian art with glorious photographs.

Milne, J. Grafton. "The Sanatorium of Dier-el-Bahri." *Journal of Egyptian Archaeology* 2, part 1 (1914): 96 –98. Lends an insight into ancient "miracle" cures.

Montet, Pierre. *Everyday Life in Egypt During the Days of Ramesses the Great.* (Philadelphia: University of Pennsylvania Press, 1981). A survey of everyday life during one of the great periods of ancient Egypt.

Moodie, Ray L., ed. *Studies in the Paleopathology of Egypt.* (Chicago: University of Chicago Press, 1921). A technical discussion of disease in ancient Egypt, based on autopsies of mummies.

Numm, John F. *Ancient Egyptian Medicine.* (London: British Museum Press, 1996). The latest and best book on medical practice in ancient Egypt.

Nutley, R. C., et al. "Palaeoepidemiology of Schistosoma Infection in Mummies." *British Medical Journal* 304 (1992): 355 –56. All that the title promises.

Partridge, Robert. *Transport in Ancient Egypt.* (London: Rubicon Press, 1987). How the Egyptians moved objects, on both land and water.

Petrie, Flinders. *Arts and Crafts of Ancient Egypt.* (London: T. N. Foulis, 1909). A legendary early Egyptologist describes finds that relate to Egyptian crafts.

Piankoff, Alexandre. *The Pyramid of Unis.* (Princeton, N.J.: Princeton University Press, 1968). A thorough discussion of the oldest Egyptian religious writing.

Quirke, Stephen, and Jeffrey Spenser, eds. *The British Museum Book of Ancient Egypt.* (London: Thames and Hudson, 1992). A solid, quick reference book.

Remler, Pat. *Egyptian Mythology A to Z.* (New York: Facts on File, 2007). Written for young adults, this book lists all the gods of Egypt and describes them in detail. Good illustrations.

Robins, Gay, and Charles Shute. *The Rhind Mathematical Papyrus.* (London: British Museum Press, 1987). A detailed discussion of the most important Egyptian mathematical work ever found.

Romer, John. *The Great Pyramid.* (Cambridge: Cambridge University Press, 2007). The most detailed discussion of this building, including some new theories. Illustrated.

Ruffer, Marc Armand. "Note on the Presence of 'Bilharzia haemotobia' in Egyptian Mummies of the XXth Dynasty." *British Medical Journal* 1 (1910): 16. Shows that one medical problem was more common in ancient times than it is today.

Sameh, Waley-el-dine. *Daily Life in Ancient Egypt.* (New York: McGraw-Hill, 1964). Some informative illustrations.

Sandars, N. K. *The Sea Peoples: Warriors of the Ancient Mediterranean.* (London: Thames and Hudson, 1978). A discussion of these enigmatic people with an attempt to discover who they were.

Sauneron, Serge. *Un Traité Égyptien d'Ophiologie.* (Cairo: L'Institut Français d'Archéologie Orientale, 1989). Translation of the Egyptian treatment of snake bites.

Scheel, Bernd. *Egyptian Metalworking and Tools.* (Aylesbury, England: Shire Publications, 1989). A concise, illustrated discussion of metallurgy in ancient Egypt.

Simpson, William Kelly. *The Literature of Ancient Egypt.* (New Haven, Conn.: Yale University Press, 1972). A fine collection of short stories, myths and religious texts of ancient Egypt.

Smith, W. Stevenson. *Art and Architecture of Ancient Egypt.* (New York: Penguin Books, 1958). A basic but extensive survey of all Egyptian arts.

Steuer, Robert O., and J. B. de C. M. Saunders. *Ancient Egyptian & Cnidian Medicine.* (Berkeley: University of California Press, 1959). A technical work on the Egyptian theory of disease.

Stocks, Denys A. *Experiments in Egyptian Archaeology: Stoneworking technology in Ancient Egypt.* (London and New York: Routledge, 2003). Discovers how ancient Egyptians worked stone through actual experiments.

Trigger, B. G., B. J. Kemp, D. O'Connor, and A. B. Lloyd. *Ancient Egypt: A Social History.* (New York: Cambridge University Press, 1983). Technical essays by authorities on various aspects of Egyptian society.

Tydesley, Joyce. *Daughters of Isis: Women of Ancient Egypt.* (London: Penguin Books, 1995). An excellent account of the situation of women in ancient Egypt.

———. *Hatchepsut: The Female Pharaoh.* (New York: Viking, 1996). A good, scholarly biography of the queen who became pharaoh.

———. *Nefertiti: Egypt's Sun Queen.* (New York: Viking, 1999). Written by an Egyptologist, this is a scholarly but readable biography of a famous queen.

Walker, James H. *Studies in Ancient Egyptian Anatomical Terminology.* (Warminster, England: Aris and Phillips, 1996). The hieroglyphs used by ancient Egyptians for various parts of the human body.

Watson, Philip J. *Costume of Ancient Egypt.* (New York: Chelsea House, 1987). Some good illustrations of clothing.

Weeks, Kent. *The Anatomical Knowledge of the Ancient Egyptians and the Representation of the Human Figure in Egyptian Art.* (Ann Arbor, Mich.: University Microfilms, 1970). A very technical discussion of the understanding of anatomy in ancient Egypt as shown by the words and drawings of the Egyptians themselves.

Westendorf, Wolfhart. *Painting, Sculpture and Architecture of Ancient Egypt.* (New York: Abrams, 1968). A chronological survey of Egyptian art with fine pictures of the masterpieces.

Wilkinson, J. Gardner. *The Ancient Egyptians, Their Life and Customs.* (New York: Crescent Books, 1988 [1854]). This reprint of the first book on the everyday life of ancient Egyptians still contains the most extensive illustrations from tomb paintings.

Wilkinson, Richard H. *Readings in Egyptian Art.* (London: Thames and Hudson, 1992). A clear introduction to hieroglyphs and how they were used in Egyptian art.

Winlock, H. E. *Models of Daily Life in Ancient Egypt: From the Tomb of Meket-Re at Thebes.* (Cambridge: Harvard University Press, 1955). Clear pictures of ancient models that show what the real things must have been like.

Woldering, Imgard. *The Art of Egypt.* (New York: Greystone Press, 1963). A basic illustrated history of Egyptian art.

Yadin, Yigal. *The Art of Warfare in Biblical Lands.* 2 vols. (New York: McGraw-Hill, 1963). Abundant pictures and descriptions of wars in the ancient world, involving both Egypt and other countries.

Egypology Websites

Thousands of websites deal with ancient Egypt, some good, some not so good. Below are some of the best, but by following links you will have access to hundreds of others.

http://www.aeraweb.org/
> Mark Lehner presents the latest findings of his excavations at the workmen's village below the Giza Plateau.

http://www.britishmuseum.org/default.aspx
> The British Museum in London has one of the largest collections of ancient Egyptian objects in the world. Many of its most important artifacts are online with informative descriptions.

http://www.brooklynmuseum.org
> Images of much of the superior Brooklyn Museum collection.

http://www.egyptology.com
> Provides links to most of the better websites along with topical articles.

http://oi.uchicago.edu/research/projects/epi/
> The University of Chicago's Oriental Institute has been working at Luxor for more than 75 years and has accumulated a vast archive of images and records. This is a wonderful source for details on excavations.

http://www.osirisnet.net/e_centra.htm
> Pictures and a good discussion of most of the tombs of nobles at Thebes.

http://www.oxfordexpeditiontoegypt.com/
> Click on "Database." Oxford University's site displays the latest finds of their expeditions.

http://www.petrie.ucl.ac.uk
> The Petrie Museum at University College London has a unique collection of daily life objects, many of which are pictured online.

http://www.thebanmappingproject.com/
> Website for the Theban Mapping Project. Dr. Kent Weeks has spent 25 years mapping the Valley of the Kings and this site provides descriptions and short films of all the tombs.

INDEX

(*continued on next page*)

PICTURE CREDITS

ABOUT THE AUTHORS

Bob Brier is Senior Research Fellow at the C. W. Post Campus of Long Island University in Brookville, New York. Recognized as one of the world's foremost experts on mummies, he conducts pioneering research in mummification practices and has investigated some of the world's most famous mummies. He has studied pyramids and tombs in 15 countries and has hosted award-winning television specials for TLC. He is the author of over 100 articles and many books, including *The Murder of Tutankhamen* (1998), *The Encyclopedia of Mummies* (1997), *Egyptian Mummies* (1994), and *Ancient Egyptian Magic* (1980).

Hoyt Hobbs is Professor of Philosophy and Chair of the Department at the C. W. Post Campus of Long Island University in Brookville, New York. He is author of *Fielding's Complete Guide to Egypt and the Archaeological Sites* (1983) and *A Complete Guide to Egypt and the Archaeological Sites* (1981). His research interests include epistemology, logic, Egyptology and history.